Radical Ethnic Movements in Contemporary Europe

Studies in Ethnopolitics

General Editors: **Timothy D. Sisk**, University of Denver, and **Stefan Wolff**, University of Bath

This new series focuses on the growing importance of international and external influences on ethnopolitical issues, such as diplomatic or military intervention, and the increasing effects of the forces of globalisation on ethnic identities and their political expressions.

Disputed Territories: The Transnational Dynamics of Ethnic Conflict Settlement
Stefan Wolff

Peace at Last? The Impact of the Good Friday Agreement on Northern Ireland
Edited by **Jörg Neuheiser** and **Stefan Wolff**

Radical Ethnic Movements in Contemporary Europe
Edited by **Farimah Daftary** and **Stefan Troebst**

Radical Ethnic Movements in Contemporary Europe

Edited by
Farimah Daftary and Stefan Troebst

Berghahn Books
New York • Oxford

First published in 2003 by

Berghahn Books

www.BerghahnBooks.com

©2003 Farimah Daftary and Stefan Troebst

Library of Congress Cataloging-in-Publication Data

Radical ethnic movements in contemporary Europe / edited by Farimah
Daftary & Stefan Troebst.
  p. cm. -- (Studies in ethnopolitics)
Includes bibliographical references and index.
ISBN 1-57181-622-4 (alk. paper)
  1. Social movements--Europe. 2. Ethnic groups--Europe. 3. Ethnic
conflict--Europe. 4. Political violence--Europe. 5. Europe--Ethnic relations.
6. Europe--Social conditions. 7. Europe--Politics and government. I.
Daftary, Farimah. II. Troebst, Stefan. III Series.

HM881.R33 2004
303.48'4'094--dc21   2002043680

British Library Cataloguing in Publication Data

A catalogue record for this book is available from the British Library

Printed in the United States on acid-free paper
ISBN 1-57181-622-4 hardback

CONTENTS

Foreword   vi
Preface and Acknowledgements   viii
Notes on Contributors   ix
List of Abbreviations   xiv

Introduction   1
Stefan Troebst and Farimah Daftary

PART ONE: COMPARISONS
1. Regionalism in Western Europe   21
   Peter Alter

2. Conflicts Between East European States and Minorities in an
   Age of Democracy   31
   Tom Gallagher

PART TWO: CASE STUDIES
3. Ethnoradicalism as a Mirror Image of State Centralisation:
   the Basque Paradigm in Franco's Spain   57
   Daniele Conversi

4. Chechnya and the Caucasus   71
   Helen Krag

5. International Dimensions of the Northern Ireland Conflict
   and Settlement   84
   Adrian Guelke

6. Explaining Ethnic Violence in Bosnia-Herzegovina   105
   Marie-Janine Calic

PART THREE: LESSONS
7. The Use of Force in Minority – Majority Relations:
   An International Law Perspective   133
   Rainer Hofmann

8. Third Party Mediation in Violent Ethnic Conflicts   150
   Norbert Ropers

PART FOUR: CONCLUSION
9. In Quest of Peaceful Coexistence – Strategies in Regulating
   Ethnic Conflicts   165
   Ulrich Schneckener and Dieter Senghaas

Index   201

FOREWORD

The recent history of Europe has introduced, or reintroduced, into the diplomatic lexicon a term that is as frightening to historians and political scientists as it may be reassuring to practical politicians. This is the term 'ancient hatreds'. It is a frightening concept, because it implies the historical inevitability of ethnic conflict. Such conflict will always persist, whatever the state of historical development of a given society, because that society, by virtue of its ethnic composition and violent tradition, is simply given to inevitable armed discourse. True, this armed confrontation can be forcibly repressed for a time. This happened in the centralist-communist states of the Warsaw Pact where national unity was rigorously enforced. But such a period of ethnopolitical calm can only last as long as the repression that generates it is maintained. Once the repressive mechanism collapses – as was the case with the dissolution of the Warsaw Pact, of the Soviet Union and of the Socialist Federal Republic of Yugoslavia – the cycle of violence returns to its natural pattern of conflict and destruction.

This dim view of human history is, of course, not persuasive. It cannot explain why some multiethnic societies managed the post-communist transition without violence. It fails to take account of the fact that ethnopolitical violence also occurs in regions that have not been subjected to a radical political transformation, including Western Europe. And it fails to note that, over time, ethnic division can be overcome and replaced by a concept of ethnic diversity. The principal attraction of the concept of 'ancient hatreds' therefore seems to lie in its utility to politicians. They can blame the failings of ethnopolitical conflict prevention or conflict management on the inevitable forces of history that cannot, it is claimed, be arrested through the application of reason and of reasoned dialogue.

This volume offers a far more sophisticated analysis of the causes of ethnopolitical violence. It locates the topic within the current literature and then offers detailed and nuanced case studies covering both Eastern and Western Europe. It also includes references to non-European cases, where appropriate, in order to provide a broad range of examples relevant to the topic. The cross-cutting analyses that follow substantially add to the lessons that can be drawn from the individual case studies. Of course, there is no single and simple formula that determines the factors that turn a national or ethnic struggle into a violent ethnopolitical

conflict. But the book brings us nearer to an understanding of this question in its many facets. As well as that, it offers an initial assessment of
the remedies that can be brought to bear on ethnopolitical violence.

In this way, this study exemplifies a typical concept of many of the
publications of the European Centre for Minority Issues (ECMI) in
combining novel conceptual thinking with a practice-oriented
approach. This closely mirrors ECMI's own working methods, be they
related to its research or its constructive conflict management ventures.
The Centre was founded under the impression of ethnopolitical conflict
in Europe during the 1990s. It was located in the German-Danish border
region to emphasise that ethnic tension, even if reinforced through war,
can be overcome and that different ethnic groups can live together
peacefully.

Marc Weller
ECMI Director
Flensburg, Germany, January 2002

PREFACE AND ACKNOWLEDGEMENTS

On 4 December 1996, the European Centre for Minority Issues was opened in Flensburg, the 'capital' of the multicultural German-Danish border region. In addition to conducting practice-oriented research, providing information and offering advisory services concerning minority-majority relations in Europe, the Centre started organising scholarly conferences on various aspects of ethnopolitics. The first of these academic events was the international conference 'Ethnoradicalism and Centralist Rule: Western and Eastern Europe at the End of the Twentieth Century'. It was held from 17 to 19 October 1997 at the University of Aarhus's course centre, the Sandbjerg Estate, located on the Sound of Als in Denmark's southernmost province of Sønderjylland. This conference provided the inspiration for the present volume, which contains nine of the thirteen contributions to the conference. These have been rewritten and revised since. However, when it comes to ethnic conflict, new developments occur by the day and one cannot always be entirely up-to-date. It is hoped that by providing an analytical framework for the understanding of these conflicts, these contributions will remain useful references for some time to come.

The editors are indebted to Walker Connor, Georg Elwert, Kinga Gál, Maj-Britt Risbjerg Hansen, Marita Lampe, John Loughlin, Gazmend Pula, Jacques Rupnik, James Sullivan, Sven Tägil and Marc Weller for their input in the conference and/or this collection of essays. The late H.P. Clausen (1928–98), Danish Consul General in Flensburg and member of the ECMI Board, was particularly helpful in bringing about this conference. This volume is therefore dedicated to him.

Flensburg/Leipzig, Germany, January 2002
Farimah Daftary, ECMI (Senior) Research Associate 1997–2002
Stefan Troebst, ECMI Director 1996–8

NOTES ON CONTRIBUTORS

Professor Peter Alter teaches Modern and Contemporary History at the University of Duisburg, Germany. He has published extensively on German, Irish and British history. His publications in English include: *The Reluctant Patron: Science and the State in Britain 1850–1920* (1987); *Nationalism* (2nd edition 1994); *Out of the Third Reich: Refugee Historians in Post-War Britain* (1998); and *The German Question and Europe: A History* (2000).

Dr Marie-Janine Calic is Senior Researcher at the German Institute for International and Security Affairs, Berlin. From 1999 to mid-2002 she held the position of Political Adviser to the Special Coordinator of the Stability Pact for Southeastern Europe in Brussels. She has lectured extensively about Yugoslavia and its successor states at the Universities of Munich, Berlin and Basel. She has published numerous articles and books on the Balkans, including *Krieg und Frieden in Bosnien-Herzegovina* [War and Peace in Bosnia-Herzegovina] (1996; revised edition 2002). She is a regular commentator on Balkan affairs for the German and Swiss media.

Dr Daniele Conversi received his PhD in Sociology at the London School of Economics. He taught in the Departments of History and Government at Cornell and Syracuse Universities and, as an Associate Professor, at the Central European University, Budapest. He is now Senior Lecturer at the University of Lincoln. He has published several works on ethnic politics, nationalism and sociolinguistics, including *German-Bashing and the Breakup of Yugoslavia*, Seattle: University of Washington/ Henry M. Jackson School of International Studies (The Donald W. Treadgold Papers in Russian, East European and Central Asian Studies no. 16, March 1998) and his internationally acclaimed *The Basques, the Catalans, and Spain: Alternative Routes to National Mobilization* (London: Hurst/Reno: Nevada University Press, 1997/2000). More recently he has edited a large volume on *Ethnonationalism in the Contemporary World: Walker Connor and the Theory of Nationalism* (London: Routledge, 2002).

Farimah Daftary is currently a Minority Protection Program Officer at the Open Society Institute's EU Accession Monitoring Program (EUMAP) in Budapest. Until March 2002, she was affiliated with the European Centre for Minority Issues (ECMI) in Flensburg. She obtained her Masters in International Affairs with a specialisation in East-Central Europe in 1991 from the School of International and Public Affairs (SIPA), Columbia University, New York. Her recent publications include: 'Conflict resolution in FYR Macedonia: Power-sharing or the "civic approach"?,' *Helsinki Monitor* 12:4 (2001), pp. 291–312. Forthcoming publications include: 'Insular Autonomy: A Framework for Conflict Settlement? A Comparative Study of Corsica and the Åland Islands,' in: *Managing and Settling Ethnic Conflicts: Comparative Perspectives from Africa, Asia, and Europe*, Ulrich Schneckener and Stefan Wolff (eds), and *Nation-Building, Ethnicity and Language Politics in Transition Countries*, Farimah Daftary and François Grin (eds), Budapest: LGI/OSI, 2003.

Professor Tom Gallagher holds the Chair of Ethnic Conflict and Peace at Bradford University in the United Kingdom. He has published widely on the role of nationalism in Southeastern Europe, experimenting with democracy and on the security concerns of individual countries, particularly Romania. *Outcast Europe: The Balkans, 1789–1989. From the Ottomans to Milošević*, was published in 2001 by Routledge. *Distrusting Democracy: Romania Since 1989*, and *From Tyranny to Tragedy: The Balkans Since The Cold War*, are due to be issued in 2003.

Professor Adrian Guelke is Professor of Comparative Politics in the School of Politics at Queen's University, Belfast. He is the director of the Centre for the Study of Ethnic Conflict (within the School of Politics). He was the Jan Smuts Professor of International Relations at the University of the Witwatersrand, Johannesburg in 1993, 1994 and 1995. He edited *The South African Journal of International Affairs* between 1995 and 1998. In 2000, Manchester University Press published *A farewell to arms?: From 'long war' to long peace in Northern Ireland*, a collection of pieces on the Irish peace process, which he jointly edited with Michael Cox and Fiona Stephen. Other publications include the following single-authored works: *South Africa in Transition: The Misunderstood Miracle* (1999); *The Age of Terrorism and the International Political System* (1995); and *Northern Ireland: The International Perspective* (1988). In addition, he coauthored (with John Brewer, Ian Hume, Edward Moxon-Browne and Rick Wilford) *The Police, Public Order and the State* (2nd edition 1996), and edited *New Perspectives on the Northern Ireland Conflict* (1994).

Professor Rainer Hofmann is the Director of the Walther Schücking Institute for International Law, University of Kiel. He is also President of the Advisory Committee established under the Council of Europe

Framework Convention for the Protection of National Minorities and Member of the Board of the European Centre for Minority Issues (ECMI), Flensburg. His publications include (with J.A. Frowein and S. Oeter, eds): *Das Minderheitenrecht europäischer Staaten, Vol. I* [Minority-Related Legislation of European States] (1993) and *Vol. II* (1994); *Minderheitenschutz in Europa: völker- und staatsrechtliche Lage im Überblick* [Minority Protection in Europe: an Overview of the Situation of International and Constitutional Law] (1995); 'Die Rolle des Europarates beim Minderheitenschutz' ['The Role of the Council of Europe in Minority Protection'], in: M. Mohr (ed.), *Friedenssichernde Aspekte des Minderheitenschutzes* (1995), pp. 159–211; 'Minority Rights: Individual or Group Rights,' *German Yearbook of International Law* 40 (1998), pp. 356–82; 'Das Überwachungssystem des Rahmenkonvention des Europarates zum Schutz nationaler Minderheiten' ['The Monitoring System of the Council of Europe Framework Convention for the Protection of National Minorities'], *Zeitschrift für europarechtliche Studien* 2:3 (1999), pp. 379–92; 'Der Schutz von Minderheiten in Europa' ['The Protection of Minorities in Europe'], in: W. Weidenfeld (ed.), *Europa Handbuch* (first edition 1999), pp. 823–46.

Dr Helen Krag is Associate Professor in Minority Studies at the University of Copenhagen, Denmark. In her research, she takes a strong interest in majority-minority relations in East European and Russian Studies. She has published on minority, multiethnicity and foreign policy related topics, lately primarily on the Caucasus and on Jewish relational issues. Helen Krag is a Member of the Board of the Danish Center for Holocaust and Genocide Studies and of the corresponding Programme in Uppsala, Sweden, as well as of the Danish Association for Research on the Caucasus and the Danish Chechnya Committee. She has published (together with L. Funch Hansen) 'The North Caucasus: Minorities at a Crossroads' (1994) (an edited and updated version in Russian was published in St. Petersburg in 1996); *Amol is geven. Jewish Culture and History in Eastern Europe* (together with M. Warburg, 2001) (in Danish); and *The North Caucasus: People and Politics in a European Border Region* (together with L. Funch Hansen, 2002) (also in Danish).

Dr Norbert Ropers is Director of the Berghof Research Center for Constructive Conflict Management, a Berlin-based nongovernmental institution dedicated to developing and testing constructive models for dealing with ethnopolitical conflicts and to creating peace constituencies in crisis zones. As a facilitator, trainer, consultant and researcher, Dr Ropers concentrates on the contributions by civil society actors and development agencies to peacebuilding and on strategies to improve the interlinkage of 'Track 1' and 'Track 2' approaches to conflict resolution. He is currently engaged in developing a 'Resource Network on Conflict Studies and Transformation' in Sri Lanka. His recent publications include: 'Enhancing the Quality of NGO Work in Peacebuilding,' in: *Peacebuilding: A Field Guide*, Luc Reychler and Thania Pfaffenholz (eds) (2001), pp. 520–32; 'Ziviles Krisenmanagement: Handlungsebenen, Arbeitsfelder und Zeit-perspektiven' ['Civilian Crisis Management: Phases of Action, Fields of Work and Perspectives on Time'], in: *Europas Beitrag zum Frieden: Vom militärischen zum zivilen Krisenmanagement*, Österreichisches Studienzen-trum für Frieden und Konfliktlösung (ed.) (2000), pp. 29–43; 'Konfliktbearbeitung in der WeltbürgerInnengesellschaft. Friedens-förderung durch Nichtregierungs-organisationen' [Constructive Conflict Management in a Global Civil Society: Promoting Peace Through NGOs], in: *Vom ewigen Frieden und vom Wohlstand der Nationen. Dieter Senghaas zum 60. Geburtstag*, Ulrich Menzel (ed.) (2000), pp. 70–101; (together with Diana Francis) 'Peace Work by Civil Actors in Post-Communist Societies,' *International Negotiation* 4:3 (1999), pp. 529–47.

Dr Ulrich Schneckener is a Senior Research Fellow at the German Institute for International and Security Affairs (Stiftung Wissenschaft und Politik), Berlin. His recent publications include: *Auswege aus dem Bürgerkrieg: Modelle zur Regulierung ethno-nationalistischer Konflikte in Europa* ['Escape from Civil War: Models for Regulating Ethnonational Conflicts in Europe'] (2002); 'Minority Governance between Self-rule and Shared-Rule,' in: *Minority Governance in Europe*, Kinga Gál (ed.) (LGI/OSL2002), pp. 349–371; 'Making Power-Sharing Work: Lessons for Successes and Failures in Ethnic Conflict Regulation,' *Journal of Peace Research* 39:2 (2002), pp. 203–227; 'Regulierung ethnischer Konflikte in Südosteuropa' ['Regulating Ethnic Conflict in Southeastern Europe'], *Internationale Politik* 54: 9 (1999), pp. 7–20.

Professor Dieter Senghaas holds the chair for Peace, Conflict and Development Studies at Bremen University, Germany, and is co-director of the Institute for Intercultural and International Studies (InIIS). His publications include: *The Clash Within Civilisations: Coming to Terms with Cultural Conflicts* (2001); and *The European Experience: A Historical Critique of Development Theory* (1985). Professor Senghaas is also the editor of '*Frieden machen*' [Making Peace] (1997) and '*Den Frieden* *denken. Si vis pacem, para pacem'* [Thinking the Peace: If You Want Peace, Prepare for Peace] (1995).

Professor Stefan Troebst teaches East European cultural studies at the University of Leipzig, Germany and is Deputy Director of the Leipzig Centre for the History and Culture of Eastern Europe (GWZO). His fields of research are international and interethnic relations in modern Eastern Europe. From 1992 to 1995 he served on the CSCE Spillover Monitor Mission to Macedonia and the CSCE/OSCE Mission to Moldova. From 1996 to 1998 he was director of the European Centre for Minority Issues (ECMI), Flensburg. Among his recent publications are *Conflict in Kosovo: Failure of Prevention? An Analytical Documentation, 1992–1998* (1998); *Handelskontrolle – 'Derivation' – Eindämmung. Schwedische Moskaupolitik 1617–1661* [Trade Control – 'Derivation' – Containment. Sweden's Policy Toward Muscovy, 1617–1661] (1997); and *Bugarsko-jugoslovenskata kontroverza za Makedonija 1967–1982* [The Bulgarian-Yugoslav Controversy over Macedonia, 1967–1982] (1997). He is co-editor (together with Heinz-Dietrich Löwe and Gönther H. Tontsch) of *Minderheiten, Regionalbewußtsein und Zentralismus in Ostmitteleuropa* [Minorities, Regional Identity and Centralism in Eastern Europe] (2000), and of *Südosteuropa. Gesellschaft, Politik, Wirtschaft, Kultur. Ein Handbuch* (together with Magarditsch Hatschikjan) [Southeastern Europe: Society, Politics, Economy, Culture. A Handbook] (1999).

LIST OF ABBREVIATIONS

ANC	African National Congress
BCP	Bulgarian Communist Party
BiH	Bosnia-Herzegovina
CEFTA	Central European Free Trade Area
CIS	Commonwealth of Independent States
CSCE	Conference on Security and Co-operation in Europe
DUP	Democratic Unionist Party
ECHR	European Convention on the Protection of Human Rights and Fundamental Freedoms/European Convention on Human Rights
ECMI	European Centre for Minority Issues
ETA	Euzkadi 'ta Askatasuna Euskadir 'ta Askatasuna (Basque Land and Freedom)
EU	European Union
FRY	Federal Republic of Yugoslavia
HDZ	Hrvatska demokratska zajednica (Croatian Democratic Union)
HVO	Hrvatsko Veče Odbrane (Croatian Defence Council)
ICRC	International Committee of the Red Cross
ICTY	International Criminal Tribunal for the former Yugoslavia
INC	Irish National Caucus
IRA	Irish Republican Army
JNA	Jugoslovenska Narodna Armija (Yugoslav People's Army)
KLA	Kosovo Liberation Army
MRF	Movement for Rights and Freedoms
NATO	North Atlantic Treaty Organisation
NGO	Nongovernmental Organisation
OSCE	Organization for Security and Co-operation in Europe
PACE	Parliamentary Assembly of the Council of Europe
PLO	Palestine Liberation Organization
RUC	Royal Ulster Constabulary
SCR	(UN) Security Council Resolution
SDA	Stranka demokratske akcije (Party of Democratic Action)
SDLP	Social Democratic and Labour Party
SDS	Srpska demokratska stranka (Serb Democratic Party)
SECI	South-East European Cooperation Initiative
SNP	Scottish National Party

UDMR	Uniunea Democrată Maghiară din România (Democratic Alliance of Hungarians in Romania)
UDP	Ulster Democratic Party
UFF	Ulster Freedom Fighters
UKUP	United Kingdom Unionist Party
UN	United Nations
UNESCO	United Nations Educational, Scientific and Cultural Organization
UNGA	United Nations General Assembly
UNHCR	United Nations High Commissioner for Refugees
USSR	Union of Soviet Socialist Republics
UUP	Ulster Unionist Party
VRS	Vojska Republike Srpske (Army of the Republika Srpska)

In memoriam H.P. Clausen (1928–1998)

Introduction

Stefan Troebst and Farimah Daftary

Among the means nation-states and minorities have at their disposal to safeguard and to pursue political and other interests, violence figures prominently. This is valid for central governments and ethnic peripheries in today's Western Europe as well as in Eastern Europe, including the Balkans and the Commonwealth of Independent States (CIS). Yet, whereas in the European Union area separatist terrorism in Northern Ireland, the Basque Provinces and Corsica is safely fenced in inside the United Kingdom, Spain and France respectively, ethnopolitical conflicts in Eastern Europe still have the potential to trigger off interstate wars – Bosnia-Herzegovina being the most recent example, and Kosovo, the Caucasus and Cyprus at or beyond the threshold of ethnic warfare. Accordingly, in Europe ethnic conflict is an almost ubiquitous phenomenon; it is, however, not a predominant one. Although there are a few instances where political struggles for power and participation between minorities and majorities lead to interethnic warfare, in the majority of cases they do not. We know of ethnonational conflicts being successfully transformed, even solved, by efficient power sharing models, and we know of ethnoregional movements that have withered away during what Miroslav Hroch would call their 'A phase' (Hroch 2000). We even find cases where the ethnic entrepreneurs of a movement, after having turned to violent means, switch back to nonviolent forms of action. The key questions therefore are:

1. What makes minorities turn to violence in putting forward their demands to the authorities of the state they are living in and/or what makes them defend themselves against the demands directed to them by this state?
2. What makes governments and other official actors use violent means in trying to control minorities on their territory, to assimilate them, or even to expel them?
3. Are minority actors turning to violence only as a last resort or do they make deliberate use of violence as a factor which strengthens ethnic identity, polarises, mobilises, and in particular radicalises the in-group?
4. How does the turn to violence change the relationship between 'ethnic entrepreneurs' and their target group?
5. What are the factors of escalation – that is, for an ethnic conflict to turn violent – and of de-escalation ?

6. What are the remedies outside actors have at their disposal to put an end to the spiral of violence, to transform protracted ethnopolitical conflicts into nonviolent ones and even reverse them into dialogues?

7. And finally, is there a theoretical framework to provide an explanation for all this?

These are by no means new questions, as the more than 4,000 articles listed in the *Social Science Citation Index* under 'ethnic conflict' as well as the recent proliferation of collections of essays on ethnopolitical conflict and interethnic violence, demonstrate (Ther 2001: 3).[1] Generally speaking, three schools of thought can be identified among those currents in the social sciences and the humanities that deal with the intricate relationship between ethnicity and violence as well as between nationalism and warfare, and thus try to detect 'method in the madness' (Bardhan 1997: 1381; Hägel 2001: 246): first, a historicist one interpreting both phenomena as two sides to the same coin; secondly, an intermediate one depicting ethnonationalism as at least potentially violent; and thirdly, a differentiated one which distinguishes between nonviolent ethnic conflict on the one hand and violent ethnic conflict on the other.

The first school of thought is best represented by the historian Lewis Namier, who in 1946 summarised his famous account of the 1848 revolutions in Europe in a single sentence:

> States are not created or destroyed, and frontiers drawn or obliterated, by argument and majority votes; nations are freed, united, or broken by blood and iron, and not by a generous application of liberty and tomato-sauce; violence is the instrument of national movements. (Namier 1946: 36)

Among historians, the causal link between nationalism and violence soon became commonplace. For instance, for Namier's German colleague Peter Alter – the author of an authoritative summary on the topic and represented in this volume[2] – nationalism is a 'synonym for intolerance, inhumanity and violence' (Alter 1995: 16). And the Swiss political scientist Bruno Schoch categorically stated: 'Violence and nationalism belong together' (Schoch 1995: 189). Other authors point to the fact that the emergence of almost all nation-states was accompanied, if not facilitated, by considerable degrees of violence.

The second school of thought perceives violence as an instrument of *some* but not all national movements. Accordingly, in 1995 David Laitin in an article on 'National Revivals and Violence' asked: 'Why should

---

1 For recent collections of essays on the topic, see Scheffler (1991); Trotha (1997); Koehler and Heyer (1998); Elwert et al. (1999); Höpken and Riekenberg (2001); Ther and Sundhaussen (2001); Chirot and Seligman (2001). See also the study by Wimmer (2002).

2 See Chapter 1, 'Regionalism in Western Europe.'

one nationalist movement be marked by terrorism, and the other by political negotiation?' and 'Why [do] certain nationalist movements become arenas for terror and others for peaceful bargaining?' (Laitin 1995: 9, 41). By comparing four case studies in Eastern and Western Europe Laitin arrived at the following conclusion:

> 'Nothing inherent in nationalism leads to violence; but since national revivals compel people to make important changes in how they live their lives, violence and terror become an available tool for those supporting or those suppressing the national project. The tool of violence is not historically or culturally determined; it is triggered by factors incidental to macrosociological factors and to the prevailing nationalist idea.' (Laitin 1995: 41)

Violent ethnic conflict is here depicted as a stage of escalation of ethnic conflict. In another article on 'Explaining Interethnic Cooperation,' coauthored by Laitin, a 'theory that can account for ethnic violence without over-predicting its occurrence' is put forward while the possibility of de-escalation is stressed: 'We argue that decentralized, nonstate institutional mechanisms may often arise to mitigate problems of opportunism in interaction between individuals from different ethnic groups' (Fearon and Laitin 1996: 715). What Laitin exemplified in his article 'National Revivals and Violence' through the cases of the Basque Country, Catalonia, Ukraine and Georgia,[3] two Danish authors, Søren Rinder Bollerup and Christian Dons Christensen, tested in the cases of Estonia, Moldova, Croatia and Czechoslovakia. They, too, interpret violent ethnic conflict as an escalated stage of ethnic conflict. The quintessence of their study reads:

> 'The potential for intense (and ultimately violent) national conflict is highest when the opposing nation-groups perceive strong primordial and instrumental interest with both or all groups perceived as conflicting with the interest of the opposing group(s).' (Bollerup and Christensen 1997: 263)

The third school of thought is the youngest one. It makes a clear distinction between ethnic conflict and violent ethnic conflict. Both types of conflict are put on the same hierarchical level, i.e. not in a causal connection of escalation or de-escalation. Here, ethnic violence is not classified as a mere means to an end and accordingly as an epiphenomenon, but as a social fact *sui generis*. Interestingly enough, David Laitin recently emerged as a protagonist of this line of thought. In an article on 'Ethnic and Nationalist Violence' written jointly with Rogers Brubaker and published in 1998, Laitin stated: 'Violence is not a quantitative degree of conflict but a qualitative form of conflict, with its own dynamics' (Brubaker and Laitin 1998: 426). In doing so, he implicitly criticised positions he himself had held until rather recently:

---

3   For more post-Soviet case studies, see Laitin (1998) and Laitin (2001) as well as Kaufman (2001) and Chapter 4, 'Chechnya and the Caucasus,' in this volume. The (post-) Yugoslav cases are covered by Calic (1996), Melčić (1999) and Höpken (2000). See also Chapter 6, 'Explaining Ethnic Violence in Bosnia-Herzegovina,' in this volume.

Violence has generally been conceptualised – if only tacitly – as a *degree* of conflict rather than as a form of conflict, or indeed as a *form* of social or political action in its own right. [Emphasis in the original – S. T.] (Brubaker and Laitin 1998: 425)

Brubaker and Laitin summarised the results of their review of what they call 'the largely non-intersecting literature on ethnic conflict and political violence' by stating:

'We lack strong evidence showing that higher levels of conflict (measured independently of violence) lead to higher levels of violence. Even where violence is clearly rooted in pre-existing conflict, it should not be treated as a natural, self-explanatory outgrowth of such conflict, something that occurs automatically when the conflict reaches a certain intensity, a certain 'temperature.' … The study of violence should be emancipated from the study of conflict and treated as an autonomous phenomenon of its own right.' (Brubaker and Laitin 1998: 426)

This perception is strongly derived from sociologist Peter Waldmann's pioneering comparative study of 1989 on ETA, the IRA and the *Front de Libération du Québec*. Waldmann interprets ethnic violence or, in his words, 'ethnic radicalism', not as 'the inevitable result of an extreme state of tension, but as an autonomous mode of conflict, whose application is primarily determined by the interests and available resources of the adversaries' (Waldmann 1989: 267).[4] In his view, this mode of carrying on a conflict is particularly attractive to those nonstate actors that see a gross imbalance between their means of political and material power and those of their opponent. Waldmann therefore depicts violence 'as an emergency resource of social groups that would otherwise be resource-weak' (Waldmann 1989: 34). In other words: violent ethnic conflict is not an escalation of nonviolent ethnic conflict. Instead, it is a deliberately chosen mode of operation, a specific form of political, social, economic, cultural or other action.

In Waldmann's footprints, the political scientist and Near East specialist Thomas Scheffler has come up with an elaborate concept explaining the rationale of what he calls 'ethnoradicalism', which he defines as follows: ' "Ethnoradical" I call all political efforts which construct friend-foe patterns along ethnic lines and which pursue their aims by violent means' (Scheffler 1995: 12). Scheffler follows Waldmann in stressing the attractiveness of violence to the smaller party in an asymmetric ethnic conflict. In particular, he perceives violence as a way of compensating for a lack of resources, strength or numbers by tapping 'the source of an international public.' This pattern, known since the 'Turkish atrocities' and 'Bulgarian horrors' of the nineteenth century, looked (and still looks) like this: the pinpricks of a minority movement in sensitive areas dramatically heighten the sense of danger,

---

4 For an attempt to apply Waldmann's approach to interwar Eastern Europe – here on the Internal Macedonian Revolutionary Organisation, the Croat Ustaša, and the Ukrainian Military Organisation/Organisation of Ukrainian Nationalists in Poland, see Troebst (1996); for a similar perspective on twentieth century Macedonia, see Troebst (2001).

with the intention of provoking an overreaction by the central government against the minority. The hope is that the outside world will intervene on behalf of the victims and/or that the victims will be polarised, solidarised, radicalised and ultimately mobilised to the extent that they turn to large-scale armed resistance. The cases of Armenia at the end of the nineteenth century, Macedonia at the beginning of the twentieth, and even more so that of Kosovo at the end of the previous millennium, illustrate just how risky this tactic can be – notwithstanding globe-spanning communication and international mass media (Troebst 2000).

So, according to this latter school of thought, represented by Waldmann and Scheffler as well as by Brubaker and Laitin, the crucial question is not what causes escalation and de-escalation in ethnic conflict. They speak of two different forms of ethnic conflict – nonviolent and violent. Still, '[w]hy are some nationalist movements peaceful in strategy and outcome while others create carnage?' (Laitin 1995: 3). Laitin himself comes up with a number of factors present in the violent case such as 'dense rural structure', 'codes of honour' or 'weak but tenacious central states' (Laitin 1995: 14, 41). Laitin, together with Brubaker, also puts forward two more general explanations: first, 'the decline ... in states' capacities to maintain order by monopolising the legitimate use of violence in their territories and the emergence in some regions ... of so-called quasi-states' (Brubaker and Laitin 1998: 424), and secondly, 'the eclipse of the left-right ideological axis that has defined the grand lines of much political conflict – and many civil wars – since the French Revolution' (Brubaker and Laitin 1998: 424–5). What used to be framed 'in the language of the grand ideological confrontation between capitalism and communism' is now reframed ethnically (Brubaker and Laitin 1998: 425). It seems that, at least with regard to Eastern Europe, this second argument is considerably weaker than the first one.

The loss of legitimacy of states is also stressed by Waldmann as a key factor in violent ethnic conflict, since it enables ethnic entrepreneurs to build up their own counter-legitimacy and to present themselves to their addressees as the nucleus of a future state. In addition, Waldmann identifies two more factors to which he attributes primary importance. These are the degree of territoriality of an ethnic conflict on the one hand, and the social composition of the ethnic entrepreneurs on the other. The more important territorial aspects are in an ethnic conflict, the higher is the likelihood that the conflict will be carried out using violent means. And the stronger the impact of middle-class groups is on an ethnic movement, the smaller is the likelihood that it will turn to violent action. For this latter point in particular Waldmann comes up with strong arguments derived from the examples of the Catalan and Quebecois movements, both of which at times have turned to violence but due to their predominantly middle-class elites switched back to nonviolent forms. One could probably also put South Tyrol (Trentino-Alto Adige) into this category, whereas Northern Ireland and the Basque Country accordingly represent cases of violence-prone lower-class elites.

To summarise: it is the actors in an ethnic conflict who consciously take the decision whether to carry out the conflict with violent or nonviolent means; there is no automatic spiralling into ethnic warfare. It is, of course, sufficient that one of the two or more parties to the conflict opt for violence, although there are instances when both sides take simultaneous and analogous decisions in this direction – as, for example, in early 1998 and again in early 1999 in the case of the Milošević regime and the Kosovo Liberation Army (KLA).

Turning from theory to practice, the question remains, however: what means do outside actors have at their disposal to contain ethnic violence and ultimately to transform protracted violent ethnic conflicts into nonviolent ones? Is there a theory-driven 'open sesame' to prevent or de-escalate violent ethnic conflict? Most likely not, and for several reasons. According to the first school of thought portrayed here, *all* ethnic conflicts sooner or later turn violent. Thus, to change, so to speak, the course of history through a conflict-prevention strategy seems to be impossible. The second school holds that it is the specific constellation of a particular conflict which determines whether it turns violent or not. This means, however, that *a priori* no generalising theory can be applied. The third school stresses the importance of the political will for violence by the actors in an ethnic conflict. That means that successful outside intervention in the conflict is faced with the task of talking one or more parties to the conflict out of violence – also not a very promising enterprise.

What, then, can be done? Probably the same as what Ruth Lapidoth undertook in her ambitious study, *Autonomy: Flexible Solutions to Ethnic Conflicts*. Having set out to develop what she called 'a model or some models of autonomy,' she soon realised that 'due to the great diversity of the various cases, it would not be feasible to formulate a practical general model' (Lapidoth 1997: 4). Taking this as a new starting-point, she restricted herself 'to highlight[ing] the features of autonomy and to indicating the principal options,' as well as to painstakingly analysing a large number of cases ranging geographically from Puerto Rico to Eritrea, passing through the Faeroe Islands. Since theory does not provide us with a golden key to the de-escalation of violent ethnic conflict, the precondition to all constructive conflict management is to carefully analyse each conflict separately in order to come up with tailor-made proposals for de-escalation. In doing so, however, theory can be of considerable help, particularly when it is based on comparisons. To put it in a nutshell: conflict-ridden interethnic relations strongly resemble conflictual interfamily relations – there is a structural resemblance of the 'harmonic' cases while the less 'harmonic' ones are as they are, due to very specific, and in each case different, reasons. Or – as Leo Tolstoy put it in the very first sentence of his *Anna Karenina*: 'Happy families are all alike; every unhappy family is unhappy in its own way.'[5]

This volume applies the Tolstoy-Lapidoth approach to a selection of European cases, ranging from the Basque Country to Chechnya, from Northern Ireland to Bosnia-Herzegovina. It tries to demonstrate that, when it comes to violent conflict between ethnoradical movements and centralist states, the 'Western' perception of 'Eastern Europe' is inaccurate, even misleading. As Jacques Rupnik has pointed out, 'ethnic violence in post-1989 Eastern Europe is the exception to the rule, whereas in Western Europe we have ongoing violent conflicts.'[6] In other words: violent ethnic conflict is a European phenomenon, not just an East European one. Still, Rupnik sees a major difference between Western and Eastern Europe concerning the context and risk of such conflicts: 'The problems may be just as acute in the West, but they do not occur in a context which poses a serious threat, nor do they pose the same risk thanks to four features: (1) power sharing mechanisms, (2) a developed civil society, (3) rule of law, and (4) a European framework.'[7] While Eastern Europe is slowly but steadily approaching these four aims, it remains to be seen whether Western Europe will eventually succeed in de-escalating its violent ethnic conflicts.

The volume is organised in three sections – comparisons, case studies and lessons. The first section on *Comparisons* seeks to generalise across, on the one hand, the case studies from Western Europe and, on the other hand, the case studies from Eastern Europe. Peter Alter highlights the diversity of situations in Western Europe (Chapter 1) and then presents an overall assessment. Of all Western countries, he judges Belgian federalism to be the most successful response to demands for regionalisation. The difficulties in France, Italy, Spain and Britain demonstrate that those nation-states were never united and homogeneous. France has been singled out as the most reluctant to respond to its regions' demands for autonomy. Italy had already offered a special status in 1948 to Sicily, Sardinia, the Aosta Valley (South Tyrol and Friuli-Venezia were added later). Democratic Spain granted cultural and political autonomy to Catalonia, the Basque Country and Galicia. However, in Alter's opinion, Britain is the most interesting due to the attempts to devise a solution to Scottish and Welsh regionalism through devolution. Also, parliament reserves the right to take back the powers, as it did in 1972 when it revoked the autonomy of Northern Ireland. Scottish demands

---

5 URL http://www.ccel.org/t/tolstoy/karenina/karenina.txt.
6 Jacques Rupnik, 'Minorities at Risk and the Risks Posed by Minorities.' Presentation given at the ECMI conference 'Ethnoradicalism and Centralist Rule: Western and Eastern Europe at the End of the Twentieth Century,' Sandbjerg Estate, Denmark, 18 October 1997.
7 Ibid.

being stronger than those in Wales, the British government has devised a different approach, granting different competencies to the new Scottish Parliament. The difference in intensity of regionalism in Scotland and Wales can be explained, according to him, by the historical ties between Britain and Wales being stronger than between Britain and Scotland. He concludes with a general observation on Western Europe: that we have witnessed the emergence of two new forms of regionalism where the historical dimension is absent – the Euro-region phenomenon, and regionalism in Northern Ireland.

In turn, Tom Gallagher (in Chapter 2) tackles the difficult task of comparing the cases in Eastern Europe. He distinguishes two phases of European nationalism: the communist era and the post-1989 period. The communist period was characterised by ethnic homogenisation, and nationalism was discredited as a tool of the bourgeois forces. When deep structural problems emerged, minorities found themselves under pressure. Radical efforts at homogenisation produced a desire for a radical settlement of accounts at the end of the communist era. Furthermore, a new phenomenon emerged – 'nomenklatura nationalism' – whereby nationalism was used to 'provide a new rationalisation and legitimisation of the old but threatened power of the apparatus.' 'Ethnic entrepreneurs' realised that the revival of ethnic grievances could divert attention from the injustices of privatisation and the formation of new economic oligarchies around the old nomenklatura. Ethnic nationalism also provided avenues for social mobility. Another feature of the new wave of nationalism in post-1989 Eastern Europe, according to Gallagher, is that it is most prominent among the anti-communists. This confirms the view of the Hungarian specialist on minority issues Oscar Jaszi that 'the political morals of an oppressed nation change when it comes to power' (in Bookman 1994: 68). Often, the new elites turn against their minorities whom they see as tools of the former communist rulers. The case of Croatia shows how nationalism can be transformed from an emancipating force to an oppressive ideology against the Serb minority which is pressured to assimilate or leave. Gallagher criticises the complacency of the international community, which he believes encourages discriminatory policies, and expresses concern about anti-minority discourse affecting the Roma in the Czech Republic. He then examines the various responses by minorities, noting that in contrast to Western Europe, violence is actually the exception rather than the rule in Eastern Europe (leaving aside the Caucasus and parts of former Yugoslavia). The absence of a tradition of bearing arms, fear of the majoritarian state, and greater state violence are among the explanations advanced for minorities' nonviolent response. The placing of minority rights on the European and world agenda is another positive factor. Indeed, Gallagher sees the Council of Europe and the Organization for Security and Co-operation in Europe (OSCE) as an

international constraint on state behaviour and 'nomenklatura nationalism'. Better communications technology, improved sophistication of
voters, and the rise of new political forces on the left are also positive
factors. Still, he singles out a few countries that seem to be the exception
to these trends: Serbia, Slovakia (under Mečiar) and Belarus. In conclusion, Gallagher outlines two factors which might decide the future of
majority-minority relations in Eastern Europe: (1) the speed and extent
to which the region overcomes its chronic economic difficulties, and (2)
the fate of European integration. If the latter fails, he foresees that disillusionment could boost radical nationalism in Eastern Europe.

The *Case Studies* section is opened by a study on the Basque Provinces
by Daniele Conversi (Chapter 3), in which he argues that state centralisation in the 1950s led to ethnopolitical radicalisation as well as
'ethnogenesis', illustrating this theory through the prism of the Basque
experience. Nationalism can thus be seen both as an attempt to seize
control of the state as well as a reaction to state interference and expansion. Looking at the early days of ETA (*Euzkadi 'ta Askatasuna*), he
claims that its radicalisation occurred because of attempts by the
Spanish state to crush it. He demonstrates that the increasing centralisation of the state in turn led to more sophisticated forms of mobilisation
within the Basque nationalist movement, resulting in a reinvention of
Basque identity and propagation of nationalist politics. Whereas in
Catalonia nationalism concentrated on the recovery of language, in the
Basque context commitment to the nationalist cause could only be
measured by the degree of the individual's involvement in political
violence. Conversi concludes that, as a direct consequence of state
repression under Franco, a new Basque nation was born. This phenomenon was linked to the collapse of state legitimacy in *Euskadi* and a
heightening of the conflict. He also observes that a similar process can
be seen in Northern Ireland, Chechnya and Turkish Kurdistan.

In Chapter 4, Helen Krag analyses the first conflict in Chechnya
during the period 1994–6 to illustrate the role of the 'ethnic' factor in
the transformation of the USSR and the process of ethnic mobilisation
vis-à-vis centralist rule. Because of Gorbachev's misjudgement that the
ethnic question had been solved, she argues, the nationality question
was not addressed during the process of *glasnost* and *perestroika* and soon
massive protests against Russian/Slavic dominance surfaced. Intervention did not solve the problems – on the contrary. In all five Caucasian
conflicts (Nagorno-Karabakh, Abkhazia, South Ossetia, Prigorodny
rayon and Chechnya), disagreements over political issues became ethni-
cised. These were minority conflicts, in the sense that they questioned
previously unquestioned minority–majority relations and the legitimacy
of majority rule on minority territory. Krag then focuses on who uses
force and why. By refusing to accept the Chechens as potential negotiation partners and isolating them politically and economically, Moscow

contributed to the popularity of the independence movement. Krag's explanation as to why Chechnya chose a unique path relates to several distinguishing features: a simple ethnic majority, a leader who was disciplined and goal-oriented, and a reputation for continuous opposition to Russian governance. Krag argues that the real reason for radicalisation can be better understood by looking at other armed conflicts in the Caucasus where the spiral of violence was set in motion by the violent reaction of central authorities and a colonial Russian mentality. While several contextual reasons have been set forth, none of them explains the choice of violence by Moscow as a legitimate means of governance. Krag claims that perceived stability and balance of power appear more important to Russian authorities than democracy and human rights, and that post-Soviet society still lacks the preconditions for consensus- or dialogue-based conflict resolution. In conclusion, Krag warns against the growing strength of groups within Chechnya seeking support outside European circles and especially from Muslim states, and an accompanying radicalisation as a result of neglect by the international community. She therefore calls for urgent action to assist Chechnya on the path of developing a democratic society.

In Chapter 5, Adrian Guelke examines the background to the Northern Ireland conflict and the Good Friday Agreement of 10 April 1998 which, he argues, was facilitated by changes in the international context of the conflict and the positive impact of certain external actors (e.g. Clinton and Blair). The Agreement appears all the more remarkable at a time when Northern Ireland's domestic politics were sharply polarised. Guelke then proceeds to identify obstacles to the implementation of the Agreement, such as divergences between Unionists and Republicans as well as within Unionist opinion. He also looks at the important issue of weapons 'decommissioning'. Guelke rejects the perception that the conflict has recently become internationalised, arguing instead that it has become internalised. Internationalisation, which he traces back to the beginning of the problems in 1968, involves five broad areas: (1) a territorial dispute between the United Kingdom and the Republic of Ireland; (2) the involvement of countries outside the British Isles in the conflict; (3) the international affiliation of the parties to the conflict; (4) the impact of the conflict on the outside world; and (5) the influence of international opinion on the conflict. Guelke also looks at the impact of developments in the international political system on the Northern Ireland conflict, highlighting the consequences of the break-up of Yugoslavia and the successful completion of the South African transition on the interpretation of international norms invoked by the conflict parties in Northern Ireland. Indeed, Guelke argues that the international community's hostility towards secession has weakened, resulting in less rigidity in the territorial interpretation of self-determination and a greater legitimacy of minorities' demands for better treatment within the state. He concludes with a sober assessment of prospects for success of the Good Friday Agreement. Still, he believes that, despite numerous delays, it can serve as the basis for a durable settlement of the conflict.

In the final case study (Chapter 6), Marie-Janine Calic refutes popular explanations for the outbreak of war in Bosnia-Herzegovina in 1992. Instead, she argues that the armed conflict was caused by a combination of political, economic, legal, constitutional, military and psychological events. She identifies five factors that are important for understanding strategies of violence in the Bosnian conflict: (1) the disintegration of Yugoslavia, (2) growing nationalism, (3) the emergence of a new class of ethnic entrepreneurs, (4) the availability of weapons, and (5) a political and legal vacuum. The Bosnian conflict had elements of both a traditional war and a new type of military conflict in which ethnic and religious factions battle not only for power and territory but also for national or religious identities. This was an international and a civil war at the same time, where the coercive methods used to carry out 'ethnic cleansing' did not reflect a culturally defined behavioural pattern or a remnant of a Balkan 'state of mind'. Rather, massive violations of human rights were part of a policy, a rational means to a specific end. The violence of ethnic cleansing was particularly brutal when the percentage of the ethnic group to be evicted from a certain area was high and when the defending political and military side was poorly organised. The way the Bosnian war was fought was derived from the Yugoslav military doctrine of all-peoples' defence and the partisan-led resistance against the German and Italian occupation during the Second World War. This doctrine was intended to mobilise all possible resources from the bottom up; in other words, people were educated to take defence matters into their own hands. However, with the political, administrative and military structure splitting along ethnic lines, partisan warfare turned against the civilian population itself. Calic warns, though, that the degree of rationality should not be overstated, for there were also strong elements of nationalistic passions and historical traumas. She then briefly looks into the dynamics of civil war and how cultural traditions were instrumentalised. Calic notes that many other societies have a tradition of idealisation of war and warriors without leading to violent conflict; it is therefore not folk tradition that guides national leaders like Radovan Karadžić, but rather the other way around. Calic concludes that one cannot attribute the behaviour of the Yugoslavs primarily to historical or psychocultural factors, but that these have been utilised to mobilise public support and to confuse Western observers. There exists a specific array of culturally inherited instruments and strategic interests – which she calls a 'culturally defined menu' – which determines the range of behavioural patterns in a war situation. She therefore cautions the reader not to allow excessive historical and psychocultural analysis to skew her/his understanding of conflicts.

The section on *Lessons*, as is evident from its title, seeks to draw lessons from the studies on the appearance and the use of violence in ethnic conflict in order to arrive at strategies in resolving these conflicts. Rainer Hofmann provides a detailed international law perspective in Chapter 7. He notes that the fundamental principle of prohibition of the use of force, enshrined in Article 2(4) of the UN Charter, is not applicable to minority–majority relations since it only pertains to interstate relations. However, in the recent practice of the UN Security Council, some internal situations where extreme violence was involved have been considered as a threat to international peace and security, thereby justifying international intervention. 'Humanitarian intervention,' i.e. 'third party intervention into a state without a prior pertinent decision by the UN Security Council and with the aim to prevent or to discontinue massive violations of fundamental human rights,' is also possible. However, this type of intervention is not lawful for it constitutes a clear violation of the territorial integrity and sovereignty of states as well as of the principle of the prohibition of the use of force. When minority–majority relations deteriorate to the point of internal armed conflict, common Article 3 of the 1949 Geneva Red Cross Conventions is the basic norm. Unfortunately, it is not clear whether the more extensive 1977 Additional Protocol Relating to the Protection of Victims of Non-International Armed Conflicts (Protocol II) is applicable. In any case, Hofmann underlines that governments must abide by their treaty and customary law obligations; this is relevant especially in situations where minority–majority relations have escalated but have not yet reached the point of armed conflict. A state may limit the rights of its citizens according to international human rights law in order to maintain a nonviolent public order or in situations of public emergency. Concerning the right to secession, Hofmann observes that minorities do not have such a right under current international law because they do not possess the right to self-determination – a right granted to peoples only. Nor does international minority rights law require the state to grant territorial autonomy to a minority. There are, however, certain instances where a minority can justifiably claim to constitute a people and therefore may possess the right to self-determination. Even in these cases, this right would be limited to internal self-determination because of what is considered a necessary balance between the right of peoples to self-determination and the right of states to territorial integrity (specific arrangements under domestic constitutional law or a negotiated dissolution are, of course, not excluded). In conclusion, Hofmann observes that it is increasingly being argued that international law allows a minority which constitutes a people to secede, if it is the subject of systematic human rights violations by its government.

Chapter 8 by Norbert Ropers addresses the possibilities for and limits to peaceful intervention by outside actors in violent ethnopolitical conflicts. Having set the preconditions for 'third party' mediation, i.e. neutrality and impartiality (or rather 'omnipartiality'), Ropers defines various types of mediation, opting for a flexible combination of reward and punishment. He observes that there has been a recent 'mediation boom' because traditional instruments for conflict resolution are ill fitted to deal with new ethnopolitical conflicts and because of the emergence of an 'alternative dispute resolution movement.' Despite the multiplicity of actors – from government representatives, diplomats and representatives of multilateral organisations ('Track 1' level) to representatives of churches, human rights activists, nongovernmental organisations (NGOs) and academics ('Track 2' level), the results have been modest. While he acknowledges a few cases of success (e.g. the efforts of the OSCE High Commissioner on National Minorities and other international organisations concerning the citizenship conflict in Estonia and Latvia), Ropers notes that the number of failures is greater. This is due to the fact that the study of mediation has concerned itself chiefly with preconditions for successful intervention, such as minimum fragmentation amongst actors, minor power differentials between disputants, no prior serious conflicts, a low number of victims, and security or sovereignty not being at stake. However, these preconditions are missing in current conflicts, where territorial integrity is usually at stake. He therefore proceeds to highlight important factors to be borne in mind by mediators for successful intervention, such as an understanding of the deeper processes involved in conflict (what Ropers terms 'content- and relation-based mediation'), and the awareness by the mediators of the heterogeneity of a conflict party, for to prioritise extremes entails the risk of further 'ethnicising' the conflict. He also notes that the increased demand for third party mediation has led to increased supply and thereby tougher competition for funds. Negative effects of this phenomenon include the desire to show spectacular success, unfair attribution of resources to 'bungee NGOs' and quick-result projects. In conclusion, Dr Ropers calls for replacement of the traditional peace maxim *si vis pacem, para bellum* ('If you want peace, prepare for war') with *si vis pacem, para pacem* ('If you want peace, prepare for peace'), i.e. large-scale mobilisation and training of third parties to tackle the challenges of ethnopolitical conflict management.

As a *Conclusion*, the volume is wrapped up with a systematic as well as analytical contribution by Dieter Senghaas and Ulrich Schneckener which forms Chapter 9. The authors identify three strategies for dealing with ethnonational minorities in Europe: *elimination, control* and *recognition* of cultural differences. Unlike the first two, *recognition* is the only policy which aims to achieve coexistence through negotiation processes. Focusing on the range of constructive means by which ethnonational

conflicts may be brought to an end, the authors first examine the requirements for peaceful coexistence in ethnonational conflicts, such as the
establishment of confidence building measures, of empathy, the broadening
of the actors' intellectual 'horizon' and the adoption of a problem-solving
orientation. These are the pillars of what they call a 'productive conflict
culture,' i.e. 'the ability to contain and manage conflicts in a constructive
and nonviolent manner through institutional arrangements accepted by all
parties involved.' This approach, based on recognition rather than rejection of cultural difference, allows for several modes of coexistence and
ethnic conflict regulation. Granting *minority rights* is the most basic form of
recognition but it raises the problem of reconciling special protection and
the principle of equality of all citizens. The authors argue in favour of such
special rights although they view it as insufficient. They also note that it is
where minority rights are most needed that governments are least willing to
grant them. *Bilateral minority protection* might provide a solution when there
is a 'patron state' and where internal minority conflicts threaten to degenerate into interstate wars. The numerous attempts at bilateral minority
protection in Central and Eastern Europe (which, with a few exceptions,
have stopped short of granting territorial autonomy) are significant for they
have elevated the minority issue to an international level. However, they
might also have a negative effect in asymmetric cases, when they fail to
agree on little more than the lowest common denominator (e.g. the
Slovak-Hungarian Basic Treaty). *Territorial autonomy* and *federalism* offer a
higher degree of self-government rights and seek to reconcile geographic
and ethnic boundaries. However, because each new border creates a new
minority, this might aggravate the conflict. Such territorial logic might also
motivate 'ethnic cleansing' or be perceived as encouraging separatism. The
authors go into great detail on how to ensure that such solutions succeed,
paying special attention to power sharing or *consociationalism*. Senghaas
and Schneckener raise a particularly important question: can one transfer a
successful model to another multiethnic society? Key preconditions for
success are the renunciation of separatist intentions and especially the existence of an overarching loyalty shared by all groups, such as the sense of
belonging to the same 'nation'. This limits the possibilities for transferring
models. The authors also examine the most radical modes of recognition:
secession and *partition* which can be peaceful provided that the conflict has
not yet turned violent and if all parties accept this as a legitimate means of
conflict resolution. In conclusion, Senghaas and Schneckener underline
the importance of a cooperative attitude, especially in difficult situations
such as Northern Ireland, Bosnia, Cyprus, Kosovo or the Trans-Dniester
region where a combination of the different modes outlined might be the
answer. However, they see willingness to cooperate not as an *a priori* condition but as the result of recognition, emphasising the importance of a
collective learning process which can take place thanks to the institutional
framework provided by a particular mode of conflict regulation.

The papers of this volume demonstrate that the emergence of the use of violence in ethnopolitical conflicts, whether by government actors or by ethnic groups, can be traced to various causes and must be linked to the specific historical, psychological and social conditions of the region in question. Unilateral explanations and generalisations should be avoided and a whole range of factors should be taken into account. However, certain common features can be distinguished. First, violence, whether in the form of 'ethnic cleansing' or psychological violence, has emerged as the main instrument of modern warfare in Eastern Europe's ethnopolitical conflicts, which have broken with classical definitions of international or civil wars. Once unleashed, violence seems to follow a logic and imperatives of its own. Second, this may also apply to certain forms of violence in Western Europe, which albeit reined in by the governments of France, Britain or Spain, has persisted, moving through cycles of cease-fires and renewed attacks on symbols of the centralised state. Third, comparing East and West, traditional views regarding the propensity for conflict in Eastern Europe are challenged by the assertion that, in contrast to Western Europe, violence in Eastern Europe is the exception rather than the rule. One also notes that the distinction between separatist struggle and economically motivated entrepreneurship is often blurred. There are many strategies for resolving ethnopolitical conflicts, especially given the recent 'mediation boom' and proliferation of third party mediation and NGOs involved in conflict resolution. Strategies may be combined, and models may serve as an inspiration. However, a key element to bear in mind is that the aim of conflict resolution should be to provide the right institutional framework for the development of a cooperative attitude between parties in a dispute. One should not expect quick or spectacular results. Rather, mediators should allow for a collective learning process. Finally, a crucial element in stemming the wave of violent conflict in Eastern Europe will be the speed and success of economic reform and democratisation and the institutionalisation of traditional channels for political mobility.

References

ALTER, Peter (1995). 'Einleitung'. In: *Nationalismus. Dokumente zur Geschichte und Gegenwart eines Phänomens*, Peter Alter (ed.). München: Piper, pp. 15–35.

BARDHAN, Pranab (1997). 'Method in the Madness? A Political-Economy Analysis of Ethnic Conflicts in Less Developed Countries.' *World Development* 25:9, pp. 1381–98.

BOLLERUP, Søren Rinder, and Christian Dons CHRISTENSEN (1997). *Nationalism in Eastern Europe: Causes and Consequences of the National Revivals and Conflicts in Late Twentieth-Century Eastern Europe.* London: St. Martin's Press.

BOOKMAN, Milica Zarcovic (1994). *Economic Decline and Nationalism in the Balkans.* New York: St Martin's Press.

BRUBAKER, Rogers, and David D. LAITIN (1998). 'Ethnic and Nationalist Violence.' *Annual Review of Sociology* 24, pp. 423–52.

CALIC, Marie-Janine (1996). *Der Krieg in Bosnien-Hercegovina. Ursachen – Konflikt-strukturen – Internationale Lösungsversuche.* Frankfurt am Main: Suhrkamp (revised edition 2002).

CHIROT, Daniel, and Martin E. P. SELIGMAN (eds) (2001). *Ethnopolitical Warfare. Causes, Consequences, and Possible Solutions.* Washington, DC: American Psychological Association.

ELWERT, Georg, Stephan FEUCHTWANG and Dieter NEUBERT (eds) (1999). *Dynamics of Violence: Processes of Escalation and De-escalation in Violent Group Conflicts.* Berlin: Duncker & Humblot.

FEARON, James D., and David D. LAITIN (1996). 'Explaining Interethnic Cooperation.' *American Political Science Review* 90: 4, pp. 715–35.

HÄGEL, Peter (2001). ' "Methoden im Wahnsinn?" Sozialwissenschaftliche Erklärungsansätze zu Nationalitätenkonflikten.' In: Ther and Sundhaussen (eds) (2001), pp. 247–64.

HÖPKEN, Wolfgang (2000). 'Das Dickicht der Kriege: Ethnischer Konflikt und militärische Gewalt im früheren Jugoslawien 1991–1995.' In: *Wie Kriege entstehen. Zum historischen Hintergrund von Staatenkonflikten.* Bernd Wegner (ed.). Paderborn, München, Wien, Zürich: Ferdinand Schöningh, pp. 319–67.

HÖPKEN, Wolfgang, and Michael RIEKENBERG (eds) (2001). *Politische und ethnische Gewalt in Südosteuropa und Lateinamerika.* Köln/Weimar/Wien: Böhlau.

HROCH, Miroslav (2000). *Social Preconditions of National Revival in Europe: A Comparative Analysis of the Social Composition of Patriotic Groups Among the Smaller European Nations.* New York: Columbia University Press (3rd edition).

KAUFMAN, Stuart (2001). *Modern Hatreds: The Symbolic Politics of Ethnic War.* Ithaca, NY/London: Cornell University Press.

KOEHLER, Jan, and Sonja HEYER (eds) (1998). *Anthropologie der Gewalt: Chancen und Grenzen der sozialwissenschaftlichen Forschung.* Berlin: Verlag für Wissenschaft und Forschung.

LAITIN, David D. (1995). 'National Revivals and Violence.' *Archives européennes de sociologie* 36: 1, pp. 3–43.

——— (1998). *Identity in Formation: The Russian-Speaking Populations in the Near Abroad.* Ithaca, NY/London: Cornell University Press.

——— (2001). 'Secessionist Rebellion in the Former Soviet Union.' *Comparative Political Studies* 34, pp. 839–61.

LAPIDOTH, Ruth (1997). *Autonomy: Flexible Solutions to Ethnic Conflicts.* Washington, DC: United States Institute of Peace Press.

MELČIĆ, Dunja (ed.) (1999). *Der Jugoslawien-Krieg. Handbuch zu Vorgeschichte, Verlauf und Konsequenzen.* Opladen: Westdeutscher Verlag.

NAMIER, L.B. (1946). '1848: The Revolution of the Intellectuals.' *Proceedings of the British Academy* 30, pp. 1–124.

SCHEFFLER, Thomas (1995). 'Ethnoradikalismus: zum Verhältnis von Ethnopolitik und Gewalt.' In: *Minderheiten als Konfliktpotential in Ostmittel-und Südosteuropa,* Gerhard Seewann (ed.). München: R. Oldenbourg, pp. 9–47.

——— (2002). 'Wenn hinten, weit, in der Türkei die Völker aufeinander schlagen …': Zum Funktionswandel 'orientalischer' Gewalt in europäischen Öffentlichkeiten des 19. und 20. Jahrhunderts.' In: *Europäische Öffentlichkeit. Transnationale Kommunikation seit dem 18. Jahrhundert,* Jörg Requate and Martin Schulze Wessel (eds). Frankfurt am Main/New York, NY: Campus, pp. 205–31.

SCHEFFLER, Thomas (ed.) (1991). *Ethnizität und Gewalt*. Hamburg: Deutsches Orient Institut.

SCHOCH, Bruno (1995). 'Nationalismus, Rassismus und die Wiederkehr der Gewalt in Europa.' In: *Gewalt: Kulturelle Formen in Geschichte und Gegenwart*, Paul Hugger and Ulrich Stadler (eds). Zürich: Unionsverlag, pp. 188–211.

THER, Philipp (2001). 'Nationalitätenkonflikte im 20. Jahrhundert: Ursachen von inter-ethnischer Gewalt im Vergleich.' In: Ther and Sundhaussen (2001), pp. 3–15.

THER, Philipp, and Holm SUNDHAUSSEN (eds) (2001). *Nationalitätenkonflikte im 20. Jahrhundert. Ursachen inter-ethnischer Gewalt im Vergleich*. Wiesbaden: Harrassowitz.

TROEBST, Stefan (1996). 'Nationalismus und Gewalt im Osteuropa der Zwischenkriegszeit. Terroristische Separatismen im Vergleich.' *Bulgarian Historical Review* 24: 2, pp. 25–55.

——— (2000). 'Balkanisches Politikmuster? Nationalrevolutionäre Bewegungen in Südosteuropa und die 'Ressource Weltöffentlichkeit'.' *Osteuropa* 50:11, pp. 1254–66.

——— (2001). 'Vom ethnopolitischen Schlachtfeld zum interethnischen Stabilitätspol: Gewalt und Gewaltfreiheit in der Region Makedonien im "langen" 20. Jahrhundert.' In: Ther and Sundhaussen (eds) (2001), pp. 35–55.

TROTHA, Trutz von (ed.) (1997). *Soziologie der Gewalt*. Opladen: Westdeutscher Verlag.

TURTON, David (ed.) (1997). *War and Ethnicity: Global Connections and Local Violence*. Rochester, NY: University of Rochester Press.

WALDMANN, Peter (1989). *Ethnischer Radikalismus: Ursachen und Folgen gewaltsamer Minderheitenkonflikte am Beispiel des Baskenlandes, Nordirlands und Quebecs*. Opladen: Westdeutscher Verlag.

WIMMER, Andreas (2002). *Nationalist Exclusion and Ethnic Conflict. Shadows of Modernity*. Cambridge: Cambridge University Press.

PART ONE

COMPARISONS

CHAPTER ONE

Regionalism in Western Europe

Peter Alter

If the historian takes a bird's-eye view of the changing political map of Europe since the end of the Second World War, the well-known characterisation of Europe as unity in diversity almost automatically springs to mind. From the late 1940s, under pressure from the United States in the West and the Soviet Union in the East – some of it subtle, some less so – the diversity of Europe was largely relegated to the background. The prevailing catchword was unity: in Western Europe under the banner of Western European integration (whose individual stages since the Schuman Plan was sanctioned cannot be discussed here), and in the East with the ruthless 'Sovietisation' of the broad band of states from Poland to Czechoslovakia and Hungary, right down to Bulgaria and Albania. In postwar Europe only a few states within the former Soviet Union's sphere of influence were able to avoid this process for any length of time, amongst them certainly Yugoslavia and Finland and also, to some extent, Poland, Romania and later Hungary.

Today, since the demise of the discredited communist dictatorships at the end of the 1980s, the situation in Europe has changed dramatically when compared to the two or three decades after the war. Diversity, not unity, is again at the forefront. This seemed to be the dominant theme of the political development of Europe at the end of the twentieth century – and its demands and manifestations are boundless. The consequences are obvious: modern Europe has never had as many borders and national entities as it has today. The numbers speak for themselves: in Europe today there are forty-three states, almost all of which are defined as nation-states.

A hundred years ago, however, the situation in Europe was quite different. At the end of the nineteenth century the concept of the nation-state was still at odds with the reality of huge multinational states, especially in Eastern and East-Central Europe. This was reflected in the number of European states. Between 1870 and 1914, disregarding the very tiny ones, there were only sixteen sovereign states. So, since 1914, the number of states in Europe has continually increased. The only setback to this development occurred during the seven years of National Socialist aggression between 1938 and 1945.

The increasing number of European states since the beginning of the twentieth century inevitably ran parallel with the establishment of new national borders. However, due to the Second World War and the ensuing Cold War, the old problem of borders, their permeability and arbitrariness, and the question of whether or not they made sense appeared in a new light after 1945. In other words, compared to the nineteenth and early twentieth centuries, the nature of European borders changed in many respects. After 1945, borders had different meanings and consequences, the scope of which was new. Together with the traditional borders of the nation-state, new lines of demarcation were drawn: lines denoting alliances, military allegiances, economic-political groupings, as well as internal demarcation lines within states. Some of these such as the 'Iron Curtain' across Germany made sweeping changes to the familiar political map of Europe. Then, with the end of the Cold War, the military border across the centre of Europe, and with it the ideological divisions between East and West, disappeared, but old and seemingly forgotten cultural borders and borders within states now came more sharply into focus.

This ongoing and intriguing process of removing borders and erecting new ones seems closely linked to a change in identity and loyalty amongst large population groups, which is particularly noticeable in Western Europe. Here, in the postwar years, two great movements were clearly discernible, running primarily in opposite directions. On the one hand, the greater economic, military and political integration of the nation-states restored after 1945 brought about many new forms of multinational cooperation such as the European Coal and Steel Community, the Council of Europe, the Western European Union, NATO and the European Economic Community. The other development was the crumbling of traditional political structures in nation-states hitherto centrally organised and based on the assumption of political and ethnic homogeneity.

In alternative terms, one could say that moves towards European and Atlantic integration in Western Europe during the postwar period made the boundaries between nation-states more flexible and less dividing. In many respects they lost their former significance. But this did not mean the abolition of the nation-state. On the contrary: the British historian Alan Milward has put forward the thesis that the nation-state was rescued by European integration (Milward 1992). None the less (and this is the opposite tendency mentioned) new lines of demarcation, fault-lines within states, became unmistakably more prominent. Nation-states of the past were at great pains to conceal these divisions, often by highly dubious means. In Western Europe since the 1960s and 1970s, all attempts at distancing and separatism within nation-states have generally been attributable to so-called regionalist aspirations on the part of certain groups or inhabitants of historic areas. They no longer support the concept of the centralist nation-state, perceived as an undivided political unit, and its allegedly homogeneous nation. The 'regionalists' demand autonomy, in some cases even independence. A cultural, even political identity that predates the nation-state was rediscovered and made into the basis of a political programme, although, as one would expect, the reaction to this newly defined or rediscovered identity amongst the population groups in question varies considerably.

It goes without saying that European and Atlantic integration, and also globalisation (the current buzz-word) on the one hand, and regionalism on the other, have put the nation-state under considerable pressure. However, it was relatively quick to recognise the danger to its legitimacy and continued existence. With varying degrees of hesitancy, its supporters, or governments, have developed concepts intended to counter the centrifugal forces within their states and to check the decline of centralised state authority. In Belgium, Spain, Italy, France and, most recently, the United Kingdom, there are signs that central administrations are attempting to meet the challenge of nationalist movements or regionalist aspirations within the state on the basis of their functioning parliamentary and democratic systems of government. Since 1945, the central governments of the nation-states have been, all in all, surprisingly willing to take a constructive approach towards regionalism and its fragmentary dynamics. This willingness has probably been promoted by the fact that the nation-states recognise a welcome opportunity here to relieve the centre of some of the political responsibilities and functions that overburden it. The recipe was, and is, to grant cultural and political autonomy to certain population groups or to inaugurate a systematic process of federalising the hitherto centralist nation-state.

The incentive for all these various governmental measures is the need to provide an effective institutional framework for the aspirations to cultural and political autonomy nurtured by closely-knit population groups, in order to avoid any long-term destabilisation and thus weakening of the state as a whole. In the past there have been far more radical, even extreme, statements by some regionalists which could not be ignored and served as a warning. For example, there was talk of destroying the nation-states and restructuring Western Europe in historical-cultural regions. But ultimately, these fairly utopian ideas remained little more than rhetorical warning shots. They have so far not played any serious role in the political debate, with one exception: the political movement in the Basque Country, embodied, above all, in the organisations *Herri Batasuna*[1] and ETA, whose notions of autonomy

---

1 Now called *Euskal Herritarrok* (EH) [Editors' Note].

have long since exceeded those elsewhere. Their aim is national independence for the Basque Country; therefore, the Basque movement should be regarded as a clearly national movement (Conversi 1997). Regionalism in Corsica probably belongs in the same category, although this statement requires further probing.

But apart from these two examples, in Western Europe the conflict between the centralising and homogenising nation-state on the one hand and regionalism on the other has been conducted more or less exclusively on the political level. Violence, repression and terror have been avoided by both sides, the authorities and the regionalists. This is quite remarkable. Perhaps it shows the strength and elasticity of the democratic-parliamentary systems in the countries in question. However that may be, given the pragmatic attitude of the central governments in the countries of Western Europe and their willingness to compromise, it is basically of little importance whether or not the concessions made to regionalist aspirations by proponents of the undivided nation-state were merely a tactical manoeuvre. In this context, the German political scientist Friedrich von Krosigk once spoke of a 'strategy of pacification that, in principle, is orientated towards the status quo in the nation-state system' (von Krosigk 1980: 45). This may well have been the original view in many of the nation-state capitals. Historical experience shows, however, that changes to the internal structure of the state (once they have come into effect) cannot be reversed so easily.

A glance at developments in Western Europe demonstrates this point. Of all the Western European countries, Belgium has reacted most decisively to the challenge posed by the regional question, which in the past threatened to destroy the unity of the state. The far-reaching constitutional reforms that started in the 1970s and went on until 1993 transformed the kingdom into a federation. Extensive self-administration was granted not only to Flemings and Walloons, but also to the German-speaking minority in eastern Belgium. Today it looks as if the federalist solution in Belgium has been a lasting political success.

Since the 1960s, all the large states of Western Europe have been confronted by the demands of compact social groups who consider themselves to be either national minorities or ethnically/culturally unique. These states had hitherto been regarded as the classic examples of the ethnically homogeneous nation-state, as organisational forms of the so-called 'historical nations'. Opinions differ as to the root causes of the 'uprising of the regions' (Gerdes 1980). But regionalism in France, Spain, Italy and Britain makes it quite clear that in these countries, despite all political rhetoric to the contrary, the nation-state never was completely united or homogeneous. Since the eighteenth century the nation has been, and still is, basically a fiction. Historians today see this more clearly than ever. Membership of a particular nation often came about by pure chance, and could therefore be quite arbitrary. Apart from social heterogeneity, in the classical centrally-organised nation-states, differences of a cultural/linguistic nature continued, and still continue to exist, and are often difficult to conceal. This forms the springboard for regionalism.

So far, France has to be singled out for having been most reluctant to respond to the regions' desire for autonomy, although the government in Paris has made concessions to the Corsicans, granting Corsica a fairly wide-ranging autonomous status.[2] The Italian government, on the other hand, had already created four regions with a special status as early as 1946–8, namely Sicily, Sardinia, the Aosta Valley and South Tyrol. In 1963 Friuli-Venezia Giulia was added. Only since the 1970s have the other Italian regions been given more autonomy and legislative powers. In Spain it was really only during Franco's dictatorship that the particular ethnic and cultural character of the Catalans, Galicians and Basques was called into question and violently suppressed. With its new constitution of 1979, democratic Spain granted cultural and political autonomy to Catalonia, Galicia and the Basque Country. The constitution defined Spain as a multinational state. It granted the 'nationalities' varying degrees of self-administration, to which in the meantime other Spanish regions, seventeen in all, have also laid claim.

Nowadays probably the most interesting case as far as the question of regionalism is concerned is Britain. The kingdom is, as its official name clearly states, a United Kingdom, and against this background one of the most centralised states in Europe. However, it comprises *de facto* four constituent countries of differing sizes, each with a clearly recognisable identity, which have retained certain rights to autonomy. In any case, these are regions in which the population has a marked consciousness of being, in many respects, part of a multinational state. In the last hundred years, consciousness of national independence on the part of the 'nations' of the United Kingdom, which is often competing with national feeling for Britain as a whole, or overlapping with it, has not been restricted to the cultural sphere. Instead, it has progressed to the demand for political autonomy. This demand has been stronger at some stages than others and has sometimes disappeared altogether.

In the 1920s and 1930s the urge for political autonomy in both Scotland and Wales resurfaced, though only amongst a minority of the Scottish and Welsh populations. The integrative political power of the democratic British state as a whole still proved to be greater than the particularist aspirations at its fringes. However, at this time, the two organisations which today are regarded as the most important political

---

2   Albeit limited to the sphere of administration. On 20 July 2000, following seven months of discussions with elected representatives from Corsica (the 'Matignon Process'), the French government proposed a complex set of reforms to significantly expand Corsica's autonomy. However, prospects for its full implementation are poor [Editors' Note].

standard-bearers of the concept of political autonomy and national self-determination came into existence. In 1925, *Plaid Cymru* ('Party of Wales') was founded in Wales, and in 1932 the Scottish National Party (SNP) was established in Scotland.

So when, from the 1960s onwards, the demand for more political autonomy in Scotland and Wales was revived, this was nothing new for British politicians and the public at large. What was new, however, was that there was now a far greater response to the demand amongst the population. One reason for this was that in Scotland reference to 'Scottish oil' effectively reinforced agitation by the SNP. 'Economic exploitation of Scotland by London' for the SNP was a populist slogan with great pulling-power.

From the late 1970s onwards, more and more prophets of doom in Britain predicted that the United Kingdom would split apart, even disintegrate under the barrage of national demands from the Scots and Welsh. From 1979 onwards, Conservative governments repeatedly designated Scottish and Welsh regionalism as a threat to the united British state and British identity. For them it was nationalism hardly in disguise. The Labour opposition, on the other hand, was already signalling a willingness to consider Scottish and Welsh demands for autonomy in the 1980s. Now we can see how the new Labour government is putting its concept of devolution into practice, in the context of a comprehensive modernisation of the United Kingdom. According to government statements since 1997, devolution will not weaken the British state as a whole but will permanently strengthen it.

It does not make much sense to go into the details of the early stages and implementations of devolution here. They are contained in the two White Papers on Scottish and Welsh devolution[3] and in all the newspapers. But it is worthwhile pointing out three aspects of the regionalism issue in the United Kingdom.

Firstly, there is a difference between Scotland and Wales with regard to the intensity of the demand for autonomy. So far, it has been less intense in Wales than in Scotland, as shown quite emphatically by the referenda of September 1997.

Secondly, since the nineteenth century, the aim of the majority of Scottish and Welsh regionalists has not been to break away from the British state, as was the case with Ireland. What Scotland and Wales want is political and cultural autonomy whereby important political offices are transferred from an over-powerful government in London to regional bodies. The technical term for this is 'devolution'. 'Devolution'

---

3   The Scottish Office (ed.), *Scotland's Parliament. Presented to Parliament by the Secretary of State for Scotland by Command of Her Majesty*, Cm 3658 (London: The Stationery Office, 1997). The Welsh Office (ed.), *A Voice for Wales. Presented to Parliament by the Secretary of State for Wales by Command of Her Majesty*, Cm 3718 (London: The Stationery Office, 1997).

is not another word for federalism, but means that the Westminster parliament, i.e. the parliament of the United Kingdom as a whole, devolves certain responsibilities to regional bodies in Scotland and Wales. However, parliament retains the right to take back these responsibilities if necessary. In other words: Westminster does not give up its all-embracing claim to sovereignty in principle, but gives up certain areas of legislation, on condition that they can be taken back. This has already been put into practice in the case of Northern Ireland. In 1972, as a reaction to the Troubles, London revoked the autonomy of the Northern Ireland parliament, which it had had since 1921, and reimposed direct control by central government.

Thirdly, the Labour government's concept of devolution, as publicly stated in 1997, provides for Scotland and Wales to be dealt with in different ways. Each will be given autonomous status, but the authority of their respective parliaments will differ considerably. For example, the Scottish Parliament will be given limited power to levy taxes – the Welsh Assembly will not, which, strangely enough, at no stage has ever been justified by the government in London, nor by either of the White Papers on Welsh and Scottish devolution. The fact that the devolved status of Scotland and Wales will not be the same can possibly only be explained by history. The political link between Wales and England is known (or considered) to be much stronger than between England and Scotland. Moreover, the political and cultural identity of the Scots seems to be more highly developed than that of the Welsh. Whether this difference in status will be maintained in the future remains to be seen. However that may be, now that the Welsh and Scottish parliaments have been established the political structure of the United Kingdom will become more similar to those found in the 'rest' of Europe, especially Germany, Austria, Belgium and Spain.[4]

What has been briefly hinted at in this outline of regionalism in Western Europe perhaps makes it obvious that recourse to history and cultural particularities plays a crucial role in all regionalisms. It legitimises political agitation. So, in conclusion, one should mention two forms of regionalism in Western Europe in which, interestingly, the historical dimension is almost completely absent and which, in consequence, seem at first sight to be rather artificial and constructed.

This is, firstly, the phenomenon of the Euro-regions or euregios, and, secondly, a peculiar brand of regionalism in northern Italy which, so far, is unique in Western Europe. In the case of the Euro-regions, we are dealing with a form of regionalism whose primary aim is not to loosen the political structures of the nation-state. Rather, it seeks to abolish

4 The Scottish Parliament was established in May 1999, as a result of the referendum of 11 September 1997 and the Scotland Act (1998) (see: http://www.scottish.parliament.uk). Likewise, the National Assembly for Wales was established in 1999 based on the Government of Wales Act (1998) (see http://www.wales.gov.uk) [Editors' Note].

national borders and instigate international cooperation, on the basis of the common interests of neighbouring regions. Sometimes, it is only with great difficulty that a common cultural or historical identity can be constructed for the Euro-regions, a large number of which have emerged in recent years. The demand for the creation of a Euro-region can most easily be justified by reference to common interests and a common mentality among the people who ignore political borders.

Common interests, either real or imagined, also seem to be the binding agent for north Italian regionalism. Its goal is to split up the Italian nation-state and to form a sovereign Padanian Republic (so called after the *Pianura Padana*, the Po Plain). The 'mental regionalism' of the *Lega Nord*, founded over a decade ago, cannot link up with any historical precedents since northern Italy was never politically united. With about 27 million inhabitants and a prosperous economy, it would be a political creation that invokes the common identity of the northern Italians and picks up, in some distant respects, the old divisions between northern and southern Italy. A cultural division, which has never completely disappeared, seems to be gaining ground here again. Whether 'mental regionalism', which has bolstered itself by economic arguments, will gain political significance in Italy in the foreseeable future remains to be seen. Even if it lacks a historical dimension in the traditional sense, this does not necessarily have any bearing on its chances of political success. The 'mental regionalism' of the *Lega Nord* may turn out to be a short-lived political curiosity, especially at a time when borders are being redefined almost everywhere. But in the long run it may also suggest a perspective which makes the nation-state of the nineteenth century into a complete anachronism.

At any rate, at the beginning of the twenty-first century, it looks as if the prevailing image of the ethnically homogeneous, centralist nation-state, unchallenged for so long, has now served its time, at least in Western and East-Central Europe. Its shortcomings have become too obvious. So historians and social scientists are discussing new models of state organisation that are more appropriate to the changed political circumstances and developments in Europe than the old-style principles of the nation-state inherited from the nineteenth century. In view of the increasingly evident fault-lines in every nation, the sociologist Ralf Dahrendorf has therefore pleaded for a fundamental modification of the concept of the ethnically homogeneous nation-state. In Europe, he maintains, the homogeneous nation-state has never been more than rhetoric, has never been reality. For two centuries, and to this day, all that the fiction of a homogeneous nation-state and homogeneous nation has produced is intolerance and illiberality, violence and aggression.

Dahrendorf suggests that, since for the time being we cannot do without it, the nation-state should be understood as a 'heterogeneous nation-state'. There are, he says, two simple reasons for conceiving of the state in this way: (1) The democratic nation-state is still the only effective guarantee of basic and civil rights. It encompasses the sphere of validity of a constitution, and is therefore a constitutional state, thus indispensable for the time being. (2) Heterogeneity is a characteristic of liberal polities. To quote Dahrendorf: 'Heterogeneity promotes the firm foundation of general institutions, and at the same time practical respect for cultural particularities (Dahrendorf 1993: 109).'

The concept of the heterogeneous nation-state that encompasses and respects Europe's democratic and liberal traditions as well as its national and regional particularities, as outlined by Dahrendorf, has certainly not yet been fully developed. However, it offers the prospect that within the nation-state democratic self-determination and political participation are possible for all. Advocating the heterogeneous nation-state, Dahrendorf, rather implicitly, also passes judgement on regionalism. Within the heterogeneous nation-state regionalist aspirations turn out to be among the driving forces to further tolerance, more liberalism and more political participation for the individual.

Enemies of all manifestations of regionalism, on the other hand, like to call it an anti-modern, backward-looking bunch of political ideas, directed against the main trends of the time, namely the creation of larger political entities and globalisation. Both views speculate on what the future holds. The historian cannot enter this competition because, surely, he is not a prophet.

References and Selected Bibliography

BALAKRISHNAN, Gopal (ed.) (1996). *Mapping the Nation*. London/New York: Verso.

BLOTEVOGEL, Hans-Heinrich (1993). 'Vom Kohlenrevier zur Region? Anfänger regionaler Identitätsbildung im Ruhrgebiet.' In: *Erneuerung des Ruhrgebiets. Regionales Erbe und Gestaltung für die Zukunft*, H. Dürr and J. Gramke (eds). Paderborn: Schöningh, pp. 47–52.

BOGDANOR, Vernon (1979). *Devolution*. Oxford: Oxford University Press.

BRUNN, Gerhard (ed.) (1996). *Region und Regionsbildung in Europa. Konzeptionen der Forschung und empirische Befunde*. Baden-Baden: Nomos.

CAPLAN, Richard, and John FEFFER (eds) (1996). *Europe's New Nationalism: States and Minorities in Conflict*. Oxford: Oxford University Press.

CONNOR, Walker (1994). *Ethnonationalism: The Quest for Understanding*. Princeton, NJ: Princeton University Press.

CONVERSI, Daniele (1997). *The Basques, the Catalans and Spain: Alternative Routes to Nationalist Mobilisation*. London: Hurst & Co.

DAHRENDORF, Ralf (1993). 'Die Sache mit der Nation.' In: *Grenzfälle: Über neuen und alten Nationalismus*, Michael Jeismann and Henning Ritter (eds). Leipzig: Reclam Verlag.

DUWE, Kurt (ed.) (1987). *Regionalismus in Europa. Beiträge über kulturelle und sozioökonomische Hintergründe des politischen Regionalismus*. Frankfurt am Main: Peter Lang.

FINLAY, Richard J. (1997). *A Partnership for Good? Scottish Politics and the Union since 1880*. Edinburgh: John Donald.

FITZMAURICE, John (1996). *The Politics of Belgium: A Unique Federalism*. Boulder, CO/London: Westview Press.

GERDES, Dirk (ed.) (1980). *Aufstand der Provinz: Regionalismus in Westeuropa*. Frankfurt am Main/New York: Campus Verlag.

HARVIE, Christopher (1994). *The Rise of Regional Europe*. London: Routledge.

KEATING, Michael (1988). *State and Regional Nationalism. Territorial Politics and the European State*. New York/London: Harvester/Wheatsheaf.

LEVY, Carl (ed.) (1996). *Italian Regionalism. History, Identity and Politics*. Oxford: Berg.

LOTTES, Günther (ed.) (1992). *Region, Nation, Europa*. Heidelberg: Physica Verlag.

LYNCH, Peter (1996). *Minority Nationalism and European Integration*. Cardiff: University of Wales Press.

MAR-MOLINERO Clare, and Angel SMITH (eds) (1996). *Nationalism and the Nation in the Iberian Peninsula. Competing and Conflicting Identities*. Oxford: Oxford University Press.

MILWARD, Alan S. (1992). *The European Rescue of the Nation State*. London: Routledge.

SHARPE, L.J. (1985) 'Devolution and Celtic Nationalism in the United Kingdom.' *West European Politics* 8, pp. 82–100.

STANGLER, Gottfried, and Elisabeth VYSLONZIL (eds) (1996). *Europa und seine Regionen*. Frankfurt am Main: Peter Lang.

TÄGIL, Sven (ed.) (1984). *Regions in Upheaval: Ethnic Conflict and Political Mobilization*. Kristianstad: Kristianstads Boktryckeri AB.

VON KROSIGK, Friedrich (1980). 'Zwischen Folklore und Revolution. Regionalismus in Westeuropa.' In: *Aufstand der Provinz: Regionalismus in Westeuropa*, Dirk Gerdes (ed.). Frankfurt am Main/New York: Campus Verlag.

WICKER, Hans-Rudolf (ed.) (1997). *Rethinking Nationalism and Ethnicity: The Struggle for Meaning and Order in Europe*. Oxford: Berg.

WIEDMANN, Thomas (1996). *Idee und Gestalt der Region in Europa*. Baden-Baden: Nomos.

CHAPTER TWO

Conflicts Between East European States and Minorities in an Age of Democracy[1]

Tom Gallagher

Nationalism has defined political life in Eastern Europe for well over a century. Some thirty peoples have attempted to coexist in the lands stretching from the Baltic to the Black Sea. They practise four principal religions – Roman Catholicism, Orthodoxy, Islam, and Protestantism. They speak numerous languages and use three different scripts – Latin, Greek and Cyrillic. This article mainly focuses on the Balkans and East-Central Europe (including the Ukraine and the Baltic States), but comparisons are made with the Transcaucasus and Central Asia to show how aspects of communist rule and its demolition have had destructive effects on interethnic relations across the Soviet bloc.

In the nineteenth and early twentieth centuries, most of these groups came to regard themselves as actual or potential nations which needed a state of their own to affirm their uniqueness and guarantee security. The concept of national self-determination had been popularised by the impact of the 1789 French Revolution and it seemed to acquire universal validity when the President of the United States, Woodrow Wilson, singled it out in 1917 as the new organising concept for the new Central and Eastern Europe shorn of multinational empires. Two concentrated waves of state creation, in the aftermath of the First World War and following the collapse of the Soviet Union in the early 1990s, attested to the vitality of a principle which, when applied, has often been beset with problems (Brubaker 1995: 107).

In both phases of dynamic European nationalism, state builders have usually asserted that if the new entity does not already possess a common cultural and historical heritage, steps must be taken to realise this aim

1   A comparable version of this paper has been published as 'Conflicts between East European States and Minorities in an Age of Democracy,' *Democratization* 5: 3 (1998), and is reproduced with kind permission of the publisher, Frank Cass.

(Nodia 1996a: 109). The dominant elite often chooses to define the nation in linguistic and cultural terms even if it is ethnically mixed. Most new states in fact continued to be ethnically mixed, despite the periodic warfare between 1914 and the 1990s which has seen the expulsion and even attempted extermination of several ethnic groups. In 1995 it was estimated that of the 410 million people living in Eastern Europe and the Commonwealth of Independent States (CIS), approximately one-fifth belonged to national and ethnic minorities (Brunner 1996: 62).

Insiders and Outsiders in the State-Building Era

National minorities are 'essentially collectivities that have found themselves dominated by the moral and cultural agendas of other, larger groups by having been included in nation-state formations where their relative weight is small' (Schöpflin 1991: 58). With few exceptions, minorities claim a national identity different from that of the core ethnic group in the state. It is an identity they wish to preserve and hand on to the next generation. This goal has given rise to different strategies, ranging from statehood to amalgamation of the territories they inhabit with a state dominated by their coethnics, to demands for institutions and laws which give official recognition to their identity.

The call for group rights was the customary demand of minorities in the 1990s. It was one resisted to a greater or lesser extent by the majority ethnic group. The core ethnic group may well recall that its own drive for independence and statehood originally started with demands for group rights that did not question the continued existence of the state it was then a part of.[2] A history of territorial conflict between dominant and subordinate groups means that few states are ready to accept minority demands with equanimity. The violent collapse of dynastic empires and the tendency of nation building efforts by successor states to be subverted by invasion, war and revolution, makes such reluctance to redefine majority–minority relationships understandable.

There are ample historical precedents for today's majorities becoming tomorrow's minorities. Between the 1870s and the 1990s, the reconstitution of power and opportunity among different nationalities occurred sometimes quite suddenly and with drastic results. Previously ascendant groups, such as the Hungarians and the Russians, found substantial portions of themselves reduced to minority status in the 1920s and the 1990s as a result of the contraction of their states. Majorities-turned-into-minorities

---

2 When the British Conservatives opposed home rule for Scotland after 1979, it was clear by their arguments that they shared the common East European mindset that a small measure of autonomy would inevitably give rise to demands leading ultimately to complete separation.

were often subjected to the discriminatory measures which they had exercised before such a role reversal had occurred. The transient nature of
boundaries and states thus often strengthened the predisposition of nationalist elites to impose cultural uniformity once they gained control of
territories which they regarded as their natural homelands.

Building a state identity that includes elements of minority culture
usually proves unacceptable in the heady atmosphere following independence. Instead, exchanges of population, expulsion, or the
marginalisation of minorities became normal practice in many new
states after 1918 intent on cultural uniformity. A precedent was established when Muslim populations were driven out of Serbia, Greece and
Bulgaria following their acquisition of independence (Khan 1995:
466–8). The way that religion reinforced nationalism made the presence
of large numbers of Muslims in avowedly Christian states unacceptable,
even if they sprang from the same South Slav stock as state-building
nations. The same applied in the 1990s when religious criteria were used
to justify the 'ethnic cleansing' of Bosnian Muslims by other South Slavs
driven by religious imperatives.

When the great powers were moved to protect minority rights (as they
were in pre-1918 Romania when Jews were denied full citizenship rights)
(Kellogg 1995: 39–67), they met stubborn resistance from nationalist
elites. By the early 1920s, the powers speaking for the international
community had concluded that exchanges of population of the kind
occurring between Greece and Turkey might be a more effective way of
guaranteeing a precarious international peace. The 1923 Treaty of
Lausanne legitimised the exchange of minorities in this instance. It was
approved by the League of Nations, whose existence 'marked a conceptual and political leap forward in the direction of international
government or at least international regulation' (Pearson 1983: 139).
The League of Nations attempted to regulate the tense situation arising
from the incomplete and partial application of the self-determination
concept in East-Central Europe. But it was a regulatory institution
which had modest resources, and it was ultimately unable to persuade
governments to honour the provisions for minority protection (often
vaguely expressed) in the peace treaties they had signed (Nuñez 1994:
519–20). Minorities increasingly looked to coethnics in charge of their
own state for salvation rather than a League which was known in some
revisionist states as 'the Jailer of Versailles' (Pearson 1983: 143). They
often found themselves scapegoated and dubbed 'the enemy within'
when majority state-building projects ran into trouble in the depressed
1930s. Discrimination and their own desire to escape from a subordinate
status radicalised minorities and sometimes predisposed their leaders to
combine with external forces to subvert the Versailles settlement. The
rise of totalitarian power in the Soviet Union and then in Italy and
Germany helped sweep away most of the new states of Eastern Europe

between 1938 and 1941. But their attachment to intransigent nationalism had already gravely undermined their cohesion: the alienation of
minorities and refusal to promote regional cooperation by strengthening
economic ties with neighbours, made the new states acutely vulnerable
to changes in the international system.

Communism and Minorities

On the surface, the triumph of Soviet-led communism after 1945 promised an end to debilitating interethnic conflicts. Nationalism was
dismissed as the tool of bourgeois forces, and there was the expectation
that communist modernisation would lead to the steady erosion of
national differences (Schöpflin 1991: 51). But there was a contrasting
response among peoples of the region to the brief heyday of internationalism on Soviet terms. Not surprisingly, minorities that felt
disadvantaged before 1945 showed a *relatively* high level of support. But
minority groups proved a flimsy base of support for a new social system
with vaulting ambitions, especially when the majority was historically
distrustful of the Russians (as was the case in Romania).

Minorities eventually found themselves under pressure when communist rule failed to overcome problems of structural underdevelopment
but instead exacerbated them through a reliance on antediluvian heavy
industry. When the Soviet Union relaxed its control, unpopular elites
began to appeal to the national feeling of the majority population wher-
ever this was felt to be expedient. Communism as a doctrine was suited
more to ethnic homogenisation than to promoting ethnic pluralism, so
the development may not have been merely a desperate stratagem by
elites seeking popularity. Afterwards, some nationalities were favoured
at the expense of others by the limiting of access to the ranks of the elite
and by the creation of unequal opportunities for social advancement
(Khazanov 1997: 123). This characterised Southeastern Europe in
particular, where state-led efforts to assimilate the Hungarian minority
in Transylvania had resumed by the 1960s. Thus, the nationalist variant
of Marxism-Leninism seen in Romania resulted in furious efforts by a
personalist leadership to forge a single national culture and merge
diverse populations into one single mass.

State efforts to reconfigure ethnic relations had already gone much
further in the Soviet Union. Arbitrary redrawing of boundaries in the
1920s later envenomed relations between Armenia and Azerbaijan and
between several of the Central Asian republics. The deportation of
entire peoples – the Crimean Tartars and the Chechens – also left deep
wounds that failed to heal. These brutal efforts at social engineering
created resentments which enormously complicated attempts to break

free from authoritarianism in the 1990s. Efforts at homogenisation that stopped short of forced resettlement (as in the Baltic States) also produced a desire for accounts to be settled in a radical manner. The ending of the communist era did not inaugurate an era of improved ethnic relations. The emphasis on homogenisation, and on internal and external enemies, had a negative effect on political culture as did the devaluation of civil society and emphasis on authoritarian solutions for problems large and mundane. The virtual absence of civil society and the suppression of all voluntary organisations and institutions independent of the state made the appeal of individualistic liberal ideas rather weak and abstract (Khazanov 1997: 125).

Nationalism was used in numerous parts of the former Soviet bloc to 'provide a new rationalization and legitimization of the old but threatened power of the apparatus' (Dyker 1995: 55). It was quickly realised that the promotion of a political system where competition was along ethnic lines could preserve much of the authority of communist-era figures in the context of pluralism. In most post-communist states, flawed and chaotic 'reforms' created few winners and many losers. In some instances elites, engaging in speculative and corrupt economic activity, did not hesitate to deliberately encourage violence 'to create a domestic political context where ethnicity is the only relevant identity' (Gagnon, Jr. 1994–5: 132).

States discriminating against minorities can be divided into two broad types:
1. Post-communist ones where the rulers combine ethnic nationalism with remnants of communist authoritarianism.
2. Newly independent states usually ruled by avowed anti-communists.

'Nomenklatura' Nationalism

In countries which renounce Marxism-Leninism but where there is strong continuity in leadership, obvious advantages flow from creating a political system where competition is along ethnic lines.
1. Emphasising an ethnic threat can preserve the authority of communist-era figures in the context of pluralism and block a transfer of power.
2. Attention is often diverted from abuses and injustices as privatisation occurs according to informal mechanisms and a new economic oligarchy springs up shaped around elements of the old communist *nomenklatura*.
3. In this context, electorates are often willing to put up with bad government and poorly institutionalised and corrupt regimes can survive in office for long periods despite policy failures.

In 1990 two examples of incitement to violence from opposite ends of the communist world occurred within a few months of each other, suggesting that the recourse to nationalist extremism was a natural reflex from communists under pressure.

In the Soviet Central Asian Republic of Kyrgyzstan in June 1990, traditional elements within the ruling Communist Party manipulated and revived dormant ethnic conflict between Kyrgyz and Uzbek peoples. They spread rumours of reciprocal massacres that never happened and provoked the two communities without allowing the security forces to intervene on time; these 'old guard' elements wished to present themselves as arbiters so that they could recover their role as the dominant political force (Terzani 1993: 183).

Three months earlier, remarkably similar events had unfolded in the Romanian city of Tîrgu Mureş, inhabited by ethnic Romanians and Hungarians in almost equal proportions. Hungarians, who had been in the overwhelming majority until large numbers of Romanians from other parts of the country had been resettled in Tîrgu Mureş in the 1970s and 1980s, quickly sought to reverse discriminatory policies after the downfall of the national communist regime of Nicolae Ceauşescu. As the Hungarians were demanding the return of their educational facilities, local Romanian officials, who had benefited from anti-Hungarian measures, spread unfounded rumours in several outlying villages about Hungarian attacks on children from the villages being schooled in the city. Groups of villagers, given rudimentary weapons and transportation, travelled to the city and attacked Hungarians. Days of violence in the second half of March 1990 ensued and the security forces only intervened when it appeared that the Hungarians might be getting the upper hand.[3]

President Ion Iliescu exploited these events to consolidate his hold on power. The secret police was revived because of the danger to internal security. The ruling National Salvation Front sought to use nationalism to prevent normal political competition and any peaceful transfer of power. They were successful, and a regime notorious for its policy failures and corruption was able to stay in power until 1996.

In Yugoslavia, the communist parties in each of the republics manipulated nationalism in order to preserve what they could of their privileges. The Slovene and Croat parties wished for a loose federation, while the Serbian party wished to recentralise Yugoslavia around what had been the most influential of the republics. In Serbia, there is abundant evidence that 'ethnic entrepreneurs' deliberately stoked up ethnic conflict as a means of obtaining wealth or acquiring political power.

3   For accounts of these events which agree on the essential details, see Rady (1992: 145–59); *Human Rights in Romania Since the Revolution* (New York: Helsinki Watch Report, 1991); and Gallagher (1995a: 87–88).

Under cover of patriotism, many Serb paramilitary groups in Bosnia and Croatia became 'rapacious looting machines' so that defending Serbdom 'was indistinguishable from making money' (Judah 1997: 242). Cynical manipulators of nationalism, motivated by the desire for political power or wealth, were able to incite nationalist 'true believers'. Slobodan Milošević, the Serbian ruler who was the only pre-1989 communist political chief still running his country in the late 1990s, is the arche-typal example of the ethnic entrepreneur, though he lost control of his acolytes in Serb Bosnia when they showed that they were determined to pursue their expulsion of Muslims to its murderous conclusion.

Intolerance from the Right and Centre

It is easy to overlook the fact that in Central Europe and parts of the former Soviet Union, ethnic nationalism has been promoted most avowedly by anti-communists. In the Baltic States, Croatia and Georgia – new states that had regarded themselves as forcibly incorporated into supranational entities – minorities quickly found themselves oppressed once these states acquired independence.

In these newly independent states, elites were quick to regard their minorities as tools of their former communist overlords. In the Baltic States, the evidence is unconvincing since there was massive support among the Russian minorities for the independence of the states in which they resided (Grigorievs 1996: 20–22). But in Estonia and Latvia, the Russian minority was effectively denied citizenship. New laws made place of birth and ancestry the main qualification for citizenship. Since most ethnic Russians had settled in the Baltic States after independence was lost in 1940, they were not eligible for citizenship and they could not vote in elections. One source makes a plausible case for arguing that the reasons for excluding noncitizens from the electoral rolls in Estonia and Latvia were identical: 'to boost the number of voters for the parties in power and reduce the numbers likely to vote against them' (Grigorievs 1996: 128). Ethnic survival was used to justify such measures; the Latvian draft law, debated in parliament in 1992, was entitled 'On Suspending Some Conventional Human Rights to Ensure the Survival of the Latvian Nation' (Grigorievs 1996: 134).

The Baltic experience confirms the view of Oscar Jaszi, the Hungarian specialist on minority issues, first propounded in the 1920s, that 'the political morals of an oppressed nation change when it comes to power.'[4] The Baltic experience shows all too clearly that even where minorities use the language of human rights and international liberalism to

4   Quoted in Bookman (1994: 68).

promote their cause, they are in danger of reverting to the methods of their former oppressors in order to clinch their goals.

In an even starker form, Croatia shows how nationalism can be transformed from an emancipatory force to an oppressive ideology. An ethnically exclusive state claiming to be a middle European democracy has been created against the background of war and the loss of territory (mostly since regained in 1995). The Serb minority has been under heavy pressure to assimilate or leave.[5] The nationalist leadership around President Franjo Tudjman was unwilling to treat Serbs as equal citizens whose religious, cultural and linguistic identity is respected. Government actions suggested that the Tudjman regime regarded all Serbs as tools of hardliners in Belgrade, the capital of rump Yugoslavia, even though the evidence for this was unconvincing.[6]

New states motivated by liberal values can be tempted to shape ethnicity around the majority ethnicity and reject multiculturalism if internal problems diminish their commitment to liberalism. Russia in the mid-1990s provides some confirmatory evidence of this. Some of the anti-communist reformers around President Boris Yeltsin who had encouraged the Baltic peoples to affirm their sovereignty were, by now, moving in an increasingly nationalist direction (Tairov 1995: 49). The breakaway province of Chechnya was invaded in December 1994, the prelude to two years of savage warfare which ended in the withdrawal of Russian forces and the confirmation of Chechnyan self-determination. It is probably no coincidence that the Russian leadership embarked upon this costly military adventure to compensate for internal failures which had resulted in a slump in its popularity. The nationalism of its radical opponents was borrowed in an attempt to recover some popular appeal. This strategy even led part of the Russian elite to covertly promote ethnoterritorial conflict in Georgia between Georgians and the Abkhazian and Ossetian minorities, as well as in parts of Central Asia.[7] Parts of the Caucasus were perhaps disposed to ethnic conflict owing to the highly complex ethnic composition of the

5   See the Report on Human Rights in the Republic of Croatia for 1996 (Zagreb: The Croatian Helsinki Committee for Human Rights, 1997), p. 20.

6   One expert on minority issues, however, has backed the Croatian position. Georg Brunner has written that 'the Serb rebellion in the Croat Krajina in August 1990, the war of conquest against Croatia in the second half of 1991 and the war of extermination started in April 1992 violently proved the unwillingness of the Serbs to accept their minority status even under the conditions of an adequate protection of minorities' (Brunner 1996: 79). Since Tudjman's death in December 1999, the new Croat leadership has been focusing on the return of displaced persons, including that of ethnic Serbs to the Krajina and Eastern Slavonia regions of Croatia. It has also been cooperating with the International War Crimes Tribunal in The Hague [Editors' Note].

7   For evidence and detailed analysis see the articles in Warreport 34 (June 1995), pp. 20–50, on ethnic conflict in the former Soviet Union. For the Chechnya conflict, see Gall and De Wall (1997).

region and the strength of historic grievances. But Russian attempts to reassert overlordship over outlying parts of the former Soviet empire undoubtedly exacerbated interethnic tension and led to intense localised violence, when it might have been hoped that conflict at this level could have been avoided.

Some of the most worrying instances of anti-minority discourses in Eastern Europe have emerged from the Czech Republic. There, the transition to democracy and to a market economy has probably been the smoothest in the entire former Soviet bloc. The government of Premier Václav Klaus (1991–7) had few of the problems of political legitimacy which have prompted contemporaries elsewhere to play the nationalist card. However, by the mid-1990s human rights watchdogs were cataloguing a mounting wave of discrimination and harassment directed against the Roma (or Gypsy) minority.[8] Alarm was first raised in 1993, shortly after the break-up of Czechoslovakia, when a citizenship law was passed which many believed had been crafted to exclude as many Roma as possible from citizenship (Nagle 1997: 38–39). It specified a requirement of five years without a criminal conviction, the proportion of Roma found guilty of minor crimes being much higher than that for other groups. Roma born in Slovakia who had moved to the Czech Republic when both entities had been one state, could be denied citizenship if they fell foul of the Prague authorities. The Office of the UN High Commissioner for Refugees (UNHCR) and the Council of Europe both concluded that the 1993 Czech citizenship law violated international standards (Nagle 1997: 40).[9]

Official disdain is matched by public hostility to the Roma (Pehe 1994: 52). There is a wide body of evidence to suggest that 'local police authorities in the Czech Republic have no intention of protecting Roma citizens and often their actions clear the way for further attacks' (Nagle 1997: 37). It is perhaps no coincidence that the Czech Republic harbours the largest ethnoradical party in Eastern Europe outside the former Yugoslavia, Miroslav Sládek's Republican Party, which has tirelessly promoted anti-Roma feeling (Hockenos 1993: 224–8; Pehe 1994: 51–53).

The international reaction to the discriminatory laws against minorities in the Czech Republic and the Baltic States has been a muted one. Western policy makers often assume that a government like Klaus's with a strong record on economic reform will automatically conform with other liberal-democratic norms and that there is no need to subject its

---

8   See Gomez (1995: 18); and the numerous Reuters reports carried on the web-site *Central Europe Online*, http://www.centraleurope.com, from July to September 1997.

9   In 1999, the Czech authorities adopted amendments to the citizenship law, enabling thousands of stateless Roma to gain Czech citizenship. Still, in August 2001, the UN Human Rights Committee expressed deep concern about the Czech government's treatment of Roma [Editors' Note].

record on minorities to close scrutiny. Central Europe as a whole (excepting Slovakia) is usually viewed uncritically as a haven of tolerance, certainly when compared with the Balkans. The negative image of Southeastern Europe means that the way a country like Romania treats its Roma population receives far more scrutiny than does the Czech Republic even though the evidence suggests that the Roma may even enjoy worse conditions in the Czech Republic than in proverbially xenophobic Romania. The slowness of the West to wake up to the human rights situation in the Czech Republic may indirectly be promoting anti-minority discrimination.

States actively ill-treating minorities seem to assume that the attention span of the rest of the world is limited and that even if ill-treatment arouses controversy, it will be a temporary inconvenience. Serbia's strongman, Slobodan Milošević, relied upon the myopia of the West when he orchestrated ethnic cleansing in parts of the former Yugoslavia which he wished to absorb into a Greater Serbia. The reluctance of the Western powers to act decisively until the fourth year of fighting in the former Yugoslavia suggests that the judgement was not without foundation (even though Milošević overreached himself by the scale of the bloodshed which proxy forces initially under his leadership unleashed, mainly against unarmed civilians).

Post-communist regimes of different complexions can employ a wide range of devices to make minorities feel unwelcome. Citizens' rights can be denied to them or else made subject to onerous conditions. They can be excluded from the privatisation of the state-led economy by various discretionary measures. New constitutions can refrain from acknowledging the existence of ethnic minorities and even discriminate against them by prohibiting parties based on ethnic groups, as happens in Bulgaria (Brunner 1996: 112). School textbooks can promote negative images, as in Romania where, up to 1997, history books still described Hungarians as adversaries of Romanians.[10] Demagogues who incite anti-minority violence can operate with immunity from the law and sometimes with the covert or real encouragement of the authorities. Economic pressure can be exerted to induce minorities to leave the territory they inhabit. Finally, attempts can be made by armed groups operating with the blessing of the central authorities to drive out and kill ethnic minority members, as happened from 1991 to 1995 in ex-Yugoslavia, the Serbian and Croatian states, as well as the rebel Serb authorities in Bosnia being the main proponents of what became known as 'ethnic cleansing'.

10 This was the claim of György Frunda, the ethnic Hungarian candidate in the 1996 Romanian presidential elections, in interviews with the journalist Elena Stefoi (1997: 29).

The Minority Response

Compared with Western Europe, the violent response of minorities in Eastern Europe (see Table 2.1) to situations of duress seems to be the exception rather than the rule. Movements like ETA and the IRA have been conspicuous by their absence. The correlation between minority protest and violence in Western Europe is much higher, as the periodic or long-term unrest in Corsica, the Basque Country, South Tyrol and Northern Ireland attests. Fear of the majoritarian state seems to be a strong disincentive towards using violence; there is no record of states voluntarily conceding minority demands in Eastern Europe or even showing an eagerness to negotiate. But when the state radically alters its character or new ones emerge on mixed territory, submerged groups can become more militant. It took attempted expulsions and mass killings before Bosnian Muslims spawned a state nationalism of their own. The break-up of the Soviet Union quickly led to protracted strife in the Caucasus with its complicated ethnic geography. Leaving aside the Caucasus and parts of ex-Yugoslavia, it is worth noting that there is no tradition of bearing arms across much of Eastern Europe. Minorities under pressure thus are more likely to respond with nonviolent action. Tactics which minorities normally pursue to promote their goals are:

1. Participation in state and local elections. This has resulted in minority parties being included in the government when no party has had an overall majority as, for example, in Bulgaria in the early 1990s and in Romania from 1996.[11]
2. Taking their case to European and internal fora (see below).
3. Nonviolent civil disobedience (as in Kosovo) or petitions and rallies to show their unhappiness with state behaviour towards them.

There may be additional reasons for this kind of nonviolent response:

- *Low levels of political awareness or a tradition of passivity.* The Roma lack national consciousness and a single identity. Their traditional ambivalence and flexibility about national allegiance has endangered them in many parts of ex-Yugoslavia, in a new political context defined by ethnicity and strident nationalism. Disunity may also impede a radical minority response.
- *Good-quality leadership enhances the moderate option.* The Hungarians of Romania and the Turks of Bulgaria faced the most concerted assimilationist drive in the region before 1989. Instead of meeting force with force when the state relaxed its grip, skilful and nonviolent movements emerged from the Hungarian and Turkish minorities. The pragmatic stance may have paid off: both the Democratic Alliance of

---

11 As well as in Slovakia since 1998. In Macedonia, since 1994, an ethnic Albanian party has been included in government [Editors' Note].

Hungarians in Romania (UDMR) and the (Turkish) Movement for Rights and Freedoms (MRF) entered the government at critical moments in their countries' protracted democratic transition. The Albanian population also stands out for its nonviolent response to the systematic discrimination it has encountered in Kosovo after 1989. It has adopted a strategy of nonviolence against the Milošević regime, but its aims remain radical: secession from rump Yugoslavia.

• *The placing of minority rights on the European and world agenda.* In 1992, the United Nations issued a Declaration on the Rights of Persons Belonging to National or Ethnic, Religious and Linguistic Minorities. It was the first time the UN had drawn up a declaration exclusively devoted to minority concerns. The OSCE and the Council of Europe have also issued documents containing specific standards regarding rights of persons belonging to national minorities that states have to adhere to (Hyde-Price 1994: 237; Jackson Preece 1997: 353).

Self-aware minorities subject to ill-treatment have usually been more pragmatic than their prewar counterparts. The need to attract the attention or goodwill of the international community has helped to moderate demands. Minority behaviour in the 1990s has been characterised by the following responses:

1. *Irredentism or secession has declined as a goal.*

   Since 1994 Hungary, with over 4 million coethnics in neighbouring states, has categorically rejected seeking border revisions in its favour. Albania and Russia are too preoccupied with internal problems to be tempted by irredentism. The only minority with an explicit separatist agenda are the Albanians of Kosovo (who constitute a majority in this province whose autonomy was suspended by Serb-dominated Yugoslavia in 1989). The emergence of the Kosovo Liberation Army (KLA) in 1997–8 testified to this separatist agenda.

2. *Group rights which will enable minorities to preserve their identity, are a common demand.*

   Institutions or laws are usually sought which will give official recognition and protection to their identity. Language is seen as the kernel of identity and demands for the public use of a minority language in the courts and the local administration as well as the right to be schooled in it, and to enjoy access to radio and TV broadcasts in it, are the most common ones in the minority platform.

   The advent of minority rights in post-1945 Western Europe gives East Europeans a benchmark upon which to base their claims. They often cite as models countries where there are two or more official languages (Finland, Belgium), where there is equal treatment of minority languages with the official one (parts of Italy), and where minority tongues enjoy a large share in state broadcasting (Spain, Wales).

3. *The radical wings of minority parties often call for internal self-government where their community forms a local majority.*
   The rights enjoyed by German speakers in the Italian South Tyrol (autonomy statutes of 1948 and 1972) and in the Autonomous Communities of Spain (1978) are often cited as precedents.
   The Council of Europe, in the much discussed Recommendation 1201,[12] supports the concept of territorial autonomy in regions where minorities predominate. Majoritarian states are usually opposed to the concept, which they see as preparing the way for the detachment of a minority region from state jurisdiction. Minorities themselves hesitate about embracing territorial autonomy because communist social engineering has often resulted in the dispersal of their population (e.g. the Hungarians in Romania). The concept is often viewed with unease by the international community following the numerous and sometimes violent border changes seen in Eastern Europe after 1989: the break-up of the Soviet Union and Yugoslavia in 1991 led to bitter fighting and serious loss of life in Croatia, Bosnia-Herzegovina, Azerbaijan (in the disputed Nagorno-Karabakh area), Georgia, Moldova and in the Russian autonomous area of Chechnya. By contrast, the partition of Czechoslovakia on 1 January 1993 saw the peaceful emergence of the Czech Republic and Slovakia.

Why Elites Show Restraint

International constraints on state behaviour towards minorities can now be applied in order to prevent an escalation of tension. It is probably no longer true to say that state elites have complete sovereignty over national minorities. States which join the Council of Europe have to sign the European Convention on Human Rights and Fundamental Freedoms, which imposes some limits on national state authority and gives hard-pressed citizens the chance to seek redress from state injustice through a higher transnational jurisdiction. Following the Copenhagen meeting of 1990, all OSCE states signed a declaration specifying that 'issues concerning national minorities, as well as compliance with international obligations and commitments concerning the rights of persons belonging to them, are matters of legitimate international concern and consequently, do not constitute exclusively an internal affair of a respective state' (Stan 1997: 10). Political

12 Recommendation 1201 (1993), on an additional protocol on the rights of national minorities to the European Convention on Human Rights, is a document of the Parliamentary Assembly of the Council of Europe (PACE). Article 11 reads: 'In the regions where they are in a majority the persons belonging to a national minority shall have the right to have at their disposal appropriate local or autonomous authorities or to have a special status, matching the specific historical and territorial situation and in accordance with the domestic legislation of the state [Editors' Note].'

TABLE 2.1 National and Ethnic Minorities Constituting more than 1% of the Population in Eastern Europe and the CIS

Country	Census year	National and ethnic minorities
Albania	1989	Greeks 1.8 – 4.4%[a]
Armenia	1992	Kurds 1.7%
Azerbaijan	1989	Russians 6%; Talysh 4.2%; Lezgins 4%; Kurds 2.8%; Armenians 1.41%
Belarus	1989	Russians 13.2%; Poles 4.1%; Ukrainians 2.9%; Jews 1.1%
Bosnia-Herzegovina[b]	1991	Muslims 43.7%; Serbs 31.4%; Croats 17.3%; Yugoslavs 5.5%; Roma 2.3%
Bulgaria	1992	Turks 9.4%; Roma 3.7%; Macedonians 2.9%
Croatia[c]	1991	Serbs 12%; Muslims 1%; Yugoslavs 2.2%
Czech Republic	1991	Moravians 13%; Slovaks 3%; Roma 0.3 – 2.9%
Estonia	1995	Russians 30.3%; Ukrainians 3.1%; Belarusians 1%; Finns 1.1%
Georgia	1995	Armenians 9.1%; Russians 5.4%; Azeris 5.4%; Ajarians 3.3–5.4%; Ossetians 2.9%; Abkhaz 1.9%
Hungary	1992	Roma 2.4–7.8%; Slovaks 0.1–1.2%; Jews up to 1%
Kazakhstan	1994	Russians 34%; Ukrainians 4.8%; Germans 3 – 4%; Uzbeks 2.2%
Kyrgyzstan	1994	Russians 17.1%; Uzbeks 13.8%; Ukrainians 1.8%; Tatars 1.3%
Latvia	1994	Russians 33.1%; Belarusians 4.1%; Ukrainians 3%; Poles 2%; Lithuanians 1.3%
Lithuania	1994	Russians 8.5%; Poles 7%; Belarusians 1%
Macedonia	1994	Albanians 23%; Roma 2.3%-10.3%; Turks 4%; Serbs 2%
Moldova	1992	Ukrainians 13.9%; Russians 13%; Gagauz 3.5%; Bulgarians 2%; Jews 1.5%
Poland	1994	Germans 1.9 – 2.8%; Ukrainians 0.90 – 1.3%
Romania	1992	Hungarians 7.1%; Roma 1.58– 7.9%
Russian Federation	1992	Tatars 3.7%; Ukrainians 2.9%; Chuvash 1.2%
Serbia and Montenegro	1992	Albanians 16.6 – 19%; Hungarians 3.3%; Muslims 3.1%; Roma 1.3 – 4.8%; Croats 1%
Slovakia	1992	Hungarians 10.8%; Roma 1.5–6.6%
Slovenia	1992	Croats 2.7%; Serbs 2.4%; Muslims 1.4%
Tajikistan	1994	Uzbeks 25%; Russians 1.7%; Tatars 1.4%; Kyrgyz 1%
Turkmenistan	1993	Russians 9.5%; Uzbeks 8%; Kazakhs 2.5%
Ukraine	1992	Russians 22%; Jews 0.9%; Belarusians 0.9%; Romanians/Maldovans 0.6%; Bulgarians 0.5%; Crimean Tatars 0.1%
Uzbekistan	1994	Russians 8.3%; Tajiks 4.7%; Kazakhs 4.1%; Volga Tatars 2.4%; Karakalpaks 2.1%

Source: Minority Rights Group International, *World Directory of Minorities* (London: Minority Rights Group International, 1997).

Notes:
a. The lowest and highest estimates for a minority population are given where the official figure is disputed.
b. Over half the population was displaced in the 1992–5 war in this former Yugoslav territory and the ethnic balance of the population has changed considerably.
c. The Serb population has been greatly reduced as a result of the fighting in Western Slavonia and the Krajina in 1995 as well as harassment directed against Serbs in the rest of Croatia.

will needs to be applied to give life to such declarations, but there is evidence to suggest that in countries like Romania they place a break on the advance of ethnic politics and intolerant nationalism at state level.

There are other factors which have restrained nomenklatura nationalism. It is worth recalling that some ex-communist elites have resisted the nationalist temptation. In early 1990, moderates in the still-ruling Bulgarian Communist Party (BCP) sought to contain mass anti-Turkish rallies which were mobilising larger numbers than the pre-democracy ones that had taken place at the end of 1989. In an unusual move, the pragmatic wing of the BCP deliberately promoted the nonnationalist opposition, seeing this strategy as the best way of absorbing the anti-Turkish vote into its own ranks (Drezov 1997: 8). The strategy of decompression contrasts Bulgaria with Romania, where the ex-communist elite rarely displayed similar restraint (Gallagher 1995b: 351–2).

There are also several new states, Macedonia, Moldova and Ukraine (which emerged from the break-up of the Yugoslav and Soviet federations), where the ruling elite preferred to conciliate rather than antagonise its minorities. Parties which descended from the former ruling Communist Party have retained control in usually free and open elections. A range of factors may have shaped this outcome. The need for fragile new states, each of which obtained independence in unexpected circumstances, to win international legitimacy by adhering to recognised norms of conduct in their treatment of minorities is one obvious factor. The reluctance to antagonise a powerful neighbour whose coethnics make up a large portion of the minority population is certainly a factor which weighed on the minds of the post-independence Ukrainian and Moldovan leaderships, which needed to secure the allegiance of Russian minorities whose fate is closely followed in Russia. Finally, in Macedonia, the popularity and leadership skills of Kiro Gligorov, a former communist committed to the liberal ethnic policies of his mentor, Marshall Tito, helped to keep in check tensions between the Slav majority and the growing Albanian minority which, initially, were seen as too great to allow the fledgling state much chance of survival.

In Eastern Europe, there are new factors which may make an antiminority state policy much more of a gamble than previously. The communications revolution now makes forced assimilation very difficult to accomplish (Poulton 1996: 34). Satellite television broadcasting from Hungary and Turkey now helps to preserve minority cultures. Some minorities have powerful friends abroad (e.g. the Greeks of Albania are able to rely on the backing of the powerful Greek lobby in Washington). Meanwhile, overseas Albanians are slowly turning into a mobilised diaspora, channelling funds to the 'parallel state' in Kosovo set up in the 1990s (Vickers and Pettifer 1997). There may be some grounds for thinking that the belated but firm actions of the international community in ex-Yugoslavia, culminating in NATO's 1995 intervention, may have restrained rulers with an anti-minority agenda from carrying through some of their plans.

The growing sophistication of voters can be another restraining factor. With time, it has proven less easy for nomenklatura nationalists to incite the majority against the minority. Leaderships with a record of economic incompetence (true of all ex-nomenklatura regimes, certainly in Southeastern Europe) find that inflammatory rhetoric usually has diminishing appeal. Voters assess their intentions far more sceptically and there is a growing awareness that prospects for a peaceful existence and economic improvements are jeopardised by constant references to race and nation (Nodia 1996b: 25). György Frunda, the Transylvanian Hungarian spokesman, has noticed a maturing of attitudes in his region over seven years: in 1997 he felt it would be impossible to mobilise Romanian villagers and get them to attack Hungarians, as happened in 1990 (Stefoi 1997: 26).

The rise of new political forces on the left has also weakened nomen-klatura nationalism. Ex-communist reformers keen to integrate their countries with the West and willing to accept international norms for minorities and for relations with their neighbours were elected to power in Poland and Hungary in 1993–4. In Poland, the ruling left has pursued reconciliation with Germany and stepped up state protection for the German minority.[13] Following the election of Gyula Horn and the Hungarian Socialist Party in 1994, Hungary reoriented its foreign policy even more radically. Its attitude to neighbouring states was no longer determined solely by how its coethnics were treated there. In treaties with Slovakia (1995) and Romania (1996), Hungary abandoned any claims to territory beyond its frontiers where its coethnics were a major-ity. Hungary also played a low-key role towards the conflict in ex-Yugoslavia during most of its stages even though there was no bilat-eral agreement with Serbia over the position of the Hungarian minority in Vojvodina.

Meanwhile, centre-right reformers made important strides in Romania and Bulgaria in 1996–7 which improved the conditions of national minorities. Progress was dramatic in Romania where the Hungarian minority was included in the coalition government. The desire to be included in Euro-Atlantic integration processes made the reformers far keener to accept liberal European Union norms for minor-ity rights than their predecessors had been. New laws on education and local government removed some of the main minority grievances. In Romania, President Emil Constantinescu and Premier Victor Ciorbea engaged in symbolic confidence building measures to strengthen ties between majority and minority after the politics of divide-and-rule pursued by their ex-communist predecessors. This was a totally new

<hr>

13 For Poland's increasingly liberal minority policy, see Sanford (1997: 61–64).

departure as Frunda, the ethnic Hungarian leader, noted: 'from 1918 till now no leading figure in Romanian politics ever had the courage to say "let us normalise relations with Hungary"' (Stefoi 1997: 26). The Romanian government, of course, remains a nationally minded one, but its commitment to civic rather than ethnic nationalism makes it far easier for the Hungarian minority to resist the separatist temptation and to show loyalty to a state far more responsive to its needs.

But there are a few states that resist these trends. As well as Serbia and Belarus, Slovakia under Mečiar springs to mind. Slovak leaders were not prepared to moderate their anti-minority stance even though it would have boosted their initially good chances of entering NATO. In August 1997 Premier Vladimír Mečiar even suggested the voluntary repatriation of Hungarians living in Slovakia at a summit with his Hungarian counterpart. Such a suggestion revealed the hollowness of the 1995 friendship treaty between the two states: Slovakia still has to implement many of its provisions, especially a law to protect the use of the mother tongue of the Hungarian minority.[14]

In Slovakia, a coalition of ex-communists and extreme right-wingers ruled until 1998. Interestingly, Mečiar was not himself from a nomenklatura background but was a minor dissident at an earlier stage in his career. He must have made a calculation of the advantages likely to flow to him of pursuing a politics of national assertion. The danger is that in other states, such as Romania, where reformers encounter difficulties on the economic front, attempts might be made to steal some of the nationalist clothes for the sake of political survival.

Finally, it is possible to point to two factors which have helped to moderate the behaviour of both majority and minority in societies that may remain deeply divided:

1. *The decline of religion as a variable that can be exploited by nationalists.* In Croatia and several Balkan states with Orthodox national churches, nationalists have been unable to depend on these faiths for backing to the extent that their predecessors could in the inter-war period. In Croatia, the Catholic Church has unambiguously condemned the chauvinism of the Tudjman government while in Serbia and Romania the Orthodox Church has lost much of its popular influence as a result of the close relationship it often enjoyed with the communist authorities.

2. *Intellectuals are no longer the key social group promoting radical nationalism, at least among nationalist majorities.* They appear to be more receptive to international liberal values in the 1990s than in the 1930s, when they were often exponents of authoritarian ideologies.

14 'Tongue-tied,' *The Economist*, 12 September 1997. On 10 July 1999, Slovakia adopted a Law on the Use of Languages of National Minorities. Its implementation, however, has been far from satisfactory according to domestic and international organisations [Editors' Note].

The Internationalisation of the Minority Question

In the 1990s there was a growing realisation that ethnic minority problems are a vital dimension of international security. No longer were they viewed as exclusively domestic issues unless a state goes beyond all civilised conduct in its treatment of minorities. Ingmar Carlsson, the ex-Premier of Sweden and Co-Chair of the UN Commission on Global Governance, declared in 1995 that 'in this increasingly interdependent world, it is clear that what were internal affairs now affect us all' (Carlsson 1995). The time devoted by US President Clinton to solving the Northern Ireland conflict supports this view. His challenger in the 1996 presidential election, Senator Bob Dole, provided even more striking confirmation in 1990 when he was prepared to visit the disputed and still obscure Yugoslav province of Kosovo and chide the Serbian authorities for their systematic abuse of human rights.

But leading European statesmen displayed complacency and naivety as internal conflict in Yugoslavia began spinning out of control in the late 1980s. For nearly two generations, politicians used to managing welfare capitalism had grown forgetful of how destructive conflicts of nationality could be in Europe and they lacked the conceptual tools and the basic insights to devise effective strategies to contain the unrest. There is greater backing now for early warning mechanisms or conflict prevention measures designed to forestall disputes at an early stage. The OSCE High Commissioner on National Minorities, an institution formed at the instigation of the Netherlands in 1992, has played a useful role in interposing itself between alienated minorities and intransigent majority governments, often mediating between the two.

Resourcing and defending pro-reconciliation groups is another useful role that Europe-wide bodies and concerned states can perform. The various national Helsinki Committees have played invaluable roles in countries like Romania and Croatia in documenting human rights abuses and briefing international organisations about local developments; without the protection offered to these NGOs, from Western Europe and further afield, it is sometimes hard to see how they could survive in a climate hostile to defending minority rights, such as that existing in Croatia. Similar external protection also enables newspapers and other media outlets concerned to bridge majority-minority divides to carry on their work relatively unimpeded.

Western transnational bodies have encouraged economic and military cooperation between neighbouring states sometimes estranged from one another because of the perceived ill-treatment of minorities. Indeed, such cooperation has been made a prime condition for integration with Euro-Atlantic security and economic bodies.

1. The Partnership for Peace programme launched by NATO in 1994 has facilitated military cooperation between such erstwhile rivals as Romania and Hungary.

2. The EU has promoted the establishment of regions transcending state boundaries which are to be the focus for economic and infrastructural cooperation. Romania and Poland have embraced the Euro-region concept which is helping to reduce the isolation of Hungarian and German minorities.
3. Since the end of the Bosnian war in 1995, the USA has actively promoted the South-East European Cooperation Initiative (SECI) to revive functional ties between the former Yugoslav states and between them and their neighbours. Pressure has been placed on Croatia in particular to improve ties with estranged neighbours and to protect its Serbian minority.
4. In Central Europe, ethnic nationalism is being challenged by the formation of the Central European Free Trade Area (CEFTA) which is being encouraged by the West. The prospect of ethnic peace in the Balkans would be strengthened by its extension to Southeastern Europe. In November 1997, the leaders of all the Balkan states met for the first time, at a two-day summit in Greece, but it remains to be seen what the outcome will be in terms of practical cooperation.
5. On 10 June 1999, the Stability Pact for Southeastern Europe was adopted in Cologne. The aim of this initiative of the EU, involving more than forty partner countries and organisations, is to strengthen the countries of Southeastern Europe 'in their efforts to foster peace, democracy, respect for human rights and economic prosperity in order to achieve stability in the whole region.' Euro-Atlantic integration is promised to all the countries in the region.

But ultimately it is the disposition of powerful international actors committed in principle to ensuring better protection for minorities who can make a crucial difference, by their willingness to invest energy and quality time in a situation of imminent danger and being prepared to show firmness towards forces endangering ethnic peace. In May 1997 Robin Cook, the new British Foreign Secretary, gave an indication that Britain might have a less fatalistic attitude towards nationalist intolerance in Eastern Europe when he declared that it was his intention to put human rights concerns at the centre of British foreign policy. Outside support does make a difference. In 1995, when an ex-minister of justice asked the Romanian Constitutional Court to ban the Hungarian UDMR, the Christian Democrat group on the Council of Europe speedily passed a unanimous resolution asking the Romanian government not to do so. One UDMR leader said he realised for the first time what European solidarity could mean in practice (Stefoi 1997: 149). But the Council of Europe has sometimes adopted an elastic approach towards states which it is willing to admit as full members even though their treatment of minorities leaves a lot to be desired. Grigorievs expressed concern about the admission of Estonia and Latvia, believing that restoration of citizenship to the mainly Russian minorities 'will only be achieved if the international community presses for a politics of tolerance' (Grigorievs 1996: 122). Perhaps the most worrying recent abdication of responsibility certainly by European powers occurred in the Bosnian city of Mostar: badly scarred by fighting between Croat and Muslim forces, the EU accepted a mandate to rebuild the city and try to restore communal peace. Hans Koschnick, a former mayor of Bremen, became the EU's commissioner in 1994, but he was hampered by Croat nationalists backed by the Croatian government, and he resigned after being effectively abandoned by his own government which refused to offer him the help required to resist ultra-nationalists linked to criminal elements (Sito Sutic 1996: 47). The verdict of one observer was that 'the EU's experience in Mostar suggests that the Europeans will be inclined to pursue short-term stability by pandering to nationalist politicians' (Mihalka 1996: 45).

Conclusion

Ethnoradicalism has shaped the pace and character of the transition from communist regimes to hybrid systems approximating to a greater or lesser extent to liberal democracy across the former Soviet bloc. Political systems of left and right have emerged in which ethnicity is a major organising principle. Minorities have regularly been depicted as a threat by nationalist leaderships intent on extending their tenure in office or acquiring wealth by shaping the privatisation process around nationalist criteria.

Mobilised minorities in states where they have experienced ill-treatment have been more pragmatic than perhaps might have been expected in the face of ill-treatment. Group rights remain a key objective but the demand is usually for educational, linguistic and cultural rights that can ensure the preservation of a minority identity rather than secession or territorial autonomy. Autonomy demands shaped around territory win little support from West European or global bodies prepared to use their weight to defend submerged communities. These demands bring an unavailing and sometimes violent response from majority state nationalisms. But groups like the Roma which have *not* developed a national consciousness have few champions outside the international human rights community. Similarly, the large numbers of people of mixed ethnic background in urban Bosnia also found themselves relatively friendless from 1992 to 1996 as peace plans were devised by the West that catered for populations which had a clear-cut ethnic identity. So, a national consciousness among minority groups seems to be a prerequisite for West European help, provided it is not expressed in violent or inflammatory terms.

This article starts from the premise that multiethnic states should recognise the existence of ethnic minorities and encourage conditions for the preservation of their identity where this is a clearly desired minority aspiration. It also believes that the quality of democracy is usually enhanced when minorities are able to participate on equal terms in the affairs of the country in which they live, as well as participating in decisions that affect the particular community or region in which they live. But it also recognises that demands for territorial autonomy or dual citizenship with a neighbouring state can be problematic when the minority reside in a state which they may once have dominated perhaps in association with coethnics from an adjoining one, and that no binding conventions allowing for territorial autonomy can easily be arrived at, although in some countries a surrender of sovereignty by the central organ of the state to lower tiers has enhanced its stability.

The future course of majority–minority relations in Eastern Europe may well be decided by two factors:

1. *First, the speed and extent to which the region overcomes chronic economic difficulties associated with moving from a state-led to a market economy.* Majorities are less inclined to make concessions to minorities when their economic prospects are bleak. In hard times, demagogues who insist that minority rights are a violation of national sovereignty will always find a more receptive audience than in times of economic contentment. Romania offers a fascinating example in 1997 of a society facing massive economic hardships whose government is seeking simultaneously to address minority concerns. This is a very delicate balancing-act and it is not clear at the time of writing whether ruling reformers will be able to combine austerity policies and liberal minority ones without facing a severe nationalist backlash (Gallagher 1997: 100–107).

2. *The second crucial factor is the fate of European integration processes.* If a postnationalist political model takes hold in Western Europe, it is bound to have powerful resonance in the East. The desire to belong to a common European economic and security system that will be administered by common political institutions enjoys an appeal in many Eastern lands only previously matched by extremist ideologies in the 1930s; this is especially so among intellectuals and the young. But if the European project falters or its benefits are confined to a select group of Central European states, with the Balkans relegated to an outer-Europe, then the resulting disillusionment could give a powerful impetus to radical nationalism in parts of Eastern Europe.

Majority–minority relations in states divided for longer or shorter periods along ethnic lines will probably continue to be uncertain as long as nationalism stands for a political rather than a cultural identity across Europe. Some West European states, Britain, Spain and the Netherlands, have shaped identity and citizenship around a multiplicity of identities. Others, notably France, Greece and even Germany, are more resistant to the idea of legitimising minority identities in this way. They believe that national minority rights should only be defined in terms of individual human rights and that they should remain subservient to sovereign state rights (Jackson Preece 1997: 353).[15] Collective rights for minorities in cultural, educational and religious affairs, as well as internal self-government in areas where minorities predominate, are seen by these states as endangering their territorial integrity. Such differences have long prevented the Council of Europe from agreeing on a charter of minority rights that would be legally binding on its members.[16]

A history of conflict between dominant and subordinate ethnic groups in Eastern Europe means that many states are reluctant to accept West European norms or outside supervision of majority–minority relations. However, joining Western institutions is a primary goal of most states in the area, so it is likely that greater international regulation of minorities will be accepted, albeit reluctantly.

The wars of the Yugoslav succession (1991–5) show that Europe as a whole has a big stake in preventing ethnic disputes spilling over into generalised violence. Levels of insecurity shared by majorities and minorities are often high and this reinforces their differences. A new policy agenda for Eastern Europe which emphasises the benefits to be derived from a postnationalist strategy of economic and military cooperation, following the example of West European states, offers the best prospect of defusing current disputes. But Western policy makers have been reluctant to invest the time and resources or offer sufficiently attractive incentives to persuade their former communist neighbours of the attractiveness of taking the postnationalist route. As for Southeastern Europe, there is open scepticism in Western capitals about the ability of the region to overcome legacies of socioeconomic and political backwardness which have made it a byword for instability. But the fact remains that the national question in Eastern Europe will only recede from view if the region as a whole is offered the external support which enabled the warring states of Western Europe to put aside their own not inconsiderable differences after 1945.

15 However, Germany officially recognises three national minorities – the Danes, the Sorbs and the Sinti and Roma – as well as the ethnic group of Frisians [Editors' Note].

16 On 1 February 1995, the Council of Europe opened for signature the Framework Convention for the Protection of National Minorities. As of 23 May 2003, it had been signed by forty-two out of forty-five member states and had entered into force in thirty-five of them. [Editors' Note].

References

BOOKMAN, Milica Zarcovic (1994). *Economic Decline and Nationalism in the Balkans.* New York: St Martin's Press.

BRUBAKER, Rogers (1995). 'National Minorities, Nationalizing States, and External National Homelands in the New Europe.' *Daedalus* 124 (Spring), pp. 107–32.

BRUNNER, Georg (1996). *Nationality Problems and Minority Conflicts in Eastern Europe.* Gutersloh: Bertelsmann Foundation Publishers.

CARLSSON, Ingmar (1995). *International Herald Tribune*, 25 January.

DREZOV, Kyril (1997). 'Seven Years of "Democratic Communism" in Bulgaria.' Paper presented at a conference on Democratization in the Balkans, University of Bristol (10 May).

DYKER, David A. (1995). 'Nomenklatura Nationalism: the Key to the New East European Politics?,' *Australian Journal of History and Politics* 41: 1.

GAGNON, JR., V.P. (1994–95). 'Ethnic Nationalism and International Conflict: The Case of Serbia.' *International Security* 19: 3 (Winter), pp. 130–66.

GALL, Carlotta, and Thomas DE WALL (1997). *Chechnya: A Small Victorious War.* London: Pan Books.

GALLAGHER, Tom (1995a). *Romania After Ceauşescu: The Politics of Intolerance.* Edinburgh: Edinburgh University Press.

————— (1995b). 'Democratization in the Balkans: Challenges and Prospects.' *Democratization* 2: 3, pp. 337–61.

————— (1997). 'Danube Détente: Romania's Reconciliation with Hungary After 1996.' *Balkanologie* 1: 2.

GOMEZ, Victor (1995). 'Specter of Racism.' *Transition* 1: 10 (June).

GRIGORIEVS, Alex (1996). 'The Baltic Predicament.' In: *Europe's New Nationalism: States and Minorities in Conflict*, Richard Caplan and John Feffer (eds). Oxford: Oxford University Press.

HOCKENOS, Paul (1993). *Free To Hate: the Rise of the Right In Post-Communist Eastern Europe.* London: Routledge.

HYDE-PRICE, Adrian (1994). 'Democratization in Eastern Europe: the External Dimension.' In: *Democratization in Eastern Europe*, G. Pridham and T. Vanhanen (eds). London: Routledge.

JACKSON PREECE, Jennifer (1997). 'National Minority Rights vs. State Sovereignty in Europe: Changing Norms in International Relations?' *Nations and Nationalism* 3: 3 (November), pp. 345–64.

JUDAH, Tim (1997). *The Serbs: History, Myth and the Destruction of Yugoslavia.* New Haven, CT: Yale University Press.

KELLOGG, Frederick (1995). *The Road to Romanian Independence.* Indiana: Purdue University Press.

KHAN, Mujeeb R. (1995). 'Bosnia-Herzegovina and the Crisis of the Post-War International System.' *East European Politics and Societies* 9: 3.

KHAZANOV, Anatoly M. (1997). 'Ethnic Nationalism in the Russian Federation.' *Daedalus* 126: 3 (Summer).

MIHALKA, Michael (1996). 'International Failure in Mostar.' *Transition* 2: 14 (July), pp. 45–47.

NAGLE, John (1997). 'Ethnos, Demos and Democratization: A Comparison of the Czech Republic and Hungary.' *Democratization* 4: 2 (Summer).

NODIA, Ghia (1996a). 'Nationalism and the Crisis of Liberalism.' In: *Europe's New Nationalism: States and Minorities in Conflict*, Richard Caplan and John Feffer (eds). Oxford: Oxford University Press, pp. 101–19.

NODIA, Ghia (1996b). 'Loyal or Dangerous?' *Warreport* 48 (December).

NUÑEZ, Xosé M. (1994). 'National Minorities in East-Central Europe and the Internationalisation of their Rights (1919–1939).' In: *Nationalism in Europe, Past and Present*, J. Beramendi (ed.). Santiago de Compostela: University of Santiago de Compostela.

PEARSON, Raymond (1983). *National Minorities in Eastern Europe, 1848–1945*. London: Methuen.

PEHE, Jiří (1994). 'The Czech Republic.' *RFE-RL Research Report* (Special Issue on 'The Politics of Intolerance') 3: 16 (April).

PETTAI, Vello (1996). 'Estonia's Controversial Language Policies.' *Transition* 3: 24 (November), pp. 20–22.

POULTON, Hugh (1996). 'Simmering Melting-Pot.' *Warreport* 48 (December).

RADY, Martin (1992). *Romania In Turmoil*. London: I.B. Tauris.

SANFORD, George (1997). 'Democratization and European Standards of National Minority Protection: Polish Issues.' *Democratization* 4: 3, pp. 45–68.

SCHÖPFLIN, George (1991). 'Nationalism and National Minorities in East and Central Europe.' *Journal of International Affairs* 45: 1.

——— (1994). 'The Quiet National Question.' *Warreport* 29 (October/November).

SITO SUTIC, Dario (1996). 'The Disunited Colors of Mostar.' *Transition* 2: 14 (July), pp. 42–44.

STAN, Valentin (1997). 'Democratization in the Balkans: The Role of External Forces in the Transition.' Paper presented at a conference on 'Democratization in the Balkans,' University of Bristol (10 May).

STEFOI, Elena (1997). *Drept Minoritar, Spaime Nationale*. Bucharest: Editura Kriterion.

TAIROV, Tair (1995). 'Antiwar Actions against the Odds.' *Warreport* 34 (June).

TERZANI, T. (1993). *Goodbye Mr Lenin: A Journey Through The End of the Soviet Empire*. London: Picador.

VICKERS, Miranda, and James PETTIFER (1997). *Albania: From Anarchy to a Balkan Identity*. London: Hurst & Co.

PART TWO

CASE STUDIES

CHAPTER THREE

Ethnoradicalism as a Mirror Image of State Centralisation: the Basque Paradigm in Franco's Spain

Daniele Conversi

Few cases are better suited to explore the central topic of this book than the instance of Spain. My aim is to address the relationship between state centralisation and the rise of ethnoradicalism through the prism of the Basque experience.[1] I will show the close relationship between the two, arguing that the choice of radical violence was both an *ultima ratio*, that is, a form of anguish and despair, and, at the same time, a carefully pondered decision. The latter resulted from prolonged discussions, rather than being merely a form of broadly defined 'rational choice'. A long-lasting ideological debate predated the decision to embark on the path of political violence.[2]

To understand where and why *Euskadi 'ta Askatasuna* (also Euzkadi 'ta Askatasuna, meaning 'Basque Land and Freedom') was born, we have to consider the situation in which its founders were then living: it was in the 1950s, well into over a decade of state-sanctioned silence and suppression of all political manifestations of Basque identity. The shifting tide of assimilation into mainstream Spanish culture had brought practically the totality of the Basque population to be socialised into a Spanish homogeneous 'high culture', while *Euskara* (the Basque language) was still spoken by barely 24 percent of the overall inhabitants of *Euskadi* (the Basque Country) – including Navarre, mostly in small towns and in the country-side. The urban/rural divide was slowly being supplemented by a new immigrants/natives divide. As many Basques had given up all hopes of

---

1 For a more detailed version of the events which led to the radicalisation of the conflict, see Conversi (1997). One of the central themes of the book is indeed the relationship between state centralisation and ethnopolitical violence.

2 Evidence of these long debates can be found in several documents, most of which are now collected in the eighteen volume *Documentos Y,* a collection of original ETA sources from its foundation to the early 1980s.

maintaining their culture, the fear of extinction was overwhelming – most of all among the nationalists. This apprehension has been identified by Gurutz Jáuregui Bereciartu as *sentimiento agonico* (feeling of anguish or agony).[3] The predicament was a direct consequence of the Civil War (1936–9), which had ended with the Francoist victory against the Republic, to which the Basque nationalists had been allied.

Obviously, not all aspects of Basque culture were proscribed, nor was the state interested in suppressing those areas of public culture which did not pose a reasonable threat to the regime or did not seem to lend themselves too easily to political action. As a token of 'goodwill', marginal aspects of Basque heritage, such as food, folklore and even traditional sports were pontifically tolerated (Watson 1996: 17–34). Sporting events, though, knew some occasional interdictions, being routinely visited by the *Guardia Civil* and other security forces – if only because they represented occasions of popular encounter and thus potential avenues for expressing political malaise.

Overall, people had a bleak vision of their future, but were too concerned with economic dire straits and the reconstruction of their postwar livelihood to be interested in cultural matters and identity problems. Thus, all that was left of Basqueness was tradition, and it was slowly dying out.

The first underground secret meetings were precisely inspired by a desire to reverse this situation of despair. At the beginning, it was quite a timid venture; there was neither aim nor hope to engage in any significant political action. Tired of the general impasse but also frustrated by the 'obsolete' ideology of the old nationalists, a group of students in the Jesuit University of Deusto (Bilbao) started to hold weekly meetings to study and discuss Basque history and culture. In the beginning, in 1952, there were probably fewer than ten of them, all in their early twenties. This clandestine activity 'uncovered for them an unknown world which [state] terrorism under Franco had relegated to the category of a nonexistent reality (Jáuregui Bereciartu 1981: 571).'[4] Their underground organ was an irregular bulletin, *Ekin* ('To do'), from which the group borrowed its name. What united them was 'a lively awareness of national oppression, a keen interest in the Basque language – which the majority of them initially ignored, learning it [in the process] [...] – and an ethnic vision of Euskadi (Ortzi 1977: 279).'

The main questions addressed by Ekin's members were 'who are we?' or 'what does it mean to be Basque?' The first participants of these self-articulated informal meetings, and later courses, were sons and daughters of middle-class professionals and small bourgeoisie. Ekin expanded

---

3   Otherwise translatable as 'sentiment of despair', of impending collective threat, of living on the threshold of oblivion (Jáuregui Bereciartu 1981).

4   Their first reading included mostly earlier Basque nationalist textbooks, all of which were outlawed and very difficult to obtain.

through personal contacts with friends and trustworthy acquaintances, especially in the rural heartland where the preservation of Basque culture was regarded as a guarantee of loyalty and anti-regime feelings. Since the beginning, the group had considered the possibility of armed actions as the means both to defeat Francoism and to revitalise a nation on the verge of losing its cultural identity. This second aspect, the idea of violence as a redeeming and regenerating force, was to take root slowly, almost imperceptibly and steadily. The use of violence had been sporadically advocated as early as the 1940s by fringe militant nationalists (Garmendia and Elordi 1982: 174ff.). However, the leadership of Ekin was more prone to foster some form of passive resistance at a time in which the echoes of Gandhism still rebounded. Only a few years later, ETA reversed these assumptions, holding that 'non violent methods do not seem to yield results except under relatively honest regimes. Gandhi achieved [Indian] independence from the British socialists, not from a Franco or a Stalin.'[5]

Disenchanted with the older generation's appeasing attitude, the younger one considered the erstwhile course to be ineffective – indeed steering the country towards disaster. This schism was a significant cause in the final 'formalisation' of Ekin as a full-fledged movement, leading in 1959 to the foundation of ETA.[6] With the birth of ETA, a whole new chapter of Basque history opened up. The feeling of despair had spread after the USA had decided to embrace Franco as an anti-communist ally in the new Cold War politics. This was then perceived as the American 'betrayal' of a small nation in favour of a centralist dictatorship, becoming a key ingredient in the organisation's subsequent drift towards leftist – and eventually Trotskyite – positions. The other two crucial elements of the *Marxisante* turn were *immigration* (whereby most of the non-Basque immigrants belonged to the working class) (Conversi 1997: 187–221), and *ideological diffusion* (with the leftist vogue spreading throughout Europe in the 1960s) (Conversi 1993: 245–70). Mass immigration began in 1959 (the very same year of ETA's birth), peaking around 1974, when immigrants made up over 30 percent of the population (excluding their offspring, born in *Euskadi*).

The first acts of political violence occurred in 1961, when a few explosions shattered government buildings in different cities, although responsibility for them was not claimed. On 18 July, ETA placed an

5   See *Zutik - Tercera Serie*/N.S., no. 6, 1963, p. 9 (reprinted in *Documentos Y*, vol. 2, p. 283).

6   José Mari Garmendia quotes four reasons for the birth and expansion of ETA: 1. The persistence of Basque nationalism; 2. A crisis in Basque traditional values as an after-effect of the economic development of the 1950s; 3. The more general failure and perceived inadequacy of the Basque Nationalist Party (PNV) – especially identified in its 'naive' pro-Americanism; and 4. The attraction exerted by Third World national liberation movements (Cuba, Algeria and Israel) (Garmendia 1979: vol. 1).

explosive package on a railway track, attempting to derail a train carry-ing Francoist veterans from the Civil War (Clark 1984: 35). Once the plot was preemptively discovered, a wave of arrests occurred amongst Basque activists and their sympathisers: 110 ETA members were impris-oned, many of them tortured, and another hundred or more were forced into exile (Ibarz 1980: 95). These numbers testify to the impressive growth of the organisation. In 1953, Ekin was made up of five militants in Bilbao, and as many in Donostia. By 1960, more than 300 militants had passed through its *cursillos de formación* (training courses).[7] Despite this blow, ETA continued its underground activity, inaugurating a long period of reflection. Although deeply imbued with nineteenth-century nationalist principles, ETA's intellectuals were quite knowledgeable about European progressive thought, Third World struggles and Marxist analysis. In the early 1960s, ETA's leaders started to bring to light the results of years of study and discussion. The first issue of the journal *Zutik* ('Standing up!')[8] and the circular 'Cuadernos de ETA' (also called 'Cuadernos de Formación' – 'Training Notes') began to appear respec-tively in 1961 and 1962.[9]

The first full political programme to be adopted by ETA materialised in the book *Vasconia* (1963) by Federico Krutwig, the son of a German industrialist living in Bilbao, who took on the pseudonym F. Sarrailh de Ihartza (Krutwig 1963). *Vasconia*'s framework was a stress on action. This was partly derived from Ernest Renan's voluntarist view of the nation as an 'everyday plebiscite' (Renan 1994). The concept of voluntary partici-pation is central to the evolution of postwar Basque nationalism. However, *Vasconia*'s most relevant contribution was strategic, in that guerrilla warfare was seen as the only means to liberate *Euskadi*. In this choice, Krutwig was directly inspired by the Algerian and Cuban experi-ences. A further impulse in this direction was received via Franz Fanon's (1925–61) premises, which justified anticolonial violence as a liberating and purifying principle, essential to the psychological well-being of the 'oppressed' (Fanon 1990). This 'Third World' approach was opposed to the preexistent pro-European and ethnofederalist tradition. Somehow, an underlying opposition between the two trends has continued right up to the present.

7 Interview with Txillardegi (José Luís Alvarez Emparanza), reported in *Garaia* 1:1, 1976, pp. 24–25.
8 The early 1960s were still a period of reflection and debate. *Zutik* warmly solicited its readers to submit any kind of criticism on its contents. It also issued calls for papers, projects, ideas, various information, data, etc. (*Documentos Y,* vol. 2, p. 317).
9 Every issue of the *Cuadernos de ETA* was dedicated to a single theme. As in Ekin's days, each leading member of the organisation was charged with investigating a specific topic and preparing an ensuing *cuaderno* (notebook). Each issue had an essential bibliogra-phy, on the basis of which it is possible to establish the international ideological influences exerted on the militants (see Conversi 1993).

José Luís Zalbide's *Insurrección en Euskadi* also appeared in 1963, synthesising those parts of Krutwig's programme dealing with armed struggle.[10] Conceived as a guerrilla manual, it became the cornerstone of the strategy of ETA's military branch. The shadows of Mao-Tse-Tung and Ho-Chi-Minh permeated the spirit of the pamphlet.[11] ETA's Second Assembly (1963) approved the theses of Krutwig and Zalbide, with violence figuring prominently as a means of 'empowering the powerless'. Still, in 1962, there was no agreement on the use of violence. For instance, *Zutik* that year reported that 'between Gandhi's nonviolence and a civil war there are intermediate methods of struggle [...] which we want to put in practice.'[12] ETA participated then in its first working class strikes. Despite their low-key profile and tributary organisational role, the nationalists had to bear the brunt of the repression. While the state barely permitted the venting of economic protests, it could never tolerate any form of mobilisation couched in ethnic terms. This was because the very legitimisation of the state rested on an implacable commitment to defend its territorial integrity. Since any bland form of ethnic consciousness was seen as an attack against that order, it had to be ruthlessly repressed. As we shall see, such a strategy proved to be not only futile, but counterproductive in the long run for the state itself.

State centralism bred not only ethnic consciousness, but also radical activism. In Krutwig's footsteps, the Third Assembly (1964) defined ETA as an anti-imperialist and anti-capitalist organisation working simultaneously for national liberation and working-class emancipation. In 1963, Zalbide wrote *Carta a los intellectuales* ('Letter to the intellectuals'), which postulated the basic principles to be adopted by ETA. At the same time, the founding fathers of Ekin/ETA were expelled from France and confined to exile in Belgium. Henceforth, the physical distance considerably hampered the flow of communication between the old and experienced leadership and the later generations at the 'base' who began to act single-handedly. Establishing a long-lasting pattern, ETA came under the control of young advocates' revolutionary war.

The link between social and national struggle was firmly established during the Fourth Assembly (1965). Class struggle and national liberation

10 Published anonymously as a special issue of *Cuaderno de ETA*, 20 (1964), Bayonne: Goitziri. Reproduced in *Documentos Y*, vol. 3, pp. 20–71. The bibliography includes the main works of Che Guevara, Mao-Tse-Tung, Krutwig and, especially, *La Guerre Révolutionnaire* by Claude Delmas, entire sections of which are reproduced. It may also be possible that *Insurrección en Euskadi* was written by Madariaga, ETA's first proponent of armed struggle.

11 Especially appreciated in radical milieux was the famous Maoist aphorism of the guerrilla fighter who moves among his people as a 'fish in the water', a natural element which he needs in order to survive (Krutwig 1963: 330). One of ETA's features was indeed its symbiosis with the human environment of the Basque hinterland.

12 *Zutik* 19, reprinted in *Documentos Y*, vol. 2, p. 229.

became the two faces of the same coin. Zalbide's *Insurrección en Euskadi* was adopted by ETA as the guidelines for its actions. Its central tenet was Krutwig's theory of the 'cycle of action/repression/action' which held that 'where popular protest against injustices met with oppression, the revolutionary forces should act to punish the oppressor. The occupying forces would then retaliate with indiscriminate violence, since they would not know who the revolutionaries were, causing the population to respond with increased protest and support for the resistance in an upward spiral of resistance to the dictatorship (Sullivan 1988: 42–43).' This theory was to provide the overall framework of ETA's strategy throughout its long evolution since the publication of *Vasconia*. ETA started to assume a paramilitary form.

Armed attacks began in 1965 in the form of bank robberies. During one of these (on 7 June 1968), a *Guardia Civil* (civil guard, the major state paramilitary corps) was shot, becoming the first victim of ETA.[13] However, one member of the commando, Txabi Etxebarrieta, was subsequently assassinated in what seemed to be an act of retaliation. This was the triggering event which the theorists of armed struggle were eagerly waiting for. Popular indignation over the killing of Etxebarrieta prompted mass demonstrations in every major city, town and village of *Euskadi*. Priests held masses in his memory for weeks, Etxebarrieta was now a hero and ETA's popularity dramatically increased (Clark 1984: 49).

The first premeditated political murder was carried out less than two months later, on 2 August, against the police commissioner Melitón Manzanas, commonly abhorred as a rampant practitioner of torture. Already, six years before the assassination, an article in *Zutik* (1962) had claimed that persons like Manzanas 'will pay dearly for their crimes.'[14] These accusations were frequently reiterated in ETA's proclamations and pronouncements throughout the years.[15] Hence, Manzanas was a highly selected target, a symbol of state oppression and centralism, whose killing was likely to bring new recruits and more support for ETA's violent strategists.[16]

The government response was swift and ruthless. A 'state of exception' was proclaimed, during which legions of suspected ETA sympathisers were clustered, illegally arrested, battered and terrorised. Yet, people defiantly filled the streets in mass demonstrations. This was hailed by the terrorists as the first stage of the 'action/repression/action' cycle. However, the structure of ETA was severely disrupted by a further wave of arrests in 1969. Most of the leaders were forced into exile, where

13 '*7 de junio de 1968: ETA aprieta el gatillo por primera vez*,' *La Vanguardia*, 5 June 1988, pp. 6–7 (report published on the occasion of the 20th anniversary of the beginning of armed struggle).
14 Reprinted in *Documentos Y*, vol. 3, p. 301.
15 Such as *Zutik* 2, December 1961, in *Documentos Y*, vol. 1, p. 406.
16 On these internal dynamics, see Irvin (1999).

they rejoined the other main factions. The Sixth Assembly, held in 1970, represented ETA's last serious theoretical controversy. After that date, the group became increasingly impermeable to internal debate, defiantly indifferent to 'divisive' ideological diatribes and increasingly committed to action.

The famous Burgos Trial (1970) was an historical watershed for the whole Basque movement as well as for the Spanish opposition. In Burgos, sixteen *etarras* (ETA members) charged with the murder of Manzanas were brought before a military court. For weeks, international media focused on the Basques' struggle. In a display of generosity which today would be inconceivable, mass demonstrations and solidarity committees sprang up all over Europe in support of the condemned.[17] The solidarity movement was particularly forceful and effective in post-1968 France, where Jean-Paul Sartre and the existentialist milieux became personally involved in the support campaign for the amnesty of political prisoners. In an emblematic spectacle of leftish internationalism, Sartre saw *Euskadi* as 'a colony exploited by a fascist state allied with American imperialism (Ortzi 1977: 380–1).' In comparison with other *maîtres-à-penser*, Sartre evinced considerable understanding of the problems of European national minorities. Therefore, he accused the mainstream left of uncritically assuming the French bourgeoisie's cultural Jacobinism: 'I wish to oppose the abstract universality of bourgeois humanism to the singular universality of the Basques ... A heroic people, led by a revolutionary party, has shown us another [face of] socialism, tangible and decentralising: this is the universality of the Basques ... .'[18] But Marxists, internationalists and existentialists were not the only ones mobilised in support of the prisoners. Catholics and liberals also let their voices be heard. The regime, which at least since 1959 had vowed to open up to Europe and to transform its economic practices and human rights record, felt itself under serious international pressure. In the end, all the death sentences were commuted.

As society polarised, mass mobilisations spread at the local level, beginning to attract the immigrants' offspring. Their participation in these public events encouraged the latter to share the natives' common myths and symbols. The immigrants were certainly not concerned with purely ethnic issues: what was at stake was their social peace and very existence, since all public mobilisations carried with them the risk of massive retaliation by the state. Simultaneously, left-wing nationalism conveyed a progressive message to the immigrants, while ETA's daring

17 See Jean-Paul Sartre's introduction to the radical feminist existentialist version of the event in Gisèle Halimi, Le procès de Burgos, Paris: Gallimard, 1971 [Span. transl.: El Proceso de Burgos, Caracas: Monte Avila].

18 Jean-Paul Sartre, in Halimi (1971: XXIX–XXX). Obviously, Sartre was referring to the ETA of the Burgos Trial, which surged as an international champion of resistance against oppression.

violence exercised an irresistible lure among juvenile sectors. The more ETA's *ekintzak* (armed actions) involved a direct confrontation with the state, the more ETA's star would rise among the nonnative proletariat. The great paradox is that, in these conditions, violence became a vehicle of immigrants' integration into the nationalist struggle.

The peak of ETA's legitimacy was reached with the assassination of Carrero Blanco (1973), the proposed successor of Franco. This *magnicidio* (killing of a top political leader) provoked a vacuum of power from which the regime was never to recover. Now Franco had no heir through which to perpetuate his model of authoritarian 'stability'.[19]

Situating the Nation

What has emerged in the previous section is the dawning of new forms of mass mobilisation catalysed by state centralism, authoritarianism and political repression. Governmental attacks on Basque nationalism and identity politics implied a further centralisation of the state's machinery – illustrated by the use of the notorious 'states of exception'. This quandary led to newer and more sophisticated forms of mobilisation. The result was a re-invention of Basque identity and a burgeoning propagation of nationalist politics. To put it more bluntly, extreme state centralisation led to *ethnogenesis*: a new Basque nation was being forged by the increasing interaction of social change and inadequate governmental responses. Yet, centralisation had to interact with a particular ideological and cultural *humus* in order to generate different grassroots responses (indeed, opposing ones, as in Catalonia and *Euskadi*). Given Basque nationalism's attempt to involve the immigrants, the nation could no longer be based on blood, descent or 'ethnicity' in its pristine sense. It had to be based on active participation, and this could only take place in an underground network of deepening mobilisation. In this section, I will argue that the essence of this idea can be located in Ernest Renan's 'voluntarist' notion. I will also contrast Renan's weight in *Euskadi* with the 'rival' Herderian influence in nearby Catalonia.

A centralist regime conceived the Spanish nation in organicist terms, as a holistic entity, a cohesive, complete, integral, indivisible whole. This stress on homogeneity, organicity and purity was cosubstantial to the process of state centralisation. However, this myth inevitably clashed with the rival organic visions of the ethnonations, some of which were based on organic principles as well.

In nationalist politics, Johann Gottfried Herder's (1744–1803) 'organicism' is often opposed to Ernest Renan's (1823–92) 'voluntarism'.

---

19 For an excellent synthesis on Spanish politics, with particular reference to the national question, see Heywood (1996).

The opposition is between the nation as an objective predestined entity, and the nation as a subjective ongoing process. A few catchwords are chosen, often arbitrarily, to synthesise these two approaches. The Herderian definition is that the nation is a 'distinctive cultural group', while the Renanian (even more famous) one, is that the nation is an 'everyday plebiscite'.[20] Herderianism is often associated with 'Eastern' intolerance and authoritarianism, while Renanianism is identified with Western liberalness and broad-mindedness. Yet, at least in Catalonia, the application of Herderian principles has induced the emergence of more tolerant and pluralist forms of political mobilisation, while Renanian principles have been appropriated by doctrinaire extremism amongst Basque radicals – particularly within ETA.

Theories of nationalism have traditionally failed to contemplate the organic nature of most state nationalisms. Whereas Renan's 'voluntarist' interpretation has been opposed to more 'organicist' ones, this has often been done on the understanding that the former applied to 'civic' and more democratic forms of citizenship, while the latter are representative of minority, stateless and 'ethnic' nationalism. To be fair, Renan's famous address was directed to the recovery of Alsace and Lorraine from Germany's grip. Since the large majority of Alsatians were German-speakers and ethnically Germans (or, at any rate, not ethnically French), cultural, ethnic and other 'organicist' elements, normally regarded as priorities in French discourse, had to be played down and supplanted by a vision in which 'common will' was paramount.[21]

In general, Renan's metaphor has often been used by upholders of state centralisation against autonomist pressures. For instance, the philosopher José Ortega y Gasset (1883–1955) was a fervent admirer of Ernest Renan the activist, while professing an unconditional rejection of organicist interpretations (Ortega y Gasset 1932). The latter included race and language. Yet, the Spanish (Castilian) language was singularly exempt from accusations of organicism, being a vehicle of nation building and a tool for strengthening the state. For Ortega, the state was the maker of the nation, not vice versa, and language was an instrument for that goal. As students of Spanish fascism generally know, this 'voluntarist' notion was to provide an unanticipated avenue for the legitimation of Francoism and Falangism (Payne 1995). But, as soon as the far right could manipulate it to suit its own agenda, voluntarism was in turn transfigured into an organicist conception. This proves that, rather than a Manichean dichotomy, there is a continuum between organicist and voluntarist conceptions, or between subjectivism and

20 As is known, Ernest Renan claimed that 'the existence of a nation is an *everyday plebiscite*, a perpetual affirmation of life' (Renan 1994: 17).

21 As Hans Kohn observed, Renan himself attached great importance to his patriotic address (Kohn 1945: 581–2, note 13).

objectivism. The Janus-faced vocation of nationalism is perfectly able to turn every metaphor on its head (Nairn 1997).[22] The same double-faced-ness applies to other dichotomies, such as the 'civic' and 'ethnic' dyad (Kymlicka 1995: 130–7).

Hans Kohn's distinction between Western and Eastern nationalism is based on the observation that the organicist essentialist vision is prevalent in 'Eastern' nationalism, while 'Western' nationalisms are largely exempt from it (Kohn 1945). Hans Kohn's pioneering study has often been misread as a moralistic division between 'bad' nationalisms, amongst which the German and Slavic varieties prevailed (Kohn 1953; 1960), and 'good' nationalisms, of which the USA was the herald (Kohn 1957). Similarly, Elie Kedourie, while grossly ignoring Kohn's more sophisticated contribution, attacked nationalism as a conspiracy of German Romantic intellectuals (Kedourie 1993). Yet, he was no more sympathetic to voluntarist accounts, since 'a political community which conducts daily plebiscites must soon fall into querulous anarchy, or hypnotic obedience' (Kedourie 1993: 76).

Renan's antecedents can be discerned *ante litteram* in Johann Gottlieb Fichte (1762–1814), who in his youth was a fanatical admirer of the French Revolution.[23] Renan and Fichte shared an undiluted ethnocentric posture, which was absent in Herder. However, the original Jacobin inspiration was more pronounced in Fichte than in Renan, the *prêtre manqué* (failed priest) who also was an anti-positivist and a monarchic legitimist (defender of the constitutional monarchy). The Jacobin roots of both thinkers are still open to discussion, in view of their shared racist and anti-Semitic statements. If Fichte can be recognised as the progenitor of Germany's aggressive, expansionist nationalism, Renan inspired French nationalists such as Maurice Barrès and Charles Maurras, while remaining an admirer of reactionary Germany for a long period.

Indeed, despite their differences, Renan and Fichte were both sharply dissimilar from Herder, whose pluralist vision was characterised by a sincere appreciation for all forms of cultural diversity.[24] It was rather the original Jacobin *Zeitgeist* which was characterised by an explicit, categorical, clean-cut intolerance for ethnic variety and cultural heterogeneity.

22 More than his predecessors, Nairn postulates a distinction between a 'natural' (ethnic) and a 'designed' (civic) definition of the national, the former triumphantly giving way to the latter – which is also more secular. This shift demonstrates, according to Nairn, that today's nationalism is a 'key feature of modernity'.

23 As Kedourie points out, 'national self-determination is, in the final analysis, a determination of the will; and nationalism is, in the first place, a method of teaching the right determination of the will. This indeed is the fundamental subject of Fichte's *Addresses*.' (Kedourie 1993: 76).

24 See Berlin (1976: particularly pp. 165–94) on Herder's doctrine of expression; and Barnard (1965). Herder was the inspiring muse of many secular Zionist thinkers, in particular Eliezer Ben Yehuda and other Hebrew language revivalists. See Fishman (1982: 1–14; 1985; 1997).

If this is so, the course from Jacobinism to fascism can be a promenade, while the ocean allegedly dividing French from German nationalism is not more than a rivulet. The two models – and the two sets of dichotomies attached to them – share a common *Weltanschauung*.

Turning to our case study, it should be noted that, during the postwar formative years, Catalan and Basque nationalism followed two distinct paths. Catalan nationalism concentrated on the recovery of language and other cultural expressions normally attached to language (literature, songs, theatre, etc.) as the epitome of national identity. Not only was language seen as a great unifying tool for the anti-fascist opposition, but it was also singled out as an instrument of nation building for a Catalan society which was just emerging from years of state-led oblivion.

In the Basque context, the predictable nationalist emphasis on language had to be discarded in favour of other elements. This typically occurred when the movement tried to expand in Bilbao and other urban centres where the population was virtually monolingually Spanish, particularly among the working class. This dilemma prompted a search for new inclusive models of Basque identity, away from earlier xenophobic trends. As a consequence of regime centralisation and continuous police crackdowns, participation in the struggle against fascism became a key criterion for inclusion in the Basque 'moral community'. Given the regime's dictatorial character, commitment to the national 'cause' could only be 'measured' by the intensity of personal involvement, as the individual activist put his/her own safety at stake. The most dangerous and daring actions were the most commendable and, hence, represented a distinctively prized evidence of 'Basqueness'. As political violence escalated, involvement in terrorist activities became the crucible of defining membership in the nation. Yet, a parallel culturalist vision of Basque identity emerged around Basque language schools (*ikastolak*), popular sports and other public events, but at that time was less influential in shaping popular perceptions of Basque identity, as well as in determining the regime's responses.

In other words, Catalonia opted for a Herderian-linguistic definition of the nation, while *Euskadi* adopted a Renanian-voluntarist definition. This choice derived from the interaction between state centralism and patterns of ethnic mobilisation. Contrary to widespread scholarly assumptions, the former resulted in a more moderate and peaceful form of nationalism, while the latter led to a more radical and antagonistic outcome.

Since late Francoism, the ethnoracial character of Basque nationalism was replaced by a vision in which characteristics acquired by individual choice, rather than inherited givens, played a central role. Gurutz Jáuregui Bereciartu rightly identifies this as the 'Renanian phase' of Basque nationalism (Jáuregui Bereciartu 1981: 152). Particularly relevant to the unfolding of post-1959 Basque nationalism were Renan's most activist statements, those which simply emphasised the role of sacrifice and the

importance of collective memories of suffering: in a rather disturbing statement, Renan adduced that 'common suffering is greater than happiness. In
fact, national sorrows are more significant than triumphs because they
impose obligations and demand a common effort' (Jáuregui Bereciartu
1981: 17). Lacking the power of culture as a common bond and submitted
to stern oppression by a highly centralised state, the Basque youth and
leaders became increasingly attracted by Renanian 'voluntarist' ideas –
even though the overwhelming majority of them may have never heard of
Renan's name. Finally, a widely quoted dictum among Basque radicals
became 'We fight, therefore we are,' taken *verbatim* from the repertoire of
the Zionist guerrilla leader Menachem Begin (Begin 1972).

One of the first authors to theorise the need for a continuous struggle to
revive Basque nationhood was Krutwig (Krutwig 1963). The stress on the
nation as a daily plebiscite implied a radicalisation of the conflict. Given
that the Basques themselves were not a cohesive, least of all homogeneous,
unit, internal divisions could only be bridged through a radical challenge.
In this logic, state violence and mass counter-violence were to be key
factors. Krutwig was a major proponent of the idea of a mass military revolt,
a guerrilla war to liberate *Euskadi* from the fetters of 'colonialism'. One of
Vasconia's chapters was named *Bellica* and was entirely dedicated to explor-
ing military tactics on how to best organise a popular insurrection through
the creation of guerrilla bands and cadres. As I have stressed, this became
the key source of inspiration for ETA's activists – even though Krutwig was
never a member of ETA and was rather considered as a 'free thinker'.

In short, ETA chose a Renanian route to 'nation building': what had
hitherto been an 'ethnic' nation defined by race and descent, and where
pedigree and surnames mattered more than words and deeds, was
consciously reconceived into a voluntarist one, precisely through the use of
selective violence.

Dichotomies may help to simplify what appear as confused pictures of
events, but they carry limited potentials of veracity and accuracy. Thus,
what was an original casticist vision of the nation also included a cultural
component (the rediscovery of *Euskara*, of selected traditions, and so on).
This cultural nucleus was, so to say, kept 'at bay', as an accessory tool to the
main thrust of Basque nationhood, which was conceived in terms of an
extended family (hence, in terms of what I define as 'ethnic nationalism').
In other words, culture was withheld in the background throughout
modern Basque history as a legitimising reservoir, first for a primarily racial,
subsequently for a political and military, form of nationalism – with culture
occasionally looming in the foreground. At the apex of state repression,
people were brought into the streets not in the name of defending a caste or
a race, but in the name of resistance against a state which was besetting
'them' – the same state which had destroyed traditional Basque
autonomies. The relentless response of the state caused continuous blows
in the nationalist organisation by imprisoning their leaders and leading

others into exile, but at the same time it catalysed popular resistance. For every battle won, the regime was approaching final defeat in war. Short-term calculations of ruling politicians (in other words, their irresistible eagerness to strike back in order to prove that the state was in charge), led to their long-term sink and fall. While Catalan resistance became a matter of rediscovering a forbidden language, in *Euskadi* there was no high culture which could agglutinate and 'direct' a popular response to state centralisation.

As a concluding remark, my goal has been to show how, in the Basque case, state centralisation led to ethnopolitical radicalisation. In countries pervaded by ethnic tensions, where the central state lacks legitimacy, centralisation necessarily entails a heightening of the conflict. The spiral mechanism presented herein is a familiar scenario in many highly centralised and delegitimated polities, some of which have been studied in other chapters of this book. To address the cause of centralisation itself, or to propose remedies to it, should be the work of an entirely different investigation.

References and Selected Bibliography

BARNARD, F.M. (1965). *Herder Social and Political Thought: From Enlightenment to Nationalism*. Oxford: Clarendon Press.

BEGIN, Menachem (1972). *The Revolt*. New York: Nash [Hebrew edition: Jerusalem, 1951].

BERLIN, Sir Isaiah (1976). *Vico and Herder: Two Studies in the History of Ideas*. London: Hogarth Press.

CLARK, Robert P. (1984). *The Basque Insurgents. ETA, 1952–1980*. Madison: University of Wisconsin Press.

CONVERSI, Daniele (1993). 'Domino Effect or Internal Developments? The Influences of International Events and Political Ideologies on Catalan and Basque Nationalism.' *West European Politics* 16: 3 (July), pp. 245–70.

——— (1997). *The Basques, the Catalans and Spain: Alternative Routes to Nationalist Mobilisation*. London: Hurst & Co./ Reno: University of Nevada Press.

——— (2000). 'Autonomous Communities and the Ethnic Settlement in Spain.' In: *Autonomy and Ethnicity. Negotiating Competing Claims in Multi-Ethnic States*, Yash Ghai (ed.). Cambridge: Cambridge University Press, pp. 122–44.

CRAMERI, Kathryn (2000). 'Banal Catalanism?' *National Identities* 2: 2, pp. 145–57

FANON, Frantz (1990). *The Wretched of the Earth*. Harmondsworth: Penguin. [*Les damnés de la terre*. Paris: Maspéro, 1961.]

FISHMAN, Joshua A. (1982). 'Whorfianism of the Third Kind: Ethnolinguistic Diversity as a Worldwide Societal Asset.' *Language in Society* 11, pp. 1–14.

——— (1985). 'The Whorfian hypothesis: Varieties of Valuation, Confirmation and Disconfirmation.' In: Joshua A. Fishman, *The Rise and Fall of the Ethnic Revival: Perspectives on Language and Ethnicity*. Berlin/New York: Mouton de Gruyter.

——— (1997). *In Praise of the Beloved Language: A Comparative View of Positive Ethnolinguistic Consciousness*. Berlin/New York: Mouton de Gruyter.

GARMENDIA, José Mari (1979). *Historia de ETA* (2 vols.). San Sebastián: L. Haranburu.

GARMENDIA, José Mari, and Alberto ELORDI (1982). *La resistencia vasca*. San Sebastián: L. Haranburu.

GUERIN, Daniel, and Rejean PELLETIER (2000). 'Cultural Nationalism and Political Tolerance in Advanced Industrial Societies: The Basque Country and Catalonia.' *Nationalism and Ethnic Politics* 6: 4, pp. 1–22.

HALIMI, Gisèle (1971). *Le procès de Burgos*. Paris: Gallimard. [Span. transl.: *El Proceso de Burgos*, Caracas: Monte Avila, 1976.]

HEYWOOD, Paul (1996). *The Government and Politics of Spain*. New York: St. Martin's Press.

IBARZ, Mercé (1980). *Breu història d'ETA, 1959–1979*. Barcelona: La Magrana.

IRVIN, Cynthia L. (1999). *Militant Nationalism: Between Movement and Party in Ireland and the Basque Country*. Minneapolis: University of Minnesota Press.

JÁUREGUI BERECIARTU, Gurutz (1981). *Ideología y estrategia política de ETA. Análisis de su evolución entre 1958 y 1968*. Madrid: Siglo XXI.

KEATING, Michael (1999). 'Asymmetrical Government: Multinational States in an Integrating Europe.' *Publius* 29: 1, pp. 71–86.

────── (2000). 'The Minority Nations of Spain and European Integration: A New Framework for Autonomy.' *Journal of Spanish Cultural Studies* 1: 1 (March), pp. 29–42.

KEDOURIE, Elie (1993). *Nationalism*. Oxford, UK/Cambridge, MA: Blackwell [4th expanded edn].

KOHN, Hans (1945). *The Idea of Nationalism: A Study in its Origins and Background*. New York: Macmillan Co.

────── (1953). *Pan-Slavism, Its History and Ideology*. Notre Dame, IN: University of Notre Dame Press.

────── (1957). *American Nationalism: An Interpretative Essay*. New York: Macmillan.

────── (1960). *The Mind of Germany: The Education of a Nation*. New York: Scribner.

KRUTWIG, Federico (1963). *Vasconia. Estudio dialéctico de una nacionalidad*. Buenos Aires: Narbait. [First published in 1963 under the pseudonym of Sarrailh de Ihartza.]

KYMLICKA, Will (1995). 'Misunderstanding Nationalism.' *Foundation for the Study of Independent Social Ideas* (Winter), pp. 130–7.

────── (2000). 'Nation-building and Minority Rights: Comparing West and East.' *Journal of Ethnic and Migration Studies* 26: 2 (April), pp. 183–212.

MCROBERTS, Kenneth (2001). *Catalonia*. Oxford: Oxford University Press.

NAIRN, Tom (1997). *Faces of Nationalism: Janus Revisited*. London: Verso.

ORTEGA Y GASSET, José (1932). *The Revolt of the Masses*. New York: W.W. Norton & Co. [Translation of the Spanish original, *La rebelion de las masas*, 1930.]

ORTZI (pseudonym of Francisco Letamendia) (1977). *Historia de Euskadi. El nacionalismo vasco y ETA*. Paris: Ruedo Ibérico.

PAYNE, Stanley G. (1995). *A History of Fascism, 1914–1945*. Madison: University of Wisconsin Press.

────── (2000). 'Catalan and Basque Nationalism: Contrasting Patterns.' In: *Ethnic Challenges to the Modern Nation State*, Shlomo Ben-Ami, Yoav Peled and Alberto Spektorowski (eds). New York: St. Martin's Press.

RENAN, Ernest (1994). 'Qu'est-ce qu'une nation?' In: *Nationalism. A Reader*, John Hutchinson and Anthony D. Smith (eds). Oxford: Oxford University Press, pp. 17–18. [Originally in: Ernest Renan, *Discours et Conférences*. Paris: Calmann Lévy, 1887.]

SULLIVAN, John (1988). *ETA and Basque Nationalism: The Fight for Euskadi. 1890–1986*. London: Routledge.

WATSON, Cameron (1996). 'Folklore and Basque Nationalism: Language, Myth, Reality.' *Nations and Nationalism* 2: 1 (March), pp. 17–34.

WRIGHT, Sue (ed.) (1999). *Language, Democracy, and Devolution in Catalonia*. Clevedon, England/ Philadelphia, PA: Multilingual Matters.

CHAPTER FOUR

Chechnya and the Caucasus

Helen Krag

Introduction: The War in Chechnya (1994–6)

Russia's war in Chechnya in 1994–6 was, as most Russians and Chechens would agree, a serious mistake.[1] Probably all wars fought by central powers against regions in upheaval, minorities or ethnoradical movements can be said to be mistakes in the final analysis. At least it can be seen as a sign of political maturity to admit it. Admitting, though, does not change the severe consequences. While Western media for many months – and until the end of the 1994–6 war – repeated as a fact that 30,000 had died in the war, President Yeltsin's special envoy to Chechnya, (then) Secretary of the Russian Security Council Aleksandr Lebed, and (then) Chechen President Zelimkhan Yandarbiev finally agreed in October 1996 that c. 100,000 civilians (± 20,000 depending on the source) were killed during the twenty months of regular warfare in Chechnya (Walker 1998). Chechnya was left in ruins to such a degree that international media compared post-war Grozny (the Chechen capital) of 1996 to the post-Second World War Dresden of 1945.

Troops were sent into Chechnya on 11 December 1994. Ironically, the OSCE (then CSCE) Summit in Budapest ended on 6 December 1994, less than a week prior to the invasion, with the signing of a 'Code of Conduct on Politico-Military Aspects of Security,' defining the role of armed forces in democratic societies.[2] A full-scale armed attack on the Chechen capital Grozny from the neighbouring regions of Daghestan,

1 This article was finalised for publication in Spring 1998. It was written before the second war, which started in late 1999 following another Russian invasion. The author was given an option for minor updates but time restrictions do not allow for more than that. At the time of re-editing, a new war had begun, Russian air attacks were taking place, and civilians were again fleeing Chechnya. During this new war, a radicalisation took place. Despite this return by Russia to former policies, the statement made here in principle still holds true.
2 *CSCE Budapest Document 1994. Towards a Genuine Partnership in a New Era*, pp. 11–18.

North Ossetia and Stavropol, including 40,000 Russian army and MVD (Interior Ministry) troops supported by some 500 tanks, followed in January 1995 (Tishkov 1996: 29). The Russian government by this act openly demonstrated its willingness to resolve by force a long-standing political disagreement with regional Chechen government structures. It is no secret that this model of conflict resolution resulted in an extraordinary catastrophe in terms of dead, wounded, orphans, displaced and homeless families, destroyed towns and villages, and the like. The war also changed much of Russian societal attitudes towards the use of force. The Chechen side won a military victory despite the fact that the huge Russian military machine was opposed by a small Chechen army, composed possibly of no more than 8,000 men when mobilisation was at a peak (Asuev 1996: 25). The atrocities imposed on the population of Chechnya added significantly to the vulnerability of Chechen society.

The 'Ethnic' Factor in Transition and Conflict Development in the Caucasus

So-called 'ethnic conflicts' became a major trend during the break-up of the USSR and they have accompanied the transition process from its beginning a decade ago. The Caucasus is the most conflict-stricken region in this respect, and thus offers itself to closer scrutiny concerning general and parallel dynamics in conflict development, especially with regard to the issue of ethnic mobilisation *vis-à-vis* centralist rule.[3] In this respect, Chechnya is no isolated case, neither in geographical nor in geopolitical terms. At the same time, it must be stressed that the war in Chechnya not only, or not simply, confirms a general trend but also constitutes a unique experience – particularly with respect to the Russian government's use of violence as a means of conflict resolution on its territory.

The campaign for reforms within the Soviet Communist Party, known as *glasnost* and *perestroika*, did not include the nationality or ethnic question. The last Soviet President, Mikhail Gorbachev, explicitly stated that this issue had been solved satisfactorily during the period of 'real socialism'. It did not take long before this interpretation of the prevailing social reality turned out to be erroneous, as massive protests against centralised structures and Russian/Slavic dominance surfaced. The first incident happened as early as December 1986 in the capital of Kazakhstan when

---

3   In some earlier articles the author of this paper discussed the volatility of the Caucasus
     Region prior to the war in Chechnya and the parallel dynamics of all conflicts in the
     region: e.g. 'The Caucasus – a Troubled Region at the Rim of Europe,' *Regional Contact
     1993* (1994) pp. 34–44 and 'The Break-Up of the USSR and the Dynamics of "Ethnic
     Conflict",' *Coming out of War and Ethnic Violence, Proceedings of the International
     Peace Studies Symposium '96 in Okinawa*, 1997, pp. 186–206.

youths demonstrated against the inauguration of a Russian as First Secretary of the Kazakh Communist Party. Politicians as well as the media
labelled the protesters as 'criminals', 'mafiosi', 'hooligans' and 'anti-
reformers', and many applauded when internal troops retained control,
despite several deaths and arrests.

Parallel scenarios developed in Armenia in 1988, in Georgia in 1989,
in Azerbaijan in 1990, and in Lithuania in 1991 – to mention the best-
known cases. These task force actions against the new parliaments of the
streets protesting against 'Moscow's long arm' and demonstrating for
additional regional self-expression and self-determination were ruthless
and had shocking and escalating effects.

In the years before and after the break-up of the Soviet system
(1988–92), four major conflicts evolved in the Caucasus out of initial
discontent with the Soviet system: the *Nagorno-Karabakh conflict*
between Armenia and Azerbaijan; the *Abkhaz* and the *South Ossetian
conflicts* in Georgia; and the *Prigorodny conflict* in Russia. These conflicts
resulted in hundreds of thousands killed and disabled, approximately 2.5
million refugees and internally displaced persons. They destroyed
houses, industry and infrastructure, and natural resources; left an enter-
prising population in social need and threw entire communities into
political, legal, moral and economic chaos. It is often stated as a positive
comparison with the break-up of Yugoslavia, that the break-up of the
Soviet Union into new, independent countries was a peaceful process.
Such a statement may be based on differences in Western involvement,
in conflict representation in the international media and in the influx of
refugees into West European countries. But seen against this background, it is not the whole truth.

The sequence of conflicts in the Caucasus followed similar patterns.
In the beginning, the major drive of regional and local popular movements was a desire for increased economic and cultural influence in
regional affairs, including insight into their own non-Russian cultures
and histories which, in many cases, had been made taboo, falsified or
suppressed during the Soviet period.

Former republics and autonomous regions expected that *perestroika*
would mean that rights which had been explicitly enshrined in Soviet
law would finally be implemented. When the leadership in Moscow
countered demonstrations and claims with force, the popular protest
movements regularly transformed their main slogans into claims for
sovereignty and independence, thereby triggering even more opposition
from Moscow. In all cases, political disagreements on autonomy and
legitimacy turned 'ethnic' in the course of conflict. Political claims
turned down by central authorities radicalised the popular movements
and deepened the gulf between the adversaries beyond repair.

Chronologically, the first armed conflict came to be known as the
Nagorno-Karabakh conflict, which developed into a war between

Armenia and Azerbaijan. Armenian intellectuals involved in the reform process of the 1980s included in their claims more *de facto* cultural autonomy for Nagorno-Karabakh, a primarily Armenian-populated region of Azerbaijan. When the Armenian reform movement spread to Nagorno-Karabakh, Karabakh leaders, in accordance with Soviet legislation, forwarded to the Azerbaijani as well as the Soviet leaderships an application for changing the internal administrative structures and coming under Armenian instead of Azerbaijani legislation. It was denied in both places. The Soviet State was not ready then for understanding 'ethnic conflict'. Demands for change were seen as anti-reform movements. Anti-Armenian demonstrations took place in Azerbaijan: people were killed, others had to flee. Soviet special forces became involved. The discourse between Azerbaijan and the Armenian minority became increasingly confrontational and 'ethnified'. Armenia turned against its own Azeri minority, and a flow of out-migration began. The conflict escalated until finally, in September 1989, war broke out. A political disagreement on legitimacy and autonomy had turned ethnic. Although the international community (CSCE/OSCE 'Minsk Process') became involved in resolving the conflict, no solution to the question of Nagorno-Karabakh's status has yet been agreed upon.

The *Abkhaz conflict* was the second conflict, chronologically, which turned into war in 1992. In the late 1980s, Georgia's dissident movement demanded a stronger influence in local development. Also, in Georgia, language claims were important. It was a bone of contention for those protesting against the centralised Soviet state that minorities within Georgia – one-third of the population – did not speak Georgian. Abkhazia, then an autonomous republic within Georgia, applied for separation from Georgia in order to avoid the 'Georgianisation' process. Mass demonstrations against what was perceived as Abkhazia's lack of loyalty towards Georgia's interests were brutally crushed by Soviet special forces, an event which radicalised the Georgian reform movement. When Georgia in 1990 declared its sovereignty which, in Soviet terminology, meant a lack of will to recognise the priority of Soviet legislation, Abkhazia did not wish to follow and declared sovereignty as well. This, in turn, was seen by Georgia as a threat against Georgian state integrity. After a coup and a short but bloody civil war, former Soviet Minister of Foreign Affairs Eduard Shevardnadze took over the Georgian leadership in 1992 and intervened in Abkhazia with military force. Abkhazia, helped by Russia and North Caucasians, withstood the Georgian forces. One quarter of a million Georgians fled from Abkhazia. Again, a political disagreement on autonomy and legitimacy had turned 'ethnic' and had radicalised the popular movements involved. The international community (UN) also became involved. This war, too, has ended, while no solution to the question of Abkhazia's status has yet been agreed upon.

Georgia's claim that the Georgian language be given priority on the entire territory of Georgia also inspired the Popular Movement in the Autonomous Region of *South Ossetia* to apply for an upgrading of its autonomous status. To cut a long process short: the Soviet special forces intervened to put an end to the confrontations between Georgians and Ossetians. When Georgia opted for independence from the Soviet Union, South Ossetia applied for inclusion into the Russian Federation in order to become united with its kin in Russian North Ossetia. The war was followed by a mass emigration of 100,000 Ossetians from Georgia to Russia (North Ossetia).

The South Ossetian conflict with Georgia, and the mass emigration of Ossetians to North Ossetia had an impact on a fourth violent conflict in the region – the so-called *Prigorodny conflict*, a territorial conflict over the rights of Ingush to remain settled in the Prigorodny *rayon* (district) of what was then the Autonomous Republic of North Ossetia (and is now the Republic of North Ossetia-Alania) (Krag and Funch 1994).[4] Prigorodny *rayon* had been part of Ingushetia until the Ingush people, in 1944, were collectively declared enemies of the Soviet state and deported to Asia. Their republic (which they shared with the Chechens) was given away to others. On their return, their autonomous republic was reestablished, except for the territory of Prigorodny which remained with North Ossetia. When in 1991 Boris Yeltsin became the Russian leader, he issued a 'Decree on the Rehabilitation of the Repressed Peoples', including their right to lost land – a decree which was not implemented. In October/November 1992, following armed clashes and the intervention of Russian troops, almost all Ingush fled from the Prigorodny District to Ingushetia. In this case, too, a political injustice neglected for too long had turned 'ethnic'.

There is a direct line from these conflicts and their dynamics to the latest war and conflict: Russia's military invasion of the Chechen Republic in December 1994. Also this conflict goes back to a time when it was considered 'politically correct' by the Russian leadership to take over power from communist leaders. In 1991, after the Moscow coup, former Soviet Air Force General Dzhokhar Dudaev, who while serving at Tartu Air Base in Estonia followed the Estonian Popular Front and independence movement closely, became head of the Chechen National Congress, which declared Chechnya independent, elected him President and started to abolish all symbols of Soviet and Russian power throughout the Chechen Republic. When Chechnya opted for independence, the Ingush opted for continued membership in the Russian Federation. The two groups partitioned their territory in a very undramatic manner, and Russia recognised the new Ingush Republic. Moscow,

4   See also *The Ingush-Ossetian Conflict in the Prigorodnyi Region*, A Human Rights Watch/Helsinki Report, 1996.

now under President Yeltsin, declared a state of emergency and sent special units in 1992. Although these troops were neutralised by the Chechen National Guard, the competition on political legitimacy in the Republic of Chechnya proceeded with economic and political means, among others with an economic blockade by Moscow and support to Moscow-friendly opposition groups. Chechnya, on the other hand, boycotted all Russian elections and structures, while Moscow launched an anti-Chechen campaign and ignored Chechnya's claims and complaints. In 1993, Chechnya was included in the new Russian constitution despite Chechen nonparticipation. Thus, Chechnya became *de facto* independent from 1991. Chechen President Dzhokhar Dudaev repeatedly claimed that all his attempts at discussing the issues at stake with Russian officials had been turned down.[5] Russian sources support the claim that serious attempts at talks were not undertaken at any point during the prewar phase (Tishkov 1996). Reasons given for the intervention by Moscow were the need to protect the integrity of the state from nationalist movements and criminals.

These are very generalised presentations of the conflicts in the Caucasus. All have been analysed in detail in numerous publications. The generalisations are presented here to point out the common background to the conflicts and the dynamics of their development. *Glasnost* and *perestroika* had promised new opportunities to voice desires for change with respect to political structures, reconciliation of grievances and a new order of self-determination. When such desires were voiced as complaints against earlier humiliations and as claims for stronger regional influence, they were regularly ignored or even reprimanded by the central authorities. They were then more pointedly formulated as demands for constitutional changes, which in turn were opposed by force. In the process, political claims transformed into conflicts which, increasingly, became more clearly defined in ethnic and national terms by the conflicting sides. Although all conflicts ignited on political issues (and not on ethnic issues), they were minority conflicts in the sense that they questioned formerly unquestioned minority – majority relations and the legitimacy of majority rule on minority territory. These political disagreements between region and centre increasingly developed into ethnic discourse and thus supported the insight put forward by Adam Roberts, that '[...] what binds a group together, separates it from others, and fatefully leads it into action, is [...] a sense of common vulnerability: past history and present experience teach who are one's enemies, and who one's friends. [...] Whether or not it is right to apply the term "ethnic" to all these conflicts is not very important (Roberts 1993).'

It is interesting to note that the above-mentioned conflicts, despite many differences, also have some common outcomes. E.W. Walker

5   See for instance an interview in *Der Spiegel*, no. 41/1994, p. 176.

points out that, in the case of Nagorno-Karabakh, Abkhazia and Chechnya alike, secessionists have triumphed on the battlefield and now
control their territory; that in all cases cease-fires have ended the
conflicts, while they have failed to win international recognition despite
their military success. They are also in a stalemate at home: while they
assert their right to self-determination, the governments in question
(Azerbaijan, Georgia and Russia) insist on state integrity which makes
the settlements on legal status rather difficult (Walker 1998).[6]

In no case did the use of force by the government solve the problems:
state integrity was not strengthened; peaceful and democratic developments were not promoted in the insurgent republics; the centre's
political legitimacy in the region did not grow; the issues of political
status were not solved, neither were the issues of alleged criminality –
arms trade and hostage-taking are of major concern; and, last but not
least, the nationalist or ethnic mobilisations could not be stopped – on
the contrary. As a result of these actions, any trust in the good intentions
of the centre has deteriorated. They have contributed to a process of
ethnification, i.e. of political dividing lines increasingly expressed in
ethnic terms.

The Caucasus region is economically a major source of oil and gas
deposits, which involves a multitude of geopolitical interests; ethnically, it is home to forty or fifty distinct ethnic groups – diversity
running along a range of cultural, linguistic and religious lines. Diversity, or at least the symbolic memory of it, survived the Soviet decades.
While nationality/ethnicity was verbally accepted as an essential criterion of individual, group and territorial public identity, the expression
of these identities and attachments to certain cultures and places was
discouraged in the Soviet period. The public exercise of religious
expression or the use of local languages was mostly not promoted, and
the history of smaller peoples was regularly distorted. Time and again
ethnic groups (e.g. the Chechen) were collectively and on ethnic
grounds persecuted and punished. The worst experience for the
Chechens, and an important element of Chechen self-identification,
was the collective deportation of all Chechens to Central Asia in
February 1944.

Why Separatism and Centralist Force?

Why did the Russian leadership, in the face of an intended democratic
development with an apparent need for confidence building, choose
force as a method of conflict resolution and how could it even expect to

6   Walker's statement on the cease-fire in Chechnya was made in 1998, between the two
Chechen wars.

win? When discussing this issue one must take into consideration that, at the time when the conflicts first evolved from the popular move-ments, confidence building between centre and periphery and the need for societal change was a major political motor – much more than stabil-ity and strength, which prevailed in the Soviet state and prevail again a decade later. Several contextual reasons for the use of force have been discussed widely: that the decision was not made by the President, that there was no clear military command, that the military was in bad shape, that the President was badly informed, etc. None of these arguments – which show the discrepancy of declared aims and means at the time – can explain why governmental players opted for force and violence as legitimate means for governance, as happened in all the instances of conflict mentioned above. One cannot even call on lack of experience as a plausible explanation: cruelty did not decrease with time, Russia did not learn from the experience:[7] the Chechen war, the latest of the conflicts examined, turned out to be the cruellest of them all.

One explanation imposes itself: that a very traditional, colonial mentality of power, force and strength had survived despite declarations of decentralisation and a focus on human rights. One example of the widening gap between the Russian centre and Russia's Caucasian periph-ery, in spite of declared attempts at equality, is linguistic: during the 1990s the Russian language developed the term 'person of Caucasian nationality'. This expression is modelled on an older and better-known expression in Russian: 'a person of Jewish nationality', mirroring racist or near-racist attitudes. It has not been opposed by power structures.'[8] Other examples of anti-Caucasian use of language and anti-Caucasian actions in Moscow could also be found in the media during the year preceding the war in Chechnya.[9]

There is another expression, 'Our Caucasus', exclaimed with a sigh of love and longing by Russians. It depicts the Caucasus as legitimate Russian territory, or some near-to-crown colony. It still very much mirrors strong centralist thinking when central executives talk of the relationship between Moscow and Grozny as one of civilisation versus barbarism or of the need to force Chechen youth to other regions of the Russian Federation.[10] There is adequate proof of the fact that democratic thinking has a long way to go with those who analysed the situation in Chechnya before the war and those who opted for a war.

7   This has become even more true with the new attempts at solving the 'Chechen problem' by force, as instigated in September 1999.
8   There are several analyses of 'new' Russian language (Gussejnov 1994).
9   As examples see Huttenbach (1993) and Vasilyeva (1994). Update 1999: the tone has deteriorated remarkably. Chechens and other Caucasians are hunted subjects in Moscow and other Russian cities at the time of the final editing of this article.
10 Expressed by official Russian participants during a conference on Conflicts in the Cauca-sus held in Oslo, 24–26 November 1995.

Not even to the outside world do democracy or human rights seem to have been a prime objective: despite well-developed standards on human, indigenous and minority rights and despite these rights being a concern of the international community, this did not have consequences in practice during the prewar phase. Russia was even accepted as a member of the Council of Europe in the middle of its massive warfare against the Chechen population. Perceived stability and balance of power appear to be more important than democracy and human rights – even the right to existence. Looking at the conflicts as inadequate and unsuccessful minority – majority relations, it seems adequate to say that post-Soviet society has not yet acquired the preconditions for consensus- or dialogue-based conflict resolution. If it is correct that the value of democracy lies in peaceful negotiations, in listening to and acknowledging each others' grievances and claims and finding solutions together – and not in the use of force[11] – Soviet society knew no democracy, and post-Soviet Russian society still has a lot to implement. This is not the place to discuss the Russian government's motives for retaining control in Chechnya but to look at why these motives were acted out.

Also, Chechnya is part of the post-Soviet space. But why did Chechnya opt for independence, and how was the Chechen movement mobilised to such a degree that a war against Russia could be won? There are several answers to that question. On the eve of the invasion by Russian forces, Chechnya was prepared for long-term guerrilla warfare – as an *ultima ratio* – in case of the expected Russian invasion. Most political movements in Chechnya – and also anti-Dudaev opposition forces – supported the so-called 'Caucasian Revolution' as a natural reaction to a long and cruel colonial conquest in the eighteenth and nineteenth centuries and to the humiliations of forced deportation during and after the Second World War. The Estonian parallel – the size of the population, the position at the fringes of Russia, the setting of 'colonialism' and a strong attachment to Chechnya as home territory – appeared logical to many Chechens and also to those who did not support the independence drive. The setting of being ignored as potential negotiation partners, being isolated economically and politically, being campaigned against as 'criminal devils' – nationally and internationally, or scapegoated and harassed by Moscow police or internal troops,[12] etc., did contribute to the increasing popularity of the Chechen independence movement. It was obvious to whomever wanted to visit Chechnya prior to the war that Chechens were prepared to unite loyally under the Chechen flag of President Dudaev, and to fight against Russian troops. Not only did President Yeltsin not wish to discuss peaceful solutions with President Dudaev, but even the democratic movement in the Russian capital, approached by

11 A definition according to Ross (1967: 123–33).
12 E.g. *ASN Analysis of Current Events*, December 1993, and *New Times*, October 1994.

democratic intellectuals in Chechnya,[13] was for a long time reluctant to listen to Chechen grievances.

The question has often been asked as to why Chechnya chose a path that none of the other Russian republics chose. There are several answers to that question as well. Firstly, Chechnya was one of the few republics with a simple ethnic majority and leadership after the peaceful 'divorce' from Ingushetia. Second, with a population of 1.2 million inhabitants, Chechnya's size was not unusual for independent states (e.g. Estonia). And thirdly, Chechnya had a leader who knew European traditions because he had served in Estonia – while Chechnya itself had been isolated throughout Soviet history. Furthermore, with a Soviet general as the top leader, Chechnya had a disciplined, self-conscious and goal-oriented leadership. Also, Chechens have a reputation for continuous opposition to Russian governance throughout the common Russian-Chechen history, beginning with the Russian conquest of the Caucasus at the end of the eighteenth century.

So much for Chechnya's own search for independence, but no analysis of the Chechen case independently of the other armed conflicts in the region can project the real reasons for radicalisation. As the parallel scenarios of other conflicts in the region demonstrate (Nagorno-Karabakh, Abkhazia, etc.) the spiral of violence was set in motion by the condescending reactions of central authorities, more so than by the so-called ethnic movements.

At the beginning of organised warfare on Chechen territory, aid agencies and outside observers, including the media, were prevented from assisting, informing or mediating.[14] There was little information about the situation in the region, and even less understanding of the developments. What little information existed was one-sided and Moscow-based. The Russian government insisted that it was necessary to fight a terrorist and criminal separatist local government. Shortly after the invasion, Moscow television broadcast pictures of the Russian flag on the roof of the presidential palace in the Chechen capital Grozny to prove a quick victory. The pictures were shown all over the world – until it became known that they were fake. Russia had fallen back on policies of closing the region to potential governmental, intergovernmental and nongovernmental outside players. It took some time before the global changes in information technology demonstrated that this policy of closing in a conflict could no longer be upheld. Despite Russian attempts to monopolise the information circuit around Chechnya by preventing international media access to the site of the armed clashes, the Internet made this impossible. Less than a month after the invasion, in January 1995, a discussion list was established 'devoted to', as the

13 Conversations between the author and researchers in Grozny, November 1993.
14 Chechnya was even more sealed off during the second war starting in 1999.

owner put it in his presentation, 'the current situation in Chechnya, particularly sharing the news about recent developments.' The list functioned as a major source of information throughout the war and in the postwar period. Information was supplied internationally and was at the disposal of and used by a broad range of researchers and media people. The list, one should assume, changed the information war despite the fact that Grozny could not participate directly.[15]

After the War: Strengthened Loyalties and the Role of Outside Players

As in the other Caucasian conflicts, the Chechen war as such ended, while no solution to the status question could be agreed upon.[16] Negotiations were repeatedly postponed, while the lines of disagreement sharpened. Chechnya, *de facto* independent since 1991, has strengthened its will for *de jure* independence after the military victory. Russia has not moved an inch in its unwillingness to discuss this issue. The conflict is not the same in the postwar context, though. The preconditions for economic sovereignty are much worse due to large-scale destruction; unemployment is high with allegedly 50,000 young men under arms and a breakdown in the educational system; the breakdown of the infrastructure adds to radicalisation, mounting vulnerabilities and decreasing tolerance. In the course of the war, ethnic mobilisation ran high. The value of national symbols such as the Chechen flag, the national anthem, the heroes of Chechen history, especially those of the resistance to Russian colonisation, have risen dramatically. Also, the struggle for sovereignty has intensified, as many Chechens experienced the outcome of the war as a demonstration of moral superiority to Russia: little Chechnya won a war against huge Russia; the Chechen President, who was seen by many Chechens as a national symbol, was killed by a Russian missile. Contrary to what had been used as a Russian argument, no terrorist acts were conducted in Moscow during the war, not even under the worst pressures.[17] It was also predicted that the various clan structures and political groupings would turn Chechnya into an Afghanistan scenario – which was not the case as long as Chechnya's newly elected leadership still had hopes of finding solutions with

15 The list was based on a server at the University of Warsaw (listserv@plearn.edu.pl). Since 1996, more information has been available. Books and reports have been published, and the Chechen government has its own web-site.
16 See footnote 1.
17 In August/September 1999 several bombs went off in Russian cities and many were killed. These bombs were immediately ascribed to Chechen terrorists and served as legitimisation for renewed attacks on the Chechen Republic. According to most analyses, it is by no means clear who was responsible for the bombs.

Moscow.[18] At the same time, Russia had to admit openly that the war had been a mistake. Russia's cruel and devastating war against Chechnya, i.e. against its own population, is a fact that has changed the country for many years to come.

In 1997, Chechnya stood at a crossroads concerning its future. During the war, and shortly after its end, Chechnya had a great interest in proving to the West its standard of 'civilised' behaviour – in spite of the fact that it felt let down by the international community. The elections of January 1997, which were acknowledged by the international community (OSCE) as free and fair, were a major test. Since the elections, however, Chechnya has been neglected and isolated and any prospects of foreign investment have been poor. No support was given to the devastated Chechen economy, no assistance to legalisation, education, etc., with the effect that calls for an 'alternative order' became louder. With no help from Moscow or from the West in sight, political groups seeking support in the West became weaker while groups seeking support outside European circles, and especially in Muslim states, became stronger. Chechnya became a dangerous place to go and, as hostage taking became everyday practice, most international aid organisations had to leave Chechnya. Chechnya's eagerness to prove to the West a capability to develop a democratic society is diminishing; at the same time, the support for extremist Muslim norms is increasing.

How can discursive interaction be promoted? The immediate answer would be: not by neglect. No matter what the content of negotiations, Chechnya needs guarantees by international organisations against future state violence. Chechnya needs to be listened to seriously – with direct access to international fora if future conflicts are to be avoided. As it is now, to win a war seems to be a precondition – but no guarantee – for being listened to. A minimum requirement for a future positive development is the acknowledgement of suffering during long spells of Chechen history, as well as assistance and guarantees for economic development and postwar reconstruction. The comparison of Grozny with Dresden by the media should help people to understand the issue at hand. NGOs should be involved to support the building of trust and confidence between the opponents; to provide information on good practices in the area of self-determination; to assist in developing the legislative process; to secure access to international fora (especially when central authorities do not wish this to happen). Dignity and acceptance are, undoubtedly, better ways than humiliation and neglect.

This article was written before the second war in Chechnya. During the second war relations between Russia and Chechnya further deteriorated. They are no longer at a stalemate: Russia's new president,

18 Aslan Maskhadov became President of Chechnya after the elections. He was perceived as a leader with whom compromise was possible. Still, no serious attempts to resolve the situation were undertaken after the war.

Vladimir Putin, has recently reinterpreted the war into a war on international terrorism involving Muslim fundamentalists. This can be seen as a consequence of the radicalising development described in this article.

References

ASUEV, Sharip (1996). 'Hoping for Peace, Willing for War.' *Warreport* 42 (June).

GUSSEJNOV, Gassan (1994). *Materialien zu einem russischen gesellschaftspolitischen Wörterbuch, 1992–93. Einführung und Texte*. Forschungsstelle Osteuropa an der Universität Bremen. Bremen: University of Bremen.

HUTTENBACH, Henry R. (1993). 'Counter-revolutionary "Ethnic Cleansing": Ethnic "Sweeping" in Post-October Moscow.' *ASN Analysis of Current Events* 5: 9 (December).

KRAG, Helen, and Lars FUNCH HANSEN(1994). *The North Caucasus: Minorities at a Crossroads. An MRG International Report, 94/5*. London: Minority Rights Group International .

ROBERTS, Adam (1993). 'Foreword'. In: Daniel Patrick Moynihan, *Pandaemonium: Ethnicity in International Politics*, Oxford: Oxford University Press, pp. xi–xii.

ROSS, Alf (1967). *Hvorfor Demokrati? (Why Democracy?)*. Copenhagen: Nyt Nordisk Forlag (2nd edn.).

TISHKOV, V. (1996). 'Explaining and Categorizing the Chechen War.' In: *Conflicts in the Caucasus*, Prio Report 3, Pavel Baev and Ole Berthelsen (eds). Oslo: International Peace Research Institute, pp. 27–43.

VASILYEVA, Olga (1994). ' "Devils": National in Appearance, and Criminal in Essence.' *New Times* 20 (October), pp. 20–22.

WALKER, Edward W. (1998). 'Obstacles to War and peace in Chechnya.' In: *No Peace, No War in the Caucasus: Secessionist Conflicts in Chechnya, Abkhazia and Nagorno-Karabakh*, Strengthening Democratic Institutions Project, Harvard University, John F. Kennedy School of Government, 7, no. 10.

CHAPTER FIVE

International Dimensions of the Northern Ireland Conflict and Settlement

Adrian Guelke

Few political settlements have been as unexpected as Northern Ireland's Good Friday Agreement of 10 April 1998. In the week of the settlement itself, John Taylor, the Deputy Leader of the Ulster Unionist Party (UUP), the largest party in electoral terms of the eight parties participating in the multiparty talks in Belfast, had put the odds of reaching agreement at 4 percent. Even those commentators who were optimistic that an agreement could be achieved had not expected that it would embrace all eight parties. In particular, few expected that Sinn Féin would stay the course. However, it appears that once the leaders of Sinn Féin appreciated that an agreement would be reached with or without their support, fear of the party's marginalisation and the concessions that the party was able to secure on nonconstitutional issues, such as the reform of policing and the release of prisoners, through the good offices of the Irish government, persuaded the party to go along with the Agreement and then to seek to persuade the rank and file of the party of the wisdom of this course of action.

The achievement of the Agreement is the more remarkable when viewed from the perspective of Northern Ireland's domestic politics since the start of the peace process, whether one dates its beginning from the first cease-fire by the Provisional Irish Republican Army (IRA) on 31 August 1994 or from the Joint Declaration by the British and Irish governments on 15 December 1993. Indeed, a feature of that politics has been a sharp polarisation of opinion, with a shift in support of voters to the more extreme parties on either side of the province's sectarian divide and intense intercommunal antagonism over the issue of the parades of the Orange Order during the summer months of 1995, 1996 and 1997. The actual contexts of the Agreement have been much less of a surprise. Their fundamental basis is power sharing within a devolved government of Northern Ireland, plus

an Irish dimension in the form of cross-border bodies to promote cooperation between the two parts of Ireland in a number of largely uncontroversial
policy areas. The basic thrust of the Agreement is quite similar to the
Sunningdale Agreement of December 1973. Indeed, in a widely quoted
witticism, Seamus Mallon, the Deputy Leader of the Social Democratic
and Labour Party (SDLP) – the party that represents a majority of Northern
Ireland's Catholics and Nationalists – described the basis of the current
agreement as 'Sunningdale for slow learners'.

    Factors external to Northern Ireland were very evident in the process
that led to the Agreement. Thus, a number of accounts of the achievement of the Agreement highlighted as crucial President Bill Clinton's
phone call to the Leader of the UUP, David Trimble, in the hours immediately before the announcement of the Agreement, when the UUP
appeared to be wavering as to whether to accept the deal.[1] Also widely
seen as critical to the success of the talks process was the decision of the
British Prime Minister, Tony Blair, to leave London and stay in Belfast
for the final days of the negotiations. Indeed, all the parties in the talks
praised his role in brokering the deal and that was reflected in the credit
he received in polls on the Agreement. His role appears to have been
crucial in persuading the UUP to accept a deal, both by offering reassur-
ance to the Party on a number of issues, but also by making it clear that if
Unionist opposition prevented an agreement, the British government
would take the actions it considered appropriate. An argument used by
the Ulster Unionist leadership to persuade rank-and-file members of the
party to accept the deal was that if there had been no agreement the
British government would have implemented the parts of the Agreement that the Unionists disliked most, and without the Agreement the
Unionists would not have secured what they had wanted most, the revi-
sion of Articles 2 and 3 of the Irish constitution and the replacement of
the Anglo-Irish Agreement.

    The strength of the Blair government has been a factor of immense
importance in the success of the whole peace process. The landslide that
elected Tony Blair and the success of the government in its first year
meant that Unionists were forced to come to terms with the likelihood
of Labour's being in power for much longer than five years. When Labour
came to power on 1 May 1997, the Northern Ireland peace process was
deadlocked. Immediately upon assuming office, the new government
authorised contacts with Sinn Féin at an official level. At the same time,
Blair came to Belfast to deliver an important speech, reassuring Unionists that he did not envisage a united Ireland in the foreseeable future
and making it clear that the establishment of cross-border institutions
would not be allowed to develop into a lever for pushing Unionists into a
united Ireland against their consent. However, the new government was

1 *Financial Times*, 11 April 1998.

unable to find a compromise to the demand of the Orange Order that it be allowed to parade down the Garvaghy Road in Portadown. To avoid a long-running stand-off the decision was made to force the march through against the wishes of its Catholic residents. They chanted 'no cease-fire' as the parade went ahead accompanied by a large contingent of police. Despite these ugly scenes, less than two weeks later, on 20 July, the Provisional IRA renewed its cease-fire.

The government gave three assurances to Sinn Féin to secure the cease-fire. Firstly, it agreed that the party would be admitted into the multiparty talks within a matter of weeks of a new cease-fire. The previous formula had been that the party would have to establish its bona fides over a much longer period of time before a decision on its participation was made. Secondly, May 1998 was set as a deadline for the completion of the talks. One of Sinn Féin's fears was that the process of negotiation would be stretched out indefinitely. Thirdly, the government made it clear that the issue of the decommissioning of paramilitary arsenals would not be allowed to delay negotiations on the substantive constitutional questions. Substantive talks then began in October. However, two of the Unionist parties, the Democratic Unionist Party (DUP) of Ian Paisley, and the small United Kingdom Unionist Party (UKUP) of Robert McCartney, walked out in response to Sinn Féin's inclusion in the process.

Initially, the negotiations made very little headway, with the parties reluctant to indicate areas where they would be willing to compromise. The minor parties unattached to either the Unionist or the Nationalist bloc were the most constructive in actually putting forward position papers on the issues in an attempt to move the process forward. The UUP preferred talking to the British government and to Blair himself rather than engaging with the other parties. Similarly, Sinn Féin did most of its negotiating through the Irish government, headed since the Republic's general election in June 1997 by Bertie Ahern. In December, the British and Irish governments tried to get agreement from the parties on the broad contours of a settlement, so as to provide the basis for more intensive negotiation. However, this attempt failed. In January, the two governments put forward their own 'heads of agreement' document to give the process impetus. This proposed a Northern Ireland Assembly operating on a power sharing basis, a Council of Britain and Ireland, North–South institutions and changes to the Irish constitution and to the 1920 Government of Ireland Act. This proved acceptable to all the parties except Sinn Féin. Its hostile reaction was partly influenced by a leak of the document to a national newspaper ahead of the official publication of the proposals. The leak put a strongly Unionist interpretation on their implications for the future.

By this point, the negotiations were in serious difficulty for another reason. Billy Wright, the leading figure in the Loyalist Volunteer Force – an extreme Loyalist paramilitary organisation – had been murdered just after Christmas in the Maze prison by inmates from an equally extreme Republican paramilitary organisation. As a consequence of this event, prisoners of one of the Loyalist factions taking part in the talks urged their political wing to withdraw from the negotiations. To avert this potentially fatal blow to the negotiations, the Secretary of State for Northern Ireland, Marjorie ('Mo') Mowlam, went in person into the prison to persuade the prisoners to reverse their decision. She was successful in doing so, though some were offended by her readiness to talk to prisoners who had carried out multiple killings. Further, in the event, it transpired that members of the paramilitary organisation linked to the prisoners, the Ulster Freedom Fighters (UFF), had been responsible for a number of random sectarian assassinations that had taken place in January in revenge for the killing of Billy Wright. As a consequence, the party linked to the UFF, the Ulster Democratic Party (UDP), was suspended from the talks for a period of four weeks.

A new crisis in the talks occurred at the end of February when the Chief Constable of the Royal Ulster Constabulary (RUC) concluded that the Provisional IRA had been responsible that month for two murders. These were the killing of a known drug dealer and of a member of a Loyalist paramilitary organisation who had been accused of involvement in distributing drugs. Significantly, there was no denial by the IRA of its involvement in these killings, merely a statement that the cease-fire remained intact. The point was that the IRA did not regard action it took in policing its strongholds as a breach of the cease-fire. Sinn Féin for its part argued that it did not in any event represent the IRA. Neither the governments nor the other parties were persuaded by these arguments and Sinn Féin was suspended from the talks, though for an even shorter period than the UDP had been.

The successive exclusions of the UDP and Sinn Féin and the arguments over these absorbed the energies of the parties in the talks, prompting widespread gloom over the prospects for a negotiated settlement. There was a break in the talks in the middle of March to allow the parties to take part in St Patrick's Day celebrations in the United States, during which time President Clinton strongly urged the parties to make the necessary compromises to achieve a deal. This break was followed by the talks chairman, former US Senator George Mitchell, setting 9 April as a deadline for the conclusion of the negotiations. The reason he set such an early deadline was the realisation by the two governments that unless a deal was achieved by Easter, it would prove impossible to hold the elections to the proposed Northern Ireland Assembly ahead of the climax to the Orange Order's marching season in the second week of July, since any deal would first need to be approved in referenda in Northern Ireland and the Republic of Ireland. The fear was that another confrontation on the Garvaghy Road might derail a settlement if the Assembly was not in place by this point.

The Good Friday Agreement was approved in the referenda in Northern Ireland and the Republic of Ireland. It was supported by 71 percent of those voting in Northern Ireland. However, it was already apparent that the Agreement could face difficulties in implementation. Thus, the basis for Unionist support for the Agreement was totally at odds with how the accord was being interpreted by Republicans. Further, Unionists were divided on the merits of the deal, so that barely a half of the Protestants voted 'yes' in the referendum in Northern Ireland. The division of Unionist opinion was further borne out in the elections to the Northern Ireland Assembly in June, in which roughly equal numbers of Unionist opponents and supporters were elected. As the rule for decision making in the Assembly requires the consent of representatives of both communities, the potential for deadlock is very considerable. In December 1998 the parties agreed on the policy areas that will come under the North–South institutions. However, devolution of powers to a Northern Irish Executive has been held up by disagreement between the UUP and Sinn Féin over decommissioning, with the former insisting that a start should be made to paramilitary, specifically IRA, decommissioning of illegally held weapons before an Executive is formed – a position rejected by Sinn Féin as going beyond the terms of the Good Friday Agreement, which sets out a target date for the completion of decommissioning but no starting date. A further challenge to the Agreement has been provided by the activities of violent groups on both sides of the sectarian divide opposed to the Agreement. These have included the August 1998 bombing of Omagh by the Real IRA in which twenty-nine people died, and the assassination of a prominent human rights lawyer, Rosemary Nelson, by Loyalists in March 1999. Thus, while there is no doubt that the Good Friday Agreement provides Northern Ireland with its best chance for real peace since partition, it will be a number of years before it will be possible to be certain that the Agreement has succeeded. However, its breakdown and failure may prove more sudden.

Persistence of parochialism and resistance to the influence of globalisation have formed striking features of the politics of Northern Ireland, with the notion that the province is stuck in a time-warp one of the commonest observations made about its communal divisions. Nonetheless, during the 1990s, internationalisation of the Northern Ireland problem came to be identified as a new, positive factor in the situation. One context for such references was the establishment by the European Union of a special support package for the region in the wake of the 1994 paramilitary cease-fires.[2] Another, more significant basis was President Bill Clinton's triumphant visit to Northern Ireland on 30 November 1995, highlighting America's commitment to the peace process – a degree of involvement in the domestic affairs of the United Kingdom that would have been unthinkable during the Cold War (O'Clery 1996: 4). A further basis for claims that

2   See, for example, Wilson (1997: 7).

the Northern Ireland conflict has become internationalised has been the role that outside mediators have played in the multiparty talks, as US Congressman Peter King pointed out in a speech in Belfast in October 1997.[3] However, the concept of the internationalisation of the Northern Ireland conflict itself remains problematic for a number of reasons.

Firstly, from the perspective of the academic interpretation of the problem, far from there being a process of internationalisation of the conflict, it has been internalised. Thus, one of the main themes of John Whyte's magisterial survey of the literature on the Northern Ireland problem is the growth of the dominance of internal-conflict interpretations of the conflict (Whyte 1990: 202). That is to say, whereas before the onset of the current phase of the Troubles in 1968 and in its early years, there was a preponderance of literature that blamed either British imperialism or southern Irish irredentism for the conflict, by the 1980s there was a virtual consensus among academic analysts of the conflict that the root of the problem lay in communal antagonism between Protestants and Catholics within Northern Ireland. Of course, a belief that the principal antagonists were within Northern Ireland did not preclude according a role to external factors in influencing that battle.

Secondly, while, in particular, the extent of American intervention under Clinton is unprecedented, internationalisation is not new. In important respects, it can be traced back to the very start of the current phase of the Troubles in 1968. This point will be elaborated on below.

Thirdly, confusion arises over what is meant by internationalisation because of the existence of different international dimensions of the problem. Five broad areas can be identified:
1. The ostensible territorial dispute between two states, the United Kingdom and the Republic of Ireland, over Northern Ireland.
2. The involvement of countries outside the British Isles in the conflict.
3. The international affiliations of the parties to the conflict in Northern Ireland.
4. The impact of the conflict on the outside world.
5. The influence of international opinion on the conflict.

While there has been wide variation in whichever of these areas have seemed important at particular times, it is nevertheless possible to identify different phases of the internationalisation of the conflict. Three phases in the development of the international political system had a particularly important bearing on the conflict in Northern Ireland. They were:
  (a) the end of the colonial era, exposing the province's anomalous status in the postcolonial era;
  (b) the establishment of the human rights agenda; and

3 *The Irish Times*, 3 October 1997.

(c) the end of bipolarity, in the context of which the United
Kingdom had played a crucial supporting role to the United
States in the Western alliance.

Each of these areas and phases will be examined in turn.

The Territorial Dispute between the United Kingdom and the Republic of Ireland over Northern Ireland

In formal terms there has been a conflict between the claim of the Irish
Republic's constitution that Northern Ireland is part of Ireland and the
constantly reiterated position of the British government that Northern
Ireland will remain part of the United Kingdom as long as a majority in
Northern Ireland so wishes. That stance predated the current Troubles,
though it took the slightly different form of a guarantee that Northern
Ireland would not cease to be part of the United Kingdom without the
consent of the parliament of Northern Ireland. The suspension of the
Stormont parliament in 1972 resulted in the principle of consent being
vested in the people rather than in the parliament. The formal stance of
the Republic of Ireland was enshrined in Articles 2 and 3 of the country's
1937 constitution. Article 2 asserts that 'the national territory consists
of the whole island of Ireland, its islands and territorial seas,' while
Article 3 acknowledges that in practice the jurisdiction of the Irish State
is limited to twenty-six counties 'pending the re-integration of the
national territory.' Unionists have made great play of these articles to
press the charge of irredentism against the Republic. Amendment of
these articles forms part of the Good Friday Agreement. The crux of the
amendment is the commitment that 'a united Ireland shall be brought
about only by peaceful means with the consent of a majority of the
people, democratically expressed, in both jurisdictions in the island.'[4]
Changes to the Irish constitution have to be approved by referendum
and the changes to these articles were the centrepiece of the referendum
on the Agreement held on 22 May 1998.

But what is far more striking, particularly in comparative terms, has
been the lack of enthusiasm which at times British and Irish governments and political parties have shown towards these formal
commitments. Garret FitzGerald's indiscreet political memoirs provide a
number of startling examples of the point. He explains the Irish government's concern at the beginning of 1975 over the possibility of a
unilateral British withdrawal from Northern Ireland. FitzGerald – at the

---

4   Quoted in the Agreement: Agreement reached in the multiparty negotiations, Belfast,
     1998, p. 4.

time Irish Foreign Minister – raised the matter with the American Secretary of State, Henry Kissinger, asking for the Americans to put pressure on the British government not to proceed if that proved necessary (FitzGerald 1991: 259). It does not seem to have occurred to FitzGerald quite how incongruous an argument he was advancing, considering his position as a representative of a neutral state and Britain's as America's leading ally in the Western alliance. FitzGerald also recounts Margaret Thatcher's lack of enthusiasm for his proposal that Articles 2 and 3 of the Irish constitution should be amended as part of the Anglo-Irish Agreement of November 1985 (FitzGerald 1991: 516). Admittedly, the reversal of positions described by FitzGerald is not the norm in Anglo-Irish relations. Generally speaking, disagreement between the British and Irish governments stems from conflict between positions tilted towards Unionism in the case of London and tilted towards Nationalism in the case of Dublin. An important consequence of the institutionalisation of cooperation between the British and Irish governments through the mechanisms of the Anglo-Irish Agreement was that it substantially reduced the likelihood of a serious breach in relations between the two states over the issue of Northern Ireland.

The Involvement of Countries outside the British Isles in the Conflict

The involvement of countries outside the British Isles in the conflict needs to be divided into: (1) state-level interventions; and (2) transnational exchanges at a nongovernmental level. State-level interventions can be further subdivided into: (a) direct engagement in the conflict through the supply of weapons to paramilitary organisations; and (b) diplomatic activity directed at influencing usually the British government, sometimes the Irish government and still more occasionally parties within Northern Ireland.

1. State-level Interventions

(a) Direct engagement in the conflict

Only two states have been directly implicated in supplying weapons to paramilitary organisations. They are Libya and South Africa. Libyan involvement can be dated to June 1972 when the Libyan leader, Colonel Ghadaffi, made a speech in which he declared his willingness to support Irish revolutionaries. In March 1973 the Irish navy intercepted the freighter *Claudia*, capturing five tons of arms destined for the Provisional IRA and it emerged that these had been loaded onto the ship by Libyan soldiers at Tripoli. Ghadaffi treated the conflict in Northern Ireland as an opportunity to put pressure on the British government over its approach to Middle Eastern issues. He continued to give some aid to the Provisional IRA until about 1977. What persuaded him to end this aid was the growth of trade between the Republic of Ireland and Libya (particularly imports of Irish beef) and the consequent establishment of diplomatic relations between the two countries.

A revival of Libyan involvement in Northern Ireland occurred in 1984. The context was the mysterious shooting dead of a policewoman outside the Libyan embassy in London, which led to the expulsion of Libyan diplomats from Britain. Ghadaffi's response to this humiliation was to issue a public invitation to the IRA to set up an office in Tripoli. After the Americans bombed Libya, using air bases in Britain for the raid in April 1986, Ghadaffi first said he would be resuming military aid to the IRA, then said, in an interview with the British newspaper *The Observer*, that he had already done so.[5] The full significance of Ghadaffi's rhetoric became apparent at the end of October 1987 when the French navy intercepted a Panamanian-registered ship, the *Eksund*, with 150 tons of arms and ammunition, including twenty Soviet-made surface-to-air missiles, on board. The French authorities quickly determined that the shipment had been bound for the Provisional IRA and that Libya was the source of the weapons. They also acquired information about earlier shipments that had not been intercepted.

The Irish government was shocked by the revelations. They coincided with a strong backlash against the Provisional IRA within the Republic as a result of an IRA bomb attack on a Remembrance Day ceremony in Enniskillen in November 1987 in which eleven civilians had been killed. In response, the Irish government mounted an extensive search for IRA arms in the Republic. Operation Mallard uncovered a considerable number of Provisional IRA arms caches. However, the quantity of weaponry recovered represented only a fraction of what had got through to the Provisional IRA, according to the French authorities. There were no further interceptions of arms from Libya after the *Eksund*. In 1992, in the context of seeking a de-escalation in its conflict with the international community over the investigation into the destruction of Pan Am Flight 103 over Lockerbie, Libya declared in a letter to the United Nations that it was severing its links with all groups and organisations that targeted civilians (O'Brien 1995: 256–7). The Libyan government later provided information to the British authorities on its previous links with the Provisional IRA.

The other country that provided weapons to paramilitary organisations was South Africa. The apartheid regime's intervention in Northern Ireland had its roots in the country's involvement in the civil

5 *The Observer*, 1 March 1987.

war in Angola. After the supply of sophisticated fighter aircraft to the Angolan government by the Soviet Union in the mid-1980s, South African forces became vulnerable to air attack and that was reflected in heavy casualties among white army conscripts in late 1987. South Africa became desperate to acquire surface-to-air missile technology to counter the threat. This drew South Africa into involvement in Northern Ireland because the Northern Ireland firm of Shorts Brothers, with a largely Protestant work-force, had a division producing missiles. Through links with Loyalist paramilitary organisations, South Africa hoped to acquire the technology it was looking for. This all came to light in Paris in April 1989 when the French authorities arrested three members of a Loyalist paramilitary group, Ulster Resistance, in the company of a South African diplomat and in possession of a missile display model. This case prompted further investigation of the South African connection, leading to revelations that the South African armaments corporation, Armscor, had sent a large shipment of arms to three Loyalist paramilitary organisations in January 1988. The links did not end at this point. In April 1992, agents of South African Military Intelligence were implicated with members of a Loyalist paramilitary organisation in what the British police took to be an attempt to assassinate a former member of the South African police force, who was a threat to the South African authorities because of what he had revealed about security-force involvement in the murder of anti-apartheid activists.[6]

It is significant that direct intervention at state level in the violence in Northern Ireland has been limited to two pariah states. Rather more states have become diplomatically involved in the conflict. However, its extent has been limited by the fear of other states that the appearance of intervention against British interests might damage their relations with the United Kingdom. The Irish government has lobbied for support internationally when it has believed that the British government has been pursuing policies detrimental to the Catholic minority in Northern Ireland. The purpose of such lobbying has been to mobilise international opinion so as to put pressure on the British government to change course. That was particularly the case during the hunger strike crisis of 1980–1 when the Irish government was fearful of the destabilising consequences of the radicalisation of the Catholic minority in Northern Ireland. However, while other states were often sympathetic to the Irish viewpoint and shared their concern over the likely consequences of British policy, they remained reluctant to criticise the British government publicly, though on a few occasions the exasperation of foreign leaders did become evident.[7]

6   *The Independent*, 15 July 1992.
7   On Helmut Schmidt's irritation with Britain at the time of the hunger strike crisis, see Hainsworth (1981: 14).

(b) Diplomatic activity

By far the most important source of diplomatic pressure on the British government has been the United States. In the early years of the Troubles, the United States took a strictly noninterventionist stance on the conflict in Northern Ireland. The view taken was that the problem was a domestic concern of the United Kingdom. It became clear that this stance would become difficult to sustain after Jimmy Carter became President and made human rights a foreign policy priority of the United States, since that undercut the notion that the domestic affairs of states were matters outside the purview of foreign policy. After lobbying by prominent Irish-American politicians, Carter agreed to issue a statement on Northern Ireland. Although the statement of 30 August 1977 was in the end somewhat bland and carefully couched so as not to offend the British government, which was consulted over its content, it represented a significant change in the American government's position in that it treated the conflict in Northern Ireland as a legitimate concern of American foreign policy. Furthermore, in addition to its condemnation of political violence and its promise of American support in the event of a political settlement, it endorsed the principle that another state (the Irish Republic) should be involved in any settlement.

Worse for the British government followed in August 1979 when the American State Department suspended the sale of handguns to the RUC under the rubric that the United States would not permit the sale of arms to countries or institutions that had been found guilty of violating human rights. The context was a scandal over police interrogation methods in Northern Ireland that had attracted the attention of Amnesty International, and the exploitation of Carter's domestic political difficulties by the Irish-American lobby. However, in the end, these difficulties were also to provide the British government with a measure of respite from American pressure. Reagan's victory in the 1980 Presidential elections and the conservative tide in Congress reduced the influence of the Irish-American lobby. Almost as important in limiting American pressure on the British government during the 1980s was its acceptance of a role for the Irish government, culminating in the Anglo-Irish Agreement of November 1985. When it had seemed possible that the British government might reject such a role in the wake of the British Prime Minister's abrupt rejection in November 1984 of the options outlined in the report of the New Ireland Forum, Thatcher had come under pressure from Reagan to make amends, which she did when she addressed a joint session of Congress in February 1985.[8]

The next phase of American governmental involvement in Northern Ireland came during the Clinton Presidency. In his quest for the Democratic nomination, Clinton had given qualified support to a set of

8   See Malcolm Rutherford, 'Dr FitzGerald and I,' in: *Financial Times*, 22 February 1985.

proposals being urged on candidates by a new Irish-American grouping, Americans for a New Irish Agenda. The proposals included the appointment of a peace envoy to Northern Ireland, the granting of a visa to the Sinn Féin leader, Gerry Adams, and exerting diplomatic pressure on the British government over Northern Ireland. However, after his election as President, Clinton had disappointed the Irish-American lobby, many of whom had been enlisted in 'Irish-Americans for Clinton/Gore' during the campaign itself. On the advice of the Irish government he had resisted appointing a peace envoy. It was only after differences emerged between the British and Irish governments over the handling of the peace process – launched by the two governments through a joint declaration in December 1993 – that Clinton authorised a departure from the practice of previous American governments.

Clinton granted Gerry Adams a 48-hour visa to attend a one-day conference on Northern Ireland in New York at the beginning of February 1994. It was organised by the National Committee on American Foreign Policy, the chairman of which was a prominent Irish-American, Bill Flynn. Admitting Adams ran contrary to American policy towards individuals associated with ongoing terrorism. The decision was controversial within the Clinton Administration and involved the White House overruling other agencies of government. In the words of Niall O'Dowd, the founder of the weekly newspaper *The Irish Voice*, the decision 'overturned a 50-year hegemony over Irish policy that the British government had exercised through the State Department.' There was a furious reaction from the British government to the decision, which was reflected in extremely hostile commentary on the influence of the Irish-American lobby over the Clinton Administration in the British press. At one level the row between London and Washington was somewhat artificial. Both governments shared the same objective of bringing about a Provisional IRA cease-fire. The fact that the Provisional IRA eventually called a cease-fire on 31 August 1994, and the prominent role played by Irish-American groups in the deliberations within the Republican movement leading up to the cease-fire, was widely seen as vindicating Clinton's decision on the visa.

An impasse over the issue of the decommissioning of weapons during 1995 held up progress towards all-party negotiations on Northern Ireland's future. The deadlock threatened the survival of the cease-fire. It also threatened to wreck a trip President Clinton planned to make to Northern Ireland. In the week of the visit at the end of November, the British and Irish governments, at American prompting, finally agreed to a face-saving device to break the deadlock: the appointment of an international body given the task of coming up with a formula to bridge the gap in the positions of the parties on the issue. This development was widely presented as rescuing the peace process, contributing to the hero's reception that Clinton received in Northern Ireland. However, despite the efforts of the international body, there was a breakdown of the Provisional IRA cease-fire in February 1996. The Clinton Administration called for a restoration of the cease-fire, closed its doors to Sinn Féin leaders and supported the joint efforts of the British and Irish governments to revive the peace process. However, the role played by the Clinton Administration in the run-up to the Provisional IRA's second cease-fire of 20 July 1997 was a minor one.

Diplomatic engagement with the issue of Northern Ireland by other countries has been too episodic to deserve more than passing mention, with the exception of the surprising attempt at mediation in the conflict by the new post-apartheid South African government. The South African government invited representatives of Sinn Féin and of all the parties taking part in the multiparty negotiations in Northern Ireland to South Africa for a weekend seminar in June 1997 on the lessons of the South African transition. All of the parties accepted the invitation, with the exception of the UKUP, though the other Unionist parties insisted on arrangements for the conference that kept them separated from the representatives of Sinn Féin, an ironic echo of the policy of apartheid.

2. Transnational exchanges at a nongovernmental level

Below state level, political groups in other countries outside the British Isles have had a small but not totally insignificant impact on the conflict. Unionists and Loyalists receive very little support from outside the British Isles. A few arms have been channelled to Loyalist paramilitary organisations through Canada, but in general the response of the outside world to the conflict has tended to reinforce Unionist perceptions of themselves as friendless. The most important source of support for the Nationalist cause has been the Irish-American lobby in the United States, though through the course of the Troubles there has been considerable change in the nature and priorities of Irish-American groups involved in the conflict.

In the early years of the conflict, the most important Irish-American organisation involved in the conflict in Northern Ireland was Irish Northern Aid or, as it was better known, NORAID.[9] Between its founding, in 1970, and 1991, when it ceased to report remittances, it officially remitted approximately $3.5 million to Ireland to a Sinn Féin-controlled charity that assisted the families of Republican prisoners. While this is a tiny amount in the context of political fund-raising in the United States, it represented an important source of funds for the 'Provisionals'. During the 1980s another grouping achieved greater prominence than NORAID. This was the Irish National Caucus (INC). It was founded in

9   See Warren Richey, 'The NORAID Connection,' in: *Christian Science Monitor* (international edition), 19-25 January 1985.

September 1974 to lobby in Washington for a number of Irish-American organisations, including NORAID. By the 1976 presidential campaign the main focus of the INC had become the violation of human rights in Northern Ireland. It achieved success when it persuaded the Democratic nominee, Jimmy Carter, to take up the issue in his campaign.

In September 1977 the Ad Hoc Congressional Committee on Irish Affairs was established at the initiative of the INC. Pressure from the Ad Hoc Committee was instrumental in the State Department's decision to suspend the sale of handguns to the RUC to avert Congressional hearings over British policy in Northern Ireland. The INC itself achieved most success with a campaign over the issue of discrimination against Catholics in employment in Northern Ireland. In 1984 the INC coordinated the formulation of a set of nine employment principles, modelled on American affirmative action programmes, while also drawing on the Sullivan principles, a voluntary code of conduct governing American investment in South Africa. They were named the MacBride principles after a former Minister of External Affairs in the Irish Republic. In November 1985, Massachusetts became the first state to adopt legislation requiring compliance with the MacBride principles. New York, New Jersey, Connecticut and Rhode Island followed suit in 1986 and 1987. In response, the British government enacted the Fair Employment (Northern Ireland) Act of 1989, extending the scope of its anti-discrimination measures, including empowering the Fair Employment Commission to issue affirmative action directions to employers with the goal of reducing imbalances in the employment of Protestants and Catholics.

In 1981, a group of leading Irish-American politicians who had been instrumental in persuading President Carter to issue his statement on Northern Ireland in 1977 formed the 'Friends of Ireland'. Their purpose was to promote the cause of moderate constitutional nationalism within Congress. They frequently challenged the positions taken up by the Ad Hoc Committee and the INC. In the first half of the 1980s, the 'Friends of Ireland' gave strong backing to an initiative of the Social Democratic and Labour Party (SDLP), the New Ireland Forum. The Friends welcomed the Anglo-Irish Agreement of November 1985 and helped to secure Congressional support for a package of aid to Ireland as a mark of approval for the Agreement.[10]

However, arguably the most influential Irish-American grouping in recent years has been 'Americans for a New Irish Agenda'. Their influence on Clinton was described above. Throughout the course of the Troubles, there has been a considerable evolution in Irish-American attitudes to the conflict. In its early years, a common assumption was that

10 The various components of the Irish-American lobby are described in greater detail in Guelke (1996b: 521–36).

partition was the cause of the conflict and that all that was needed to end it was British withdrawal. With greater recognition of the complexity of the Northern Ireland problem, there has been a shift in emphasis away from the necessity of British withdrawal to that of the achievement of a negotiated settlement among the parties in Northern Ireland, with the goal of peace tending to displace that of unity. However, it remains the case that there is greater support for Sinn Féin among Irish-Americans taking an interest in the conflict (admittedly a small minority of the Irish-American population), than exists in Ireland itself.

The International Affiliations of the Parties to the Conflict

Under the heading of the international affiliations of the parties can be placed the Republican movement's attempts to establish links with other nationalist movements that have been engaged in violent struggle, and the efforts of the SDLP to gain support for constitutional nationalism through its membership of the Socialist International. Once again, it is striking that Unionists and Loyalists have few such links. There has been limited cooperation between Loyalist groups and neofascist groups both in Britain and on the continent of Europe. However, only the British groups have been consistent supporters of the Loyalist cause and there has been equivocation on the Loyalist side even about these groups because of a lack of sympathy with their broader ideological objectives.

From their formation, the Provisionals sought to establish links with violent nationalist movements in other regions of Western Europe, the most important being the contacts they had with Basque and Corsican nationalists. Operational links were established between the Provisional IRA and ETA, involving a sharing of technical expertise, whereas Sinn Féin later forged a strong relationship with ETA's political wing, *Herri Batasuna*.[11] During the 1980s, the Provisionals strongly promoted comparison of the Northern Ireland conflict with the struggle by the African National Congress (ANC) against white minority rule in South Africa, and the campaign of the Palestine Liberation Organization (PLO) for a Palestinian state. The PLO played down links with the IRA as an obstacle to its diplomatic efforts to win the support of European governments.[12] Little emerged to suggest operational links between the IRA and the ANC during the 1980s, despite the efforts of the apartheid regime to play up the issue to damage the ANC's reputation in Britain. However, in the 1990s, Mandela ran into criticism in Britain for expressing sympathy for the

---

11 Now called *Euskal Herritarrok* (EH) [Editors' Note].

12 For Arafat's denunciation of stories of links as 'a big lie', see *The Irish Times*, 12 January 1980.

Republican cause.[13] That the ANC tended to view the conflict as an anti-colonial struggle was further underlined in 1995, when Sinn Féin leader Gerry Adams visited South Africa and was warmly received. The ideological sympathy between the ANC and Sinn Féin was further underlined following the Good Friday Agreement.

Thus, one of the most extraordinary aspects of the Sinn Féin leadership's efforts to convince rank-and-file members of the value of the Agreement has been its enlistment of aid from leading figures in the ANC. The first opportunity for the Sinn Féin negotiators to explain the deal to a representative group of the party's members occurred at the party's annual conference a week after the Good Friday Agreement. The only decision on the Agreement made at the conference was that it would reconvene in a month's time to debate the deal. However, the party leadership used the occasion to explain the deal in an effort to promote a positive view of the Agreement among the rank and file. They were assisted in this by an array of foreign speakers, including the Deputy Secretary-General of the ANC, Thenjiwe Mtintso. She spoke of her fears when she was a MK cadre and negotiations on the South African transition began, that the ANC leadership had sold out, and of how she had gradually been persuaded that this was not the case. That was followed by the visit of an ANC delegation to Northern Ireland at the end of April, including such senior figures as Cyril Ramaphosa and Mac Maharaj. They spoke at a number of Sinn Féin meetings, and also visited IRA prisoners in the Maze.

The Impact of the Conflict on the Outside World

The direct impact of the conflict in Northern Ireland beyond the British Isles has been slight. The Provisionals have carried out a number of attacks on British military personnel abroad, particularly in Germany, but the spill-over of the conflict onto the UK mainland and into the Republic of Ireland has been much more serious. There have been over a hundred deaths in the Republic of Ireland as a result of the conflict and a similar number on the UK mainland. Further, two Provisional IRA bombs in the City of London in 1992 and 1993 caused damage estimated as close to £2 billion. But part of the explanation why there has been relatively little spill-over from the conflict into other countries has been the enormous indirect impact of the conflict internationally in terms of media coverage. The paramilitaries have had little need to engage in activities outside Northern Ireland so as to attract attention to the existence of the conflict.

13 See, for example, 'Mandela's IRA remarks criticised,' *The Irish Times*, 21 October 1992.

The Influence of International Opinion on the Conflict

The influence of the attitudes of the outside world on the parties in Northern Ireland has been very significant. In sharp contrast to the IRA's border campaign between 1956 and 1962, which caused scarcely a ripple outside of Ireland, the current Troubles from their very outset in October 1968 attracted widespread attention, thanks in part to the inno-vation of the transmission of television pictures by satellite, which provided the basis for almost instant coverage of violent events. At the onset, opinion was sympathetic to the Catholic minority, which was seen even in Britain to have been the victim of discrimination and oppression at the hands of the Protestant majority. The reaction of inter-national opinion helped to shape the responses and strategies of the two communities. The siege mentality of the Protestant majority was strongly reinforced. Grass-roots Unionist opinion became fearful of any compromise, since it tended to see it as a slippery slope to a united Ireland. This was to undermine the efforts of moderate Unionist politi-cal leaders to reconstitute Northern Ireland as a political entity in a form capable of securing the allegiance of both communities. After the failure of power sharing in 1974 discredited liberal Unionists, Unionists focused on the need for terrorism to be defeated but they remained divided on whether the best way forward lay in the total integration of Northern Ireland into the United Kingdom or the restoration of the autonomy the province had enjoyed prior to the imposition of direct rule in March 1972.

The sympathy that the Catholic minority received emphasised the advantages from the perspective of Nationalists of the internationalisa-tion of the conflict. This led to resistance to British policy in its first phase after August 1969 when British troops were sent to the province to aid the civil power. In particular, the objective of British policy of effect-ing the reestablishment of the province's autonomy after limited reform of the province's security apparatus had a radicalising impact on Nation-alists, who feared that this would pave the way for the restoration of Unionist dominance and the neglect of their grievances for another fifty years. Their desire to internationalise the conflict to prevent such an eventuality led them to stress the lack of legitimacy of partition and therefore of Northern Ireland as a political entity, even though emphasis on the goal of a united Ireland inevitably made it more difficult for there to be a political accommodation between the two communities in Northern Ireland.

However, international opinion has not been static throughout the Troubles and in the final part of this piece, its main phases and their impact on the conflict will be traced briefly. The onset of Northern Ireland's current Troubles coincided with the completion of decolonisa-tion. The end of formal colonial rule through much of the world, with the exception of Portugal's small overseas empire, had created the basis for the universalisation of a world order based on the principle of the sovereign equality of states. While the states that made up the international system were clearly unequal in economic terms and in terms of the military power at their disposal, all appeared equal in status as fully independent sovereign states. A corollary of acceptance of the legitimacy of the struggle against colonialism was that the sovereign territorial state would be the norm of the postcolonial era. In this context, Northern Ireland's status as conditionally part of a sovereign state seemed anomalous, though there were a variety of ways in which the anomaly could be ended, including a united Ireland, the total integration of Northern Ireland into the United Kingdom, and the creation of an independent Northern Ireland.

In practice, international opinion tended to favour a united Ireland far more strongly than other solutions to the anomaly. The imposition of direct rule from London in March 1972 simply served to strengthen perceptions of Northern Ireland as an undemocratic colonial entity, lending a measure of credibility to the Provisional IRA's claim to be engaged in a struggle against British imperialism. However, the nature of the Provisional IRA's campaign of violence tended to undercut support for the organisation as bearing a closer resemblance to marginalised terrorist groups in other European societies than to the mass movements associated with the struggle against colonial rule in the Third World. However, an important change in external perceptions of the Provisional IRA occurred in the context of the 1980 and 1981 crisis in the prisons. The mass support the Republican prisoners were able to attract weakened the portrayal of the IRA as terrorists akin to the Red Army Faction in Germany or the Red Brigades in Italy.

However, by this time, the international agenda had changed and there had been a shift away from concern about unfinished business from the colonial era to the issue of human rights. From the perspective of the British government, this intensified its embarrassment over the continuation of the conflict, as well as forcing it to adopt strategies, such as criminalisation, that stressed the containment of political violence through the ordinary law, to minimise criticism of its rule in Northern Ireland. The issue of human rights provided a further basis for the internationalisation of the conflict, partly as a result of the monitoring of the conflict by nongovernmental organisations such as Amnesty International, but also as a result of Britain's involvement in European institutions and the progress of European integration. One of the British government's motives for entering into the Anglo-Irish Agreement in November 1985, giving the Republic of Ireland a right to be consulted on the policies pursued by the British government in Northern Ireland, was to reduce its exposure to international criticism. However, criticism of British policies on human rights grounds have not ceased, though in general the association of the Republic with the conduct of British rule has served to make it appear more legitimate to the outside world.[14]

The impact of the end of bipolarity on the Northern Ireland conflict has been indirect, as Soviet involvement was never a significant factor in the conflict and thus the ending of communism in Eastern Europe and the demise of the Soviet Union had no direct bearing on any of the combatants in Northern Ireland. However, the indirect effect has been considerable. The fall of the Berlin Wall was an important factor in President de Klerk's decision to liberalise the South African political system. The South African transition and the aftermath of the Gulf War were factors in the Middle East peace process, while the fact that the Provisionals had looked to the ANC and the PLO to legitimise their campaign of violence put them under pressure to develop a peace strategy so as to sustain the validity of their comparison of Northern Ireland with the situation in South Africa and the quest for a Palestinian state.[15] The end of the Cold War also increased the readiness of the Clinton Administration to intervene in the Northern Ireland problem, since the State Department was no longer able to deploy the argument that involvement in the Northern Ireland problem carried the unacceptable risk of alienating Britain, the United States' most important ally in the Western alliance. On the contrary, it could be argued that if American mediation proved successful in Northern Ireland, it would provide a boost to its role as a mediator in other conflicts around the world.

Further, the break-up of Yugoslavia and the successful completion of the South African transition have had a significant bearing on the interpretation of international norms that the parties in Northern Ireland have invoked to justify their conduct. Importantly, there has been a weakening of the international community's hostility towards secession, reflected in the recognition accorded to Slovenia and Eritrea, among others. The effect has been to reduce the rigidity of the territorial interpretation of self-determination, as well as giving greater legitimacy to the demands of minorities to be accorded better treatment within states. As a consequence, Northern Ireland's conditional status appears less anomalous. Further, in so far as the conflict between Unionism and Nationalism has come to be seen in other than 'all or nothing' terms, the prospects for political accommodation through an historic compromise between Unionism and Nationalism were enhanced, paving the way to the Good Friday Agreement. The completion of South Africa's transition has ended a conflict in which a large part of the international community endorsed the use of political

14 See, for example, *At the Crossroads: Human Rights and the Northern Ireland Peace Process*, Lawyers Committee for Human Rights, New York 1996.
15 See on the South African case, Guelke (1996a: 132–48).

violence by the ANC directed at securing the political rights of a subordinate community. But there remains less reason for any substantial section of the international community to treat the use of political violence by other groups as legitimate, now that the battle against apartheid has been won.

The changes in the international context of the conflict provide a large part of the explanation for Northern Ireland's peace process. Indeed, it can be argued that the difficulties which the peace process encountered within Northern Ireland reflected the fact that its most important sources lay in international developments. Indeed, the uncertainty that the peace process gave rise to inside Northern Ireland contributed to a polarisation of opinion. This makes the achievement of the Good Friday Agreement, with the participation of eight of the province's political parties, all the more remarkable, prompting comparison with the miracle of South Africa's transition. However, while South Africa's transition was irreversible once made, the durability of the Good Friday Agreement depends on its capacity to generate the necessary domestic political support within Northern Ireland. The initial reaction within the province was one of euphoria, since expectations of any settlement were very low. However, with the fading of the element of surprised delight, criticism of the Agreement has grown, particularly from Unionists alarmed at the absence of strong provisions on the 'decommissioning' of paramilitary arsenals,[16] and worried by the provisions for the early release of prisoners. Unionists have consequently delayed implementation of the Agreement. This has increased Nationalist distrust of Unionist intentions, creating the familiar cycle of communal polarisation. The expectation that the Agreement would become the basis of a durable settlement of the conflict in Northern Ireland has diminished. However, if, contrary to current pessimism about the Agreement's prospects, it is implemented as originally intended, it will form a very important example of the role that changed international circumstances and assumptions can play in the resolution of ethnic conflict.

16 Insufficient degree of decommissioning proved to be a major stumbling block in the peace process. However, thanks to intensive efforts by British Prime Minister Tony Blair and US envoy Robert Mitchell, a historic transfer of power to the new Northern Ireland Assembly occurred on 2 December 1999. At the same time, the Republic of Ireland signed away its constitutional claims to the North. Implementation of the Agreement continues to be very difficult, however. The Northern Ireland Assembly was suspended on 14 October 2002 and dissolved on 28 April 2003. The Secretary of State for Northern Ireland has assumed responsibility for the direction and control of the Northern Ireland departments [Editors' Note].

References

FITZGERALD, Garret (1991). *All in a Life*. Dublin: Gill and Macmillan.

GUELKE, Adrian (1996a). 'The Influence of the South African Transition on the Northern Ireland Peace Process.' *The South African Journal of International Affairs* 3: 2 (Winter), pp. 132–48.

——— (1996b). 'The United States, Irish Americans and the Northern Ireland Peace Process.' *International Affairs* 72: 3, July, pp. 521–36.

HAINSWORTH, Paul (1981). 'Northern Ireland: A European Role?.' *Journal of Common Market Studies* 20: 1 (September).

O'BRIEN, Brendan (1995). *The Long War: The IRA and Sinn Féin from Armed Struggle to Peace Talks*. Dublin: The O'Brien Press.

O'CLERY, Conor (1996). *The Greening of the White House*. Dublin: Gill and Macmillan.

WHYTE, John (1990). *Interpreting Northern Ireland*. Oxford: Clarendon.

WILSON, Robin (1997). *Continentally Challenged: Securing Northern Ireland's Place in the European Union*. Belfast: Democratic Dialogue.

CHAPTER SIX

Explaining Ethnic Violence in Bosnia-Herzegovina[1]

Marie-Janine Calic

Though this be madness,
yet there's method in't.
William Shakespeare, Hamlet.

Introduction

During four years of war, public opinion has identified Bosnia mostly with extremely violent ethnic conflicts, in which all kinds of atrocities were committed against prisoners of war and innocent civilian populations. According to UNHCR sources there were more than 200,000 war-related deaths, several hundred thousand injured or disabled and more than 2 million displaced persons. The war in Bosnia horrified the world because of the unspeakable cruelty with which the conflict was conducted. But it was the idea of 'ethnic purification' as an organising principle of state and society that came as a shock to the world public.

Tragically, many war crimes that occurred in the context of 'ethnic cleansing' were committed in the presence of foreign observers, namely members of NGOs and journalists, and even UN peacekeepers (as in Srebrenica). Military activity and human rights violations in and around Bosnia have therefore been observed in more detail than in any other civil war. Substantial investigation into the area has been undertaken under the auspices of various international organisations, first and foremost the International Criminal Tribunal for the former Yugoslavia (ICTY) in The Hague. And yet, there is still a lack of empirical research on the specific phenomenon of 'ethnic violence', especially the reasons and mechanisms of conflict escalation, and the motivation of major actors.

Even greater is the gap when it comes to interpreting these events in the light of comparative social science research. Although a substantial

1 Since this article was originally written at the end of 1997, much investigation has been undertaken regarding war crimes in the former Yugoslavia, in particular with respect to the tragic events of Srebrenica (1995). Although time restrictions do not allow for a substantial examination of recent research, the following analysis of the dynamics of ethnic violence remains valid.

amount of literature on individual violence (Kressel 1996), state-organised terror (Stohl and Lopez 1986; Harff and Gurr 1988; Bushnell et al.
1991), and genocide (Kuper 1985; Charny 1988, 1994; Chalk and Jonassohn 1990; Fein 1990; Rummel 1994, 1995; Horowitz 1997) has been
produced in recent times, few Balkan experts have made attempts to
make this theoretical knowledge available for their specific area of
expertise.

   This paper aims to delineate conditions, features and causes of 'ethnic
violence' applied during the Yugoslav war of succession. The purpose is
to provide sufficient information for making interpretations about the
phenomenon of ethnic violence in Bosnia itself. The investigations
shall, at the same time, contribute to developing clear analytical distinctions and operational definitions that will allow comparisons between
states or regions, and over time. It postulates that analytical distinction
between various forms of violence, namely repression, organised terror
and genocide, will lead to differentiated explanations. The study is based
on empirical research in the area, writings from other scholars, reports
from international organisations as well as documents and witness statements made available to me by the Office of the Prosecutor of the ICTY.

Conditions

The Yugoslav war has elicited a vast number of publications. Its origins,
military and political course, and humanitarian consequences as well as
international responses have been extensively discussed, although often
on the basis of limited, or partial, knowledge or understanding of this
event (Gow 1997). This is particularly true for those who emphasise
historical and cultural origins, tracing the roots of the Yugoslav war to
virtually every era, including the Ottoman rule, the 1912/13 Balkan
wars, and the communist period (Kaplan 1993). The main argument is
that Ottoman rule and communism had separated the Balkans during
five centuries from significant European civilisation and development,
keeping them isolated in 'a vast refrigerator'. The very essence of this
approach is that there is a peculiar 'state of mind' of Balkan people, in
the words of George F. Kennan: 'that seems to be decisive as a determinant of the troublesome, baffling and dangerous situation ... today
(Kennan 1993: 13).'

   These historical and cultural explanations are particularly popular.
However, whenever it comes to explaining the high level of savagery
with which the war was conducted, authors tend to base their argument
on historical analogy, rather than on empirical political or sociological
research into the event itself. None of the adherents of these theories
have convincingly proven how historical or cultural factors become

psychologically relevant for the individual and how they influence people's behaviour in a given conflict situation.

Moreover, the cultural theory is also contradicted by social science and psychological research, which support that all persons are potentially capable of harming others and all nations potentially capable of mass terror and even genocide (Fein 1990: 47). Authoritarian and conformist attitudes, stereotyping and prejudice, frustration and anger, the lack of formal education, the availability of aggression-related items (weapons) form the 'raw materials of mass hate' that 'can be found in almost every society on earth (Kressel 1996: 247).'

Barbara Harff, in line with Israel W. Charny and Irving Louis Horowitz, argues that only under a given array of internal conditions can people be motivated to become killers or genociders (Harff 1986: 165–87). Specifically, abrupt change in the political community, the formation of a state through violent conflict when national boundaries are redrawn, or a lost war may set the preconditions for the pursuit of genocidal policies. Structural change, however, has to go along with other factors: the existence of sharp internal cleavages prior to the emergence of the new situation, a strong 'we-group' identification among the members of the polarised groups, and the lack of external constraints in the international environment. Ted R. Gurr, in a comparative analysis, found a positive correlation between the factors of social, ethnic or religious heterogeneity, weakly institutionalised regimes, peripheral international status and state policies of violence (Gurr 1986: 45–71).

It would be going too far to discuss all the variables that have been forwarded by scholars to explain the specific case of Bosnia where political, constitutional, social, economic, military and international events played together (Cohen 1993; Woodward 1995; Bougarel 1996a; Calic 1996; Silber and Little 1996). Bearing in mind that actors always possess several options and not just politics of violence, the key question remains how various factors combine to result in mass hate and murder. It appears necessary to specify these criteria further and to distinguish three groups of variables influencing the choice of strategy in a conflict situation: (1) structural variables; (2) situational variables; and (3) dispositional variables. The three sets of conditions are complexly interrelated (Gurr 1986: 65). For systematic reasons they are presented here in a table (see Table 6.1). (4) The individual factor will also be considered.

1. Structural variables

Structural variables concern causal conditions for conflicts, such as the nature of social stratification, the relations between potential antagonistic groups, the nature of the political system, and the level of socioeconomic development.

TABLE 6.1: Hypotheses on Ethnic Violence

Structural variables	Situational variables	Dispositional variables
Ethnic heterogeneity ⇒ Ethnically plural society with nationalities living densely intermingled. ⇒ Incongruence of nation and state borders. ⇒ Superimposition of cultural or religious differences over those of ethnicity. *Political system* ⇒ Institutionalised intolerance and discrimination. ⇒ Inequality of participation in the political system. ⇒ Lack of independent evaluative and democratic institutions. *Socioeconomic factors* ⇒ Dissociation between ethnic groups (social distance). ⇒ Disparities in the levels of economic development and living standards. ⇒ Military doctrine (all-peoples' defence). ⇒ Availability of weapons.	*Political developments* ⇒ Change in the global political power structure (end of Cold War). ⇒ Collapse of the communist ideology and political system (end of Tito era). ⇒ Nationalism as a state- and power-legitimising ideology. ⇒ Trend towards ethnocratic rule. ⇒ Disintegration of state causing new problems of political participation and hierarchic relations (Republics' declarations of independence in 1991). *Socioeconomic developments* ⇒ Aggravation of a socioeconomic crisis. ⇒ Accelerated ethnic segregation. ⇒ Breakdown of the state monopoly over violence. *Military developments* ⇒ External threat (war in Croatia in the summer of 1991). *International factors* ⇒ Interference of outside actors (Croatia, FRY; JNA, HVO, paramilitary). ⇒ Role of the international community.	*Values* ⇒ Patriarchal values and traditions (family structures). ⇒ Culturally rooted latent popular support for the use of violence (heroism in the popular culture). ⇒ Past crimes committed by ethnic groups towards one another (Second World War massacres). ⇒ Strong remembrance of these crimes by the victims (role of historians). *Beliefs* ⇒ Stereotypes, scapegoats myths, hostile perceptions. ⇒ Divergent beliefs about the mutual history and current conduct and character. ⇒ Belief in an ideology or theory (Greater Serbia, Greater Croatia). ⇒ Obedience to authority and role expectations. *Attitudes* ⇒ Responsiveness to group rewards and collective definitions of the situation. ⇒ Coincidence of power and victimhood.

Many scholars stress particularly the factor of ethnic heterogeneity of a society and more precisely the social relationships between antagonists as a determinant for violent conflicts. Generally, ethnically plural societies may bear, according to Leo Kuper, the following characteristics: (1) a superimposition of cultural or religious differences over those of ethnicity; (2) differential incorporation into the political structure with inequality of participation; (3) some degree of dissociation between the different groups; and (4) a history of conflict which is expressed in stereotypes, historic memories and hostile perceptions (Kuper 1990: 19–51).

In exaggeration of this hypothesis, some authors have, in line with Huntington's famous paradigm 'clash of civilisations', assumed that sociocultural or religious incompatibilities lay at the roots of the Yugoslav war. They claim that the people in Bosnia have always hated each other and whatever tolerance and coexistence there was had been imposed by the communist regime. This assumption is by no means supported by sociological research, which has devoted much attention to ethnic relations in Yugoslavia.

According to the 1991 census, Bosnia-Herzegovina's population of 4,377,033 was composed of 43.5 percent Muslims, 31.2 percent Serbs, and 17.4 percent Croats. Many parts of the Republic were ethnically mixed. Empirical research has shown that people in Yugoslavia were usually well aware of ethnic and religious differences, especially when it came to choosing friends or a marriage partner. For instance, only 12 percent of the marriages in Bosnia were ethnically mixed (including 28 percent in Sarajevo) in the 1980s (Bougarel 1996a: 87). In an opinion poll held in 1991, 43 percent of the Muslims, 39 percent of the Croats, and 25 percent of the Serbs in Bosnia expressed the view that nationality constituted an important criterion for choosing a marriage partner. One-third of the population felt more secure if living with conationals than in a setting where their ethnic group constituted a minority.[2] However, 'attitudes depended on nationality, age and the sociocultural environment in which a person had grown up. Ethnic and national identification was usually not an issue to the generations who grew up in the fifties and sixties, while to pre-Second World War generations it often was, and it was starting to become important among young people in the eighties (Bringa 1995: 3).' Nevertheless, there is no evidence whatsoever that ethnic identities and cultural differences did inevitably become the cause of conflict, let alone war and atrocities. On the contrary, sociologists and anthropologists have demonstrated that there were many different ways in which people from different ethnic and religious backgrounds in Bosnia lived together and side by side, so that there has always been 'both coexistence and conflict, tolerance and prejudice, suspicion and friendship (Bringa 1995: 3).' To summarise: neither the idealised vision of a harmonious Bosnia nor that of a 'powder keg' is true.

Besides ethnic heterogeneity, other structural factors need to be mentioned in this context. Possibly, huge disparities in the levels of economic development and standards of living added to the effects of cultural and ethnic diversity and created profound centrifugal pressure. In addition, the communist system of self-administration, its institutional

2 *Bosna i Herzegovina izmedju rata i mira* (Beograd, 1992), p. 19.

and constitutional weaknesses, and, last but not least, the failure of trans-forming it into a democratic system based on a market economy contributed to deepening the inherited structural problems of this country.

Much more could be said about the structural variables that condition ethnic violence in conflict situations. However, it still needs to be explained how these factors inspired people or groups of people to choose a strategy of violence. This brings us to the situational variables.

2. Situational variables

It appears that the resort to massive violence is far more influenced by situational than by structural factors because the former directly affect the decision-making calculations of interest groups involved in a conflict. They include the traits of political, economic and military conflicts, external threats, considerations of the decision makers' own political resources, and other factors.

The disintegration of Yugoslavia being a result of failed politics of transforming the socialist system to democracy and a market economy is one of the key factors.[3] This process had begun with sharp economic decline and constitutional conflict in the 1980s. The general situation of social change, combined with inherited institutional weakness, tended to cause a political impasse on the federal level. Deep-rooted structural conflicts between regions, republics and peoples of Yugoslavia thus esca-lated rapidly and led to the step-by-step disintegration of governmental authority, state structures and civil order first in Yugoslavia, with Bosnia-Herzegovina coming shortly afterwards. The whole process resulted in a complete break-down of the political, institutional and military system. More fundamentally, the break-up of multiethnic Yugoslavia put several sensitive questions on the political agenda. such as the right to self-determination and the location of new borders.

The poor economic performance after the dissolution of Yugoslavia added to the problems of this area and accelerated ethnic polarisation in this multinational environment. In 1991, Bosnia's gross national product was down 45 percent from the 1990 level. At this time, the average income of a Bosnian family was far below the amount needed for subsis-tence; this was accompanied a rapid drop in the standard of living, growing unemployment and high inflation. In addition, there were serious short-ages in foodstuffs, petroleum and other staples. The fact that more and more Bosnians found themselves living below the poverty level had an extremely negative impact on the fragile, multinational republic of Bosnia-Herzegovina, especially on the ethnically mixed municipalities.

---

3   For instance, between 1980 and 1986, the GDP grew by only 0.6 percent a year, and real income was 27 percent lower than in 1979.

While there appears to be a general link between democratisation and nationalism, this was undoubtedly the case in Yugoslavia's transition from communist rule (Mansfield and Snyder 1995: 5–38). During the democratisation phase the political spectrum widened on the basis of assumed ethnic interests, which resulted in the creation of a great number of nationalistic, potentially irreconcilable political forces. The new political parties had an overwhelming incentive to mobilise mass support for which the new nationalism took on particular importance (Goati 1992: 227–38). While the Yugoslav constitution aimed at avoiding the identification of nations with territory, creating a complex system of political federalism and nationality rights, the nationalistic parties that came to power in the first multiparty elections of 1990 tended to derive political loyalties from national identities.

Specific 'national interests' were now supposed to apply to the respective ethnic community as a whole. The assumed national interest was perceived as the need to unify the respective peoples politically and to preserve or to establish independent national states (an independent and unified Bosnia on the one side, separate Bosnian Croat and Bosnian Serb republics, 'Greater Croatia' and 'Greater Serbia' respectively, on the other side). Needless to say, the attempt to force a congruence between borders and nations created overlapping claims to territory.

The weakening of central authority contributed further to polarising and antagonising these competing interest groups. Both the persisting constitutional and legal vacuum, and the factual loss of the state's monopoly over violence accelerated the division of Bosnian society along ethnic lines. Shortly after the first democratic elections in 1990 and the formation of the coalition government, the three nationalist-oriented parties (SDA, SDS, HDZ) became deadlocked over two interrelated questions: independence and the future constitutional structure of Bosnia-Herzegovina. The Serb and the Croat leaderships, having the unification of their nationals with their mother countries in mind, supported plans for the 'cantonisation' of the Republic into three or more ethnically defined regions, each of which would be dominated by either the Muslims, the Serbs or the Croats. The Muslim leadership, on the other hand, sought to preserve Bosnia-Herzegovina as a unified, multiethnic and unitary state. From the summer of 1991 onwards, ethnic polarisation occurred in the political institutions, the military, the media, the education system and public services (Smajlovic 1995: 170–95).

As the state was losing its monopoly over violence, new actors surfaced that challenged both the political and the military power elite. As in many other communist states, the Yugoslav military occupied a privileged position in the state, and the ruling elite were intertwined with military institutions (Milivojevic 1988: 15–59). This is another reason why in newly democratising states many of the interests of the ruling elite which are threatened are military in nature (Mansfield and Snyder 1995: 5–38).

The involvement of the federal Yugoslav People's Army (JNA) in the armed conflict in Bosnia proves this. The JNA had officially withdrawn from Bosnian territory on 19 May 1992. However, approximately 80 percent of the JNA forces in Bosnia-Herzegovina, armed with heavy weaponry, were integrated into a new army for the Republika Srpska. General Kadijević of the JNA wrote in his 1993 book *Moje vidjenje raspada* (My Perspective on the Collapse) that 'the units and headquarters of the JNA formed the backbone of the Army of the Serb Republic with complete weaponry and equipment (Kadijević 1993: 93).' There is evidence that the Yugoslav Army continued to be present on the territory of Bosnia and was involved in the armed conflict against it, and continued to support the Bosnian Serb armed forces militarily, financially and logistically. In parallel, the Croatian Army, from 1992 onwards, fought together with the Bosnian Croat armed forces on Bosnian territory.

One has to understand that the power vacuum on the federal and, later, on the republican level, combined with an extreme insecurity, created an environment in which uncontrolled elements could develop, while individuals took actions to defend themselves that would not have been necessary in an established system. In the volatile situation of 1991/92 the availability of weapons became crucial. According to Tito's strategy of 'all-peoples' defence', weapons were stored at the local level throughout the country to be used by the Territorial Defence of the Republics in case of war, but kept under control of the JNA. In the autumn of 1991, political parties and the JNA started to distribute weapons among the civilian population, and ethnic paramilitary groups were established.

Political party leaders and members of the military, intellectual and religious elites contributed to heightening ethnic tension to the extent that they manipulated national feelings, fuelled fears and used them to support their individual power ambitions. Besides this class of top-level personalities, a new 'middle class' of ethnic entrepreneurs emerged on the local level, many of whom were involved in arms trade, black marketing and other criminal activities. All sides relied heavily on financial and logistical support from emigrants who were able to support the parties to the conflict with donations. There was an extreme lack of money in the area so that military and civilian authorities had to rely on private persons who were able and willing to provide financial means for defence and other purposes (Bougarel 1996b: 233–68).

Tensions in Bosnia-Herzegovina increased constantly throughout the winter of 1991/92, reaching a peak after the referendum on 29 February and 1 March on the Republic's independence. Despite the boycott of the Serb Democratic Party (SDS), 66 percent of the Bosnian citizens voted in the referendum, 99 percent of whom supported an independent and sovereign Bosnia-Herzegovina. Independence was recognised on 6 April 1992 by the European Community, and on the following day by the United States. Outbreaks of violence occurred in many parts of Bosnia immediately afterwards, rapidly developing into a major armed conflict. Once the first military clashes broke out a key condition for the massive use of violence against soldiers and civilians was established. The international environment was conducive to the escalation of violence in that Western governments, international organisations and other external actors did not contribute much to change the perceptions and actions that were feeding the escalating cycle of disintegration and violence.

3. Dispositional variables

A further set of variables concerns dispositions. Dispositional variables influence how actors regard the acceptability of strategies of violence and terrorism, including norms, cultural traditions, ideologies, and historical experience with violent means of power (Chalk and Jonassohn 1990; Kuper 1990).

Social and psychological studies suggest that moral and social inhibition, under normal conditions, would keep most people from partaking in murder, rape and torture. They need to be psychologically prepared by the reinvigoration of nationalist sentiments, the reactivation of historical fears, and the stimulation of a desire for revenge (Kressel 1996: 36). Only under specific conditions can normal and law-abiding people be transformed into perpetrators.

With regard to the Holocaust it has been argued that for people to kill another large group of people the ethical and emotional constraints must be lifted by an ideology, for instance anti-Semitism or national socialism (Goldhagen 1996: 375–414). In this sense, popular explanations refer to the Serbian national ideology, tracing it back to the nineteenth century, laying particular emphasis on the role of the famous 'Memorandum' drafted by the Serbian Academy of Arts and Sciences in 1986, which seems to reflect the support of Serbia's elite for militant ethnic nationalism.[4] The underlying assumption is that had there not been extreme aggression, Bosnia would have remained the ideal example of a multiethnic and tolerant society (with its prominent symbol Sarajevo). However, there is no evidence in this text that there was an ideology from which aggression or even extermination of non-Serb groups could be derived.

Several authors hold social, cultural and socioanthropological factors such as the prevalence of patriarchal values and a popular tradition of heroism responsible for the assumed inclination of Balkan people for

---

4   'Memorandum SANU', Naše teme 33: 1–2 (1989), pp. 128–63.

violence (Kaser 1992; Höpken 1997a: 518–38). Thus, it is true that the Balkan peoples' attachment to war contains a strong emotional component which is also central to modern nationalism and folk tradition. For instance, Serb epic poetry has, since the fourteenth century, cultivated the myth of the Serbs being the immemorial defenders of Christianity against Islam. There has been, moreover, self-idealisation of several South Slavic peoples as rough and pure mountain warriors fighting wars of liberation against foreign oppressors. Balkan epic poetry is well known for its glorification of acts of revenge like torture and killing committed by warlords, e.g. the 'hajduks'. The 'hajduks' (an Arab word which means at the same time 'renegade' and 'robber') were local warlords who, throughout the centuries, fought against Ottoman rule over the Balkans. Popular folk songs have cultivated a specific 'myth of hajduks', who, in the collective memory of the Balkan peoples, became heroes.

Nevertheless, the frequent use of historical and cultural symbols during the war does not mean that the roots of violence in the Balkans can be traced back to folk tradition. Many (also Western) societies possess a tradition of idealisation of war and warriors. Cultural traditions can leave their traits on how and by which means a war is fought. But to explain the Bosnian war as a result of misguided folk tradition is to turn the story upside down. Thus, Belgrade ethnologist Ivan Čolović has demonstrated how national leaders like Radovan Karadžić or Arkan were using folk traditions to gain popularity, presenting themselves as the quasi-natural successors of popular historical figures and personalities (Čolović 1994).

We know from numerous witnesses' statements at the ICTY that during the first months of the war people of all nationalities usually did *not* expect the adversary group to behave with the extreme brutality that later was to become common use. For instance, fighters and armed civilian men believed that children and wives would be safe staying at home while they hid in the woods when the first attacks on their villages started. Instead, civilians were often mistreated in a particularly brutal manner. This leads to the conclusion that savagery probably did not belong to the culturally defined menu of behavioural patterns in a war situation which was generally shared by most people in Bosnia.

In this context, the role of historical memories calls for particular attention. While in the communist era the Second World War played a crucial role both for creating a common Yugoslav identity and legitimising the ruling party, since the 1980s, history has been virtually rewritten by nationalistic intellectuals, who replaced the former official ideology of communism with its structural opposite: nationalism (Hayden 1994: 167–201; Denich 1994: 367–90). The massacres of the Second World War were continuously recalled in the media while the number of victims among Serbs, Croats and Muslims were either overstated or diminished. Communist education had contributed to this in so far as it 'restricted itself to a fragmented and selective memory, which especially in education, deliberately did only tell those "parts of the story", affirmative to the political order and the legitimacy of its ruling party (Höpken 1997b).' Since few people in Yugoslavia understood the background of the new controversy over the number of victims, it became especially easy for propaganda to recall old grievances and historical memories and to create a climate in which a large part of the public supported nationalistic aims. Nationally oriented intellectuals and politicians argued that from the Middle Ages up to the Tito era their peoples had always been discriminated against, oppressed and threatened by others. The nationalistic propaganda proved to be quite successful in using these popular stereotypes to embody, articulate and dramatise old nationalist grievances.

The media certainly played a vital role in the rise of nationalism and the promotion of a policy of ethnic segregation. Mark Thompson, in line with many others, argues that the state-owned and private media had psychologically prepared the war (Thompson 1995; Zupanov 1995; Gow, Paterson and Preston 1996). There are many examples of how information was falsified in order to portray the respective ethnic group as being victimised. At the same time, it has been common practice to devalue the antagonists, viewed collectively as evil, threatening and subhuman.

Last but not least, the political culture and the Yugoslav military doctrine of 'all-peoples' defence' shaped patterns of using and tolerating violence. For instance, the older generation of communist elite, who had seized power following armed resistance against German and Italian occupation during the Second World War, seemed particularly habituated to its political uses. And the younger generation had been educated in the spirit of Yugoslav patriotism based on partisan-like struggle. According to the concept of all-peoples' defence that was introduced after the Soviet invasion of Czechoslovakia in 1968, all citizens were supposed to participate actively in the armed struggle. Many war-related tasks were supposed to be performed by the local political and military authorities, independently of superior command if need be. People were educated for, and used to, taking defence matters into their own hands, and they were particularly trained to apply terror-inspiring techniques of warfare such as sniping, shelling of towns, etc.[5]

All these factors did not, of course, cause the eruption of violence, but they probably increased the acceptability of strategies of repression and terrorism. And yet, many armed men, regular and irregular fighters, avoided hurting, torturing or deliberately killing prisoners of war and

---

5   Savezni Sekretarijat za Narodnu Odbranu, *Strategija opštenarodne odbrane i društvene samozaštite SFRJ* (Beograd: SSNO, COSSIS 'Maršal Tito', 1987).

civilians. Numerous witness statements on the side of the victims have confirmed this. This brings us to the question of individual responsibility.

4. The individual factor

While early interpretations, influenced by the famous Milgram studies and related research, claim that obedience to authority and the 'power of circumstances' rather than personal aggression lie at the origin of mass crime, recent research emphasises that frequently the causes are much more subtle and drawn out.[6] Social science has provided three basic answers to the question of why potential perpetrators choose a strategy of violence: first, obedience to authority and role expectations; second, responsiveness to group rewards and collective definitions of the situation, e.g. threat; and, third, belief in a theory or ideology. These motives are not necessarily explicit in the awareness of the actors (Staub 1989).

Difficult living conditions are supposed to reinforce the motivational readiness to harm others. But normally, individual differences in personality and beliefs strongly influence how a person behaves in a given situation. For instance, a 45-year-old woman who had been detained in a prisoners' camp in Central Bosnia testified at The Hague how she has been continuously trying to prevent the guards and other uniformed men from raping her by always asking the same question: 'How would you feel if your own mother was raped?' Interestingly, some potential perpetrators left discouraged, while others were not impressed at all by her argumentation.

As far as the motivation of the perpetrators is concerned, a number of gaps remain to be filled by social science research in the years ahead. What still needs to be developed is a theory of how structural, situational and cultural factors motivate potential antagonists to mandate and justify the destruction of the target group.

Intentional Use of Violence

The extreme cruelty with which the Bosnian war was conducted created a crucial moment of hesitation among external observers about whether the behaviour of the parties to the conflict followed rational calculation. The debate on causes of violence is so charged with emotion, selective perception and partiality that conceptual clarification is necessary. There is not yet consensus with regard to terminology and categorisation, and definitions vary in the nature and scope of acts conceived as

---

6   See, for example, Kelman and Hamilton (1989).

violence. Specifically, while a considerable amount of literature exists on the causes of war, the phenomenology of violence has received far less consideration (von Trotha 1997).

The particular complexity of the Yugoslav case poses specific difficulties for comparative social science research. Problems centre mainly around comparability and inference, namely the questions of whether similar violent actions imply the same motivation and intention on the part of the different actors involved – that is, although diverse acts of violence may share the same features and results (mass migration, large-scale atrocities), analytical distinctions among them might lead to differentiated explanations. Moreover, perpetrators may act out of mixed motivations, in order to achieve a variety of objectives. For instance, violent relocation of the population in a region may aim at ethnic homogenisation, but it may also be intended to secure a strategically or economically important region. Should one consider such expulsion as an act of genocide or an act of state terrorism? In addition, different parts of the perpetrators' group such as state agents, the military, warlords and individuals that act together in instilling fear in the target population may have different objectives in implementing a coercive or violent policy (Mitchell et al. 1986).

The various levels of violence applied during the Yugoslav war require analytical distinction between repression and state terrorism, and genocide.

1. Organised terror (repression, state terrorism)

'Repression' shall be defined as an 'active process of social control by neutralization or elimination of actual and potential opponents by a variety of coercive sanctions,' such as destruction of private property, suppression of political parties, physical attacks, eviction, and other tactics (Schmid 1991: 25). Repression appears when the degree of violence (physical and nonphysical) used by state actors is greater than necessary to establish control over the public order.

On the other hand, state-organised terrorism can be seen as 'a method of rule whereby some groups of people are victimised with great brutality, and more or less arbitrarily by the state or state-supported actors, so that others, who have reason to identify with those murdered, will despair, obey or comply (Schmid 1991: 31).' It uses instruments such as summary arrests, torture, disappearances and detention camps, to achieve active or passive responses from the target population through the creation of extreme fear.

Acts of terrorism are often equivalents of war crimes. They potentially involve two distinct targets: those who are physically exposed to deliberate coercion and violence, and those who observe and whose fear the perpetrator wants to increase. The latter group identifies with the victims in such a way that they perceive themselves as potential future victims. 'The act of violence therefore does not actually have to be directed at the target population. The population, however, must perceive itself at risk and as the ultimate target of the act.' Hence, 'the creation of fear must be a means toward an end (Mitchell et al. 1986: 4).'

The massive and systematic violations of human rights that happened in Bosnia from the summer of 1992 onwards occurred in the context of 'ethnic cleansing'.[7] First and foremost, they appeared as instruments to remove the civilian population from strategic areas.

'Ethnic cleansing' has, throughout history, occurred in various regional contexts and it has taken many forms (Bell-Fialkoff 1993). 'Ethnic cleansing' can be defined as 'a purposeful policy designed by one ethnic or religious group to remove by violent and terror-inspiring means the civilian population of another ethnic or religious group from certain geographic areas.'[8] This policy occurs when ethnic communities are identified with territories and the main aim is to establish a coincidence between borders and nations. The more homogeneous a region, the more easily power can be exerted. In this sense, 'ethnic cleansing' is, in the terms of the German military writer Clausewitz (1984), a rational means to a specific end.

'Ethnic cleansing' aimed at achieving various goals: first and foremost, the physical removal of a population from specific areas through threats, harassment and intimidation. Methods used include both repression and terrorist acts, such as discrimination, beatings, torture, shooting or using explosives against homes, summary executions, etc. In this line, the apparently 'irrational' destruction of houses to rubble was functional: for many people, building a new house was a life project for which families worked for years. The systematic burning of homes in rural Bosnia had, therefore, particularly devastating effects on people, and was intended to prevent refugees from returning to their places of origin.

Second, social life was to be severely damaged by 'ethnic cleansing' methods. Towns, sacred sites and city centres were continuously shelled and razed to the ground, in order to cut off local communication lines, thus making impossible the normal functioning of social life among the target community. Again, destroying houses was crucial, because a house often symbolised the social worth of a family; it was the proof of hard work and commitment to its future well-being (Bringa 1995: 86).

Third, cultural identity was at stake. Throughout Bosnia-Herzegovina, Bosnian Serb forces destroyed, quasi-systematically, the Muslim and Catholic cultural heritage, in particular sacred sites. According to

7 See the Periodic Reports on the Situation of Human Rights in the Territory of the Former Yugoslavia Submitted by Mr Tadeusz Mazowiecki to the UN Security Council and the General Assembly.

8 *Final Report of the Commission of Experts established pursuant to SCR 790* (1992), S/1994/674, 27 May 1994, p. 33.

UNESCO sources, a total of 1,123 mosques, 504 Catholic churches and five synagogues were destroyed or damaged, for the most part in the absence of military activity. Aside from mosques and churches, other religious and cultural objects such as cemeteries and monasteries were targeted.[9] Also the Serb cultural heritage was the target of attacks by military and paramilitary forces (Mileusnic 1994). The systematic destruction and levelling of religious and cultural symbols suggests that the intention was to eliminate any vestige of the opponent's presence in the respective areas.

Fourth, collective memory was jeopardised. Cultural vandalism is inherent to any culture, civilisation and historical period, as Alexander Demandt has convincingly shown (Demandt 1997). Throughout history, violence has been used to destroy buildings and monuments as the most prominent symbols of political power and historical identity of a society. Cultural assets represent sentimental values and conserve memories. Setting fire to libraries and archives will inhibit the Bosnians from writing their own history for many years to come, which, under normal conditions, is essential to forming national consciousness. In this sense, the horrendous proportions of destruction severely damaged the grounds of ethnic self-identification and national consciousness.

Finally, family relationships were in jeopardy because of the instrumental use of mass rape. The Yugoslav war of dissolution is not the only case in which gender-specific violence was applied on a large scale and systematic raping appeared as a war tool (Benard and Schlaffer 1993; Allen 1996). Rape of women belonging to enemies defeated in war has been a tool since premodern times, as these women were valued for their reproductive power. In patriarchal societies women are mainly seen as responsible for the biological reproduction and cultural preservation of their ethnic community. Hence, rape not only stigmatises individuals and families, but it also offends ethnic identities and entire social systems, especially if the role and status of men are associated with their sexuality, and the women appear as the men's possession (Eide 1997: 62).

Human rights violations were generally accompanied and reinforced by the massive humiliation of the victims, aiming at intimidating the opponent's population, forcing it to give up its resistance (Lindner 1997). Generally, aggression combined with humiliation is successful in creating a state of instability and confusion among the targeted population and their leaders, as they show that the enemy, obviously, is not capable of protecting its own ethnic community. Through individual humiliation, the opposing side will thus be intimidated and demoralised, and men especially will be offended in their social role as warriors, defenders, husbands and fathers. This behaviour is 'rational' in the sense

---

9 ICTY, *Prosecutor v. Radovan Karadžić/Ratko Mladić*, Case No. IT-95-5-R61/IT-95-18-R61, 11 July 1996.

that it intends to provoke fear and instability in order to break resistance or to deter the opposing side from taking combat action. In addition, offending the 'honour' of a supposed enemy seems, because of a long tradition of patriarchal values, to provide the offenders with particular satisfaction. The 'humiliation patterns' have also been used against members of the international community. For instance, during the UN hostage crisis in 1995, peacekeepers were presented to the world public in a most humiliating way. They were thus not only offended as individuals and as soldiers, but also as representatives of the most influential nations and the world community.

Grave human rights violations were perpetrated by all parties to the conflict, and there were victims on all sides. It should, however, be noted that these features of aggressive behaviour have been used in different regional, military and political contexts. The authors of a research project among Bosnian refugees concluded that the extent and the features of violence used in the context of 'ethnic cleansing' operations were highly dependent on the specific conditions prevailing in the area, such as ethnic composition, the distance to the line of confrontation, and political affiliations of the regional elite.

The general characteristics were as follows:
- extreme violence was used by the perpetrators if the percentage of the ethnic group to be evicted from a certain area was high;
- 'ethnic cleansing' was particularly brutally designed if the (defending) political and military authority in the area concerned was poorly organised;
- the efficiency of 'ethnic cleansing' depended on the level of political organisation and military supply of the attacking forces.

In a nutshell, 'ethnic cleansing' offended the collective identity of the targeted populations, especially the Muslims, at all levels: language, history, culture and family were violated. But again, none of the crimes committed on the territory of the former Yugoslavia were unique.

Frequently, crimes in connection with 'ethnic cleansing' were carried out by paramilitary forces. However, these irregular troops were supported, equipped and supplied by the governments they served and they usually acted in agreement with local authorities or higher military commanders. In 1994, the UN Commission of Experts to investigate war crimes in the former Yugoslavia identified more than eighty different paramilitary groups. Many of them joined in the armed conflict, operating with the regular armies and under regular army officers' command. Others operated independently in certain geographic areas from which the personnel in these units came. 'The outcome of such a structure and the strategies and tactics employed help to blur the chain of command

and conceal responsibility. This concealment may well be intended by some of the parties to provide a shield of plausible deniability.'[10]

The extent of command or influence exercised by Belgrade on the Bosnian Serb armed forces, however, is contested. The Trial Chamber of the Tadić case, by majority with the Presiding Judge dissenting, acknowledged 'the overwhelming importance of the logistical support provided by the Federal Republic of Yugoslavia to the VRS[11]' as well as 'co-ordination' between the Republika Srpska and the FRY. However, it did not recognise the 'attempt to exercise any real degree of control over, as distinct from coordination with, the VRS. So long as the Republika Srpska and the VRS remained committed to the shared strategic objectives of the war, and the Main Staffs of the two armies could coordinate their activities at the highest levels' there was no need for Belgrade to direct the actual military operations of the Bosnian Serbs.[12]

2. Genocide

While the application of state-organised terror is beyond any reasonable doubt, it appears much more difficult to determine whether or not 'genocide' took place, although atrocities committed on the territory of the former Yugoslavia were widely publicised as such (Bulajić 1993; Gutman 1993; Boyle 1994; Cekic 1994; Cigar 1995; Sells 1996; Cushman and Mestrovic 1996).[13] Again, there has been much more talk of 'genocide' in public discourse than factual and analytical research, and few scholars have devoted particular attention to the explanations and typologies presented by various social science disciplines (Gow 1997).

In contrast to state terrorism, which aims at affecting the victims' behaviour, 'genocide' implies the intention to destroy the victims' group in whole or in part. Genocide has been viewed either as the highest state of repression, a particular form of state terror, or as a phenomenon *sui generis* (Schmid 1991: 33).

Although various definitions of genocide have been put forward, many scholars have implicitly or explicitly accepted the definition

10 *Final Report of the Commission of Experts Established Pursuant to SCR 790* (1992), S/1994/674, 27 May 1994, p. 32.
11 Vojska Republike Srpske.
12 United Nations IT-94-1-T, *Prosecutor v. Duško Tadić*, 7 May 1997, opinion and judgement, pp. 220–8.
13 *Declaration to Stop Genocide Against the Serbian People* (Beograd: Agencija Dr Radulovic 1997); 'Genocid u Republici Bosni i Hercegovini 1992. godine,' *Pravna Misao* 5–8 (1992); *Genocide, Ethnic Cleansing in Northwestern Bosnia: Bosnia-Herzegovina* (Zagreb: Croatian Information Centre, 1993); United States Congress. Commission on Security and Cooperation in Europe, *Genocide in Bosnia-Herzegovina: Hearing before the Commission on Security and Cooperation in Europe, 4 April 1995* (Washington: U.S. G.P.O., 1995).

proposed by the UN Genocide Convention of 9 December 1948 (Art. 2), under which

> '...genocide means any of the following acts committed with intent to destroy, in whole or in part, a national, ethnical, racial or religious group, as such:
> (a) Killing members of the group;
> (b) Causing serious bodily or mental harm to members of the group;
> (c) Deliberately inflicting on the group conditions of life calculated to bring about its physical destruction in whole or in part;
> (d) Imposing measures intended to prevent births within the group;
> (e) Forcibly transferring children of the group to another group (Kuper 1985; Harff and Gurr 1988).'

The narrowness of this definition has been criticised in many instances. Some scholars suggested this definition be expanded to include political and social groups as victims ('politicides') and to exclude deaths resulting from warfare. According to their view, genocide is 'sustained purposeful action by a perpetrator to physically destroy a collectivity directly or indirectly, through interdiction of the biological and social reproduction of group members, sustained regardless of the surrender or lack of threat offered by the victim (Fein 1990: 24).'

Was there genocide happening on the territory of the former Yugoslavia? It is widely acknowledged that genocide is primarily a crime of the state or of another authority. However, the proof of intentional or planned mass destruction is often most problematic when killings occur during war, civil war or colonisation. Therefore, some scholars have strictly denied the interpretation that any of the acts committed in relation to 'ethnic cleansing' in Bosnia should be labelled as 'genocide', but rather as 'population transfer' aiming at the removal of a population, rather than at its extermination. The former had frequently been, to put it bluntly, a tool for building modern nation-states (Hayden 1996).

According to Helen Fein, there is a paradigm to detect genocide. It includes questions such as: Was there a sustained attack or continuity of attacks by the perpetrator to physically destroy group members? Was the perpetrator a collective or organised actor or a commander of organised actors? Were victims selected because they were members of a collectivity? Were the victims defenceless or were they killed regardless of whether they surrendered or resisted? Was the destruction of group members undertaken with the intent to kill and was murder sanctioned by the perpetrator? (Fein 1990: 25–30).

No document exists which would prove the intentions of state actors or local authorities in Bosnia to destroy partly or in whole the antagonistic groups. However, there are a number of indicators for such an intent.

First, acts of 'ethnic cleansing' have been carried out in such a systematic manner that they strongly appear to be the product of a policy:

'Indeed, the patterns of conduct, the manner in which these acts were carried out, the length of time over which they took place and the areas in which they occurred combine to reveal a purpose, systematicity and some planning and coordination from higher authorities.'[14]

Moreover, it seems that the leadership's project of creating ethnically homogeneous areas 'was inspired by a certain desire for partition,' which, consequently, led to a policy of national exclusion. For instance, as early as November 1991, Radovan Karadžić asserted in a public speech: 'Let us separate as many things as possible. Like in the days of the Turks. One Serbian town centre, one Turkish town centre, Serbian affairs, Turkish affairs, Serbian cafes, theatres, schools and everything else. This is the only solution.'[15]

On the political side, there is evidence that preparations were being made in Bosnia in order to carry out this programme in late 1991, especially with regard to the formation of the Serb Autonomous Regions. As early as September 1991, the Bosnian Serb leadership had taken steps towards forming regional autonomous areas with quasi-state powers. On 24 October 1991, a self-proclaimed Bosnian Serb parliament held the constituent meeting of an 'Assembly of the Serbian People in BiH', followed by a plebiscite on 9 and 10 November 1991 in which Bosnian Serbs voted overwhelmingly in favour of remaining in Yugoslavia. On 9 January 1992, the Assembly proclaimed the 'Republic of the Serbian People of BiH,' which on 7 April declared its independence. Its name changed in August 1992 to the Republika Srpska. At the same time, the Bosnian Croat leadership worked on the creation of a Croatian para-state. On 18 November 1991, Croat leaders founded the Croat Community of Herceg-Bosna, defined as a political, cultural, economic and regional entity. On 3 July 1992, it was officially proclaimed.

Last but not least, the constitution of the Republika Srpska made it clear that this state should be a state for Serbs exclusively. On 21 November 1991, the Assembly proclaimed as part of the territory of the federal Yugoslav state all municipalities, local communities and populated places in which over 50 percent of the Serbian population had voted to remain in that state during the plebiscite. This means that numerous municipalities with a mixed population were included in the territory of this para-state. The constitution of the Republika Srpska, however, in its article I.1 declared the Republika Srpska as 'the state of the Serb people', without mentioning citizens of other nationalities. This article suggests the conclusion that the strategic aim of the Republika Srpska was to create a purely Serbian state, and that the crimes

14 *Final Report of the Commission of Experts Established Pursuant to SCR 780* (1992), S/1994/674, 27 May 1994, p. 35.
15 ICTY, *Prosecutor v. Radovan Karadžić/Ratko Mladić*, Case No. IT-95-5-R61/IT-95-18-R61, 11 July 1996, p. 20.

committed during the armed take-over and ethnic cleansing of ethnically mixed areas were directly connected with this goal. The office of the prosecutor at the ICTY concluded in his indictments against Radovan Karadžić, President of the Bosnian Serb administration, and Ratko Mladić, Commander of the Bosnian Serb Army, that they should be charged with genocide on the grounds of internment of civilians in detention facilities and inhumane treatment therein.[16] The indictment concluded that those plans of the political and military leadership contained elements which would lead to the destruction of the non-Serb groups. 'The project of an ethnically homogenous State formulated against a backdrop of mixed populations necessarily envisages the exclusion of any group not identified with the Serbian one.'[17] In this sense, massive deportations and massacres, for instance those surrounding the events which preceded and followed the fall of the Srebrenica enclave in July 1995, could have been planned or ordered with a genocidal intent.

It has been pointed out, on the other hand, that not each and every single crime can be viewed as genocide, which is characterised by the particular intent to destroy a group 'as such'. Genocide, the 'ultimate crime', should not be diluted by too broad an interpretation, but it should be reserved only for acts of exceptional gravity and magnitude.[18] These definitely need to be distinguished from other crimes, such as crimes against humanity and war crimes, that is, grave breaches of the Geneva Conventions of 1949 and Protocols I and II as well as of customary international law of armed conflict. The prosecutor of the ICTY, in line with the UN Commission of Experts, implicitly came to the conclusion that 'genocide' did not appear as an intent to exterminate an entire group, but to eliminate particular groups in whole or in part within a specific regional context (towns, enclaves, etc.).[19]

The Affective Use of Violence

Although the use of violence in the Bosnian war was to a large extent intentional, human rights violations did not only appear in the context of armed struggle or as a purposeful policy. Besides the rational or instrumental use of violence, there were also strong elements of nationalistic

---

16 ICTY, *Prosecutor v. Radovan Karadžić/Ratko Mladić*, Case No. IT-95-5-R61/IT-95-18-R61, 11 July 1996.

17 ICTY, *Prosecutor v. Radovan Karadžić/Ratko Mladić*, Case No. IT-95-5-R61/IT-95-18-R61, 11 July 1996, p. 53.

18 UN, ICTY, *Rule 61 Hearing. Opening Statement by Mr Eric Ostberg, Senior Trial Attorney*, provisional transcript, 27 June 1996.

19 UN, Final Report of the Commission of Experts Established Pursuant to SCR 780 (1992), 27 May 1994 (S/1994/674).

passions, historical traumas and powerful feelings of revenge. For instance, revenge appeared to be a strong motivation when the Serbian Army conquered the eastern enclaves at Srebrenica because Muslim forces had been attacking Serbian villages from within these UN protected areas (Rhode 1997).

In addition, there are structural reasons why civil wars generally tend to be extremely violent (Waldmann 1997; Genschel and Schlichte 1997). First, there is the factor of time, which tends to turn internal conflicts into 'protracted wars'. The longer and more costly the conflict, the more likely it is that the reasons for which it was originally launched will be forgotten.

Secondly, civil wars in ethnically mixed regions automatically tend to turn into wars of existence because the contested territory is limited and the land that shall be conquered has to be taken away from the immediate neighbours (van Creveld 1991). In these conflicts, distinctions between civilian and soldier, individual crime and organised violence, terrorism and war, diminish (Roberts 1996). Moreover, if people involved in a civil war feel that their collective identities and physical survival are threatened, rational behaviour tends to break down. This may initiate an escalatory spiral of defensive perception and aggressive behaviour.

Thirdly, it appears that enemies hurt each other most brutally and effectively if they are on intimate terms. People who live in ethnically mixed settlements, as in Bosnia, have a mutual understanding of each other's traditions or even share the same cultural values and mentalities. This allows the perpetrators to exploit specific historical traumas or cultural taboos to instil terror in the civilian population on the victims' side. Bosnia gives us manifold examples for this, such as rape in Muslim communities, the stimulation of historical memories by repeating typical methods of killing or torturing used by the Četniks or the Ustašas during the Second World War. It was not the historical events themselves that caused nationalistic exaltation, but the way leaders had mishandled the memories of these events (Denich 1994: 370).

In some cases, ethnic violence appeared to be the result of deliberate and manipulative activities by 'conflict entrepreneurs' (Lake and Rothchild 1996). These persons can be defined as actors who use a specific situation to escalate a conflict in order to benefit from the newly emerging power relationships (Eide 1997). This may include gains in individual power, prestige or economic profit (Elwert 1997). Instigating a conflict can also be instrumental in improving the position of a (ethnic) collective in terms of protection against threats or improving living conditions. But even in this case it will help the 'conflict entrepreneur' to reach uncontested power within the we-group (Eide 1997: 44).

Janusz Bugajski described the techniques of deliberately escalating ethnic conflicts: in a politically tense situation it appears to be sufficient to capture and shoot a few members of the 'alien' ethnic group to terrorise the entire community, to create martyrs and acts of retaliation. Arming locals and encouraging them to burn houses or evict people against whom they may hold some grievance can also accelerate ethnic polarisation. This will help to make people of the same ethnic group as the perpetrators feel co-responsible and fearful of revenge. Acts committed by a few criminals will quickly be depicted as intercommunal violence, especially if supported by belligerent propaganda. Tragically, the longer the war, the greater the ethnic polarisation and perceptions of collective guilt (Bugajski 1993).

Conclusion

The Bosnian war represented a mixture of both an international and a civil war, in which regular armies were fighting side by side with the paramilitary, and in which rational calculation was sometimes accompanied by strong national passions. Hence, there is evidence for both intentional and affective use of violence.

In the light of comparative social research, the features of violence used in the Bosnian civil war did not differ significantly from those in other historical or regional environments. The events in Bosnia fit the general pattern of post-Second World War massive killing in ethnically plural societies where repression, terrorism and genocide mainly functioned to establish new political and institutional legitimacy by decimating groups who were contending for power. For instance, massacres, expulsions, deportation and flight in Algeria, Burundi, Rwanda and Zanzibar were triggered by the struggle for power, which resulted from transition towards self-determination (Kuper 1981). Like independence movements, the Yugoslav wars of succession caused a movement towards ethnocratic rule, creating massive problems of political participation and hierarchic relations. In either case, the structure of competition produced unstable coexistence and distrust, which were likely to lead to massacre and expulsion.

The resort to massive violence, therefore, seemed to be much more influenced by situational than by structural or dispositional factors, starting with the break-up of Yugoslavia, the disintegration of virtually all public institutions, and the state's loss of its monopoly over violence. These events created an environment conducive to the establishment of parallel state and military structures that functioned on the basis of repression, organised terror and (in some areas) genocidal politics to pursue their primary war aims: the creation of new national states.

In this context, all kinds of violent means were used as instruments to remove the target population from strategic areas through the creation of extreme fear. As far as it was intended to change the behaviour of the victim group rather than to eliminate it, this form of intentional violence can be viewed as organised terror. In specific regional contexts, though, such as Srebrenica, violent means were applied with a clear intent to destroy parts of the target group. Although it may not have been intended to exterminate an entire ethnic group as such, the aim was to eliminate at least particular parts of this group. In these areas, the crimes committed amount to genocide.

During four years of war, Bosnia has thus been transformed into a bitterly divided society. Even after the conclusion of the Dayton Peace Accords in late 1995, international observers continue to report 'incidents' in the form of violence, arbitrary behaviour, murder, revenge, prevention of the return of displaced persons, evictions, etc. Unfortunately, there is still no answer from the international community as to how these abuses can be stopped, nor to how future genocides can be prevented.

References

ALLEN, Beverly (1996). *Rape War: The Hidden Genocide in Bosnia-Herzegovina and Croatia*. Minneapolis: Minnesota University Press.

BELL-FIALKOFF, Andrew (1993). 'A Brief History of Ethnic Cleansing.' *Foreign Affairs* 72: 3, pp. 110–21.

BENARD, Cheryl, and Edit SCHLAFFER (1993). *Vor unseren Augen. Der Krieg in Bosnien - und die Welt schaut weg*. München: Heyne.

BOUGAREL, Xavier (1996a). *Bosnie: Anatomie d'un conflit*. Paris: La Découverte.

——— (1996b). 'L'économie du conflit bosniaque: entre prédation et production.' In: *Économie des guerres civiles*, François Jean and Christophe Rufin (eds), Paris: Hachette, pp. 233–68.

BOYLE, Francis Anthony (1994). *The Bosnian People Charge Genocide: Proceedings v. Serbia on the Prevention and Punishment of the Crime of Genocide*. Northampton: Aletheia.

BRINGA, Tone (1995). *Being Moslem the Bosnian Way: Identity and Community in a Central Bosnian Village*. Princeton: Princeton University Press.

BUGAJSKI, Janusz (1993). 'Balkan Futures: Understanding Ethnic Conflict.' In: *Armed Conflicts in the Balkans and European Security*. Ljubljana: Ministry of Defence, pp. 279–91.

BULAJIĆ, Milan (ed.) (1993). *Ratni zločini i zločini genocida 1991–1992*. Beograd: Srpska Akademija Nauka i Umetnosti.

BUSHNELL, P. Timothy, et al. (1991). *State Organized Terror: The Case of Violent Internal Repression*. Boulder, CO: Westview Press.

CALIC, Marie-Janine (1996). *Krieg und Frieden in Bosnien-Herzegovina*. Frankfurt am Main: Suhrkamp.

ČEKIĆ, Smail (1994). *Agresija na Bosnu i genocid nad Bosnjacima 1991–1993*. Sarajevo: NIPP Ljiljan.

CHALK, Frank, and Kurt JONASSOHN (1990). *The History and Sociology of Genocide: Analyses and Case Studies*. New Haven, CT: Yale University Press.

CHARNY, Israel (ed.) (1988). *Genocide: A Critical Bibliographic Review*. New York: Facts on File Publications.

—— (ed.) (1994). *The Widening Circle of Genocide*. New Brunswick/London: Transaction Publishers.

CIGAR, Norman L. (1995). *Genocide in Bosnia: The Policy of 'Ethnic Cleansing'*. College Station: Texas A&M University Press.

CLAUSEWITZ, Carl von (1984). *On War*, Michael Howard and Peter Paret (eds and transl.). Princeton, NJ: Princeton University Press.

COHEN, Lenard (1993). *Broken Bonds: The Disintegration of Yugoslavia*. Boulder, CO: Westview Press.

ČOLOVIĆ, Ivan (1994). *Bordel ratnika. Folklor, politika i rat*. Belgrade: Biblioteka XX vek.

CUSHMAN, Thomas, and Stjepan G. MESTROVIC (eds) (1996). *This Time We Knew: Western Responses to Genocide in Bosnia*. New York: New York University Press.

DEMANDT, Alexander (1997). *Vandalismus: Gewalt gegen Kultur*. Berlin: Siedler.

DENICH, Bette (1994). 'Dismembering Yugoslavia: Nationalist Ideologies and the Symbolic Revival of Genocide.' *American Ethnologist* 21: 2, pp. 367–90.

EIDE, Espen Barth (1997). ' "Conflict Entrepreneurship": On the "Art" of Waging Civil War.' In: *Humanitarian Force*, Anthony McDermott (ed.). Oslo: International Peace Research Institute, pp. 41–69.

ELWERT, Georg (1997). 'Gewaltmärkte. Beobachtungen zur Zweckrationalität der Gewalt.' In: *Soziologie der Gewalt*, Trutz von Trotha (ed.). Opladen/Wiesbaden: Westdeutscher Verlag, pp. 86–101.

FEIN, Helen (1990). 'Genocide: A Sociological Perspective.' *Current Sociology* 38: 1, pp. 104–116.

GENSCHEL, Philipp, and Klaus SCHLICHTE (1997). 'Wenn Kriege chronisch werden: der Bürgerkrieg.' *Leviathan* 25: 4, pp. 501–17.

GOATI, Vladimir (1992). 'The Political Life of Bosnia and Herzegovina.' In: *Ex Yugoslavia: From War to Peace*, Josep Palau and Raha Kumar (eds). Valencia: Generalitat Valenciana, pp. 227–38.

GOLDHAGEN, Daniel Jonah (1996). *Hitler's Willing Executioners: Ordinary Germans and the Holocaust*. New York: Little, Brown and Company.

GOW, James (1997). 'After the Flood: Literature on the Context, Causes and Course of the Yugoslav War – Reflections and Refractions.' *The Slavonic and East European Review* 75: 3 (July), pp. 446–84.

GOW, James, Richard PATERSON and Alison PRESTON (1996). *Bosnia by Television*. London: British Film Institute.

GURR, Ted Robert (1986). 'The Political Origins of State Violence and Terror: A Theoretical Analysis.' In: *Government Violence and Repression*, Michael Stohl and George A. Lopez (eds). New York: Greenwood Press, pp. 45–71.

GUTMAN, Roy (1993). *A witness to Genocide: The 1993 Pulitzer Prize-winning Dispatches on the 'Ethnic Cleansing' of Bosnia*. New York: Macmillan.

HARFF, Barbara (1986). 'Genocide as State Terrorism'. In: *Government Violence and Repression*, Michael Stohl and George A. Lopez (eds). New York: Greenwood Press, pp. 165–87.

HARFF, Barbara, and Ted Robert GURR (1988). 'Toward Empirical Theory of Genocides and Politicides: Identification and Measurement of Cases since 1945.' *International Studies Quarterly* 32: 3, pp. 359–71.

HAYDEN, Robert M. (1994). 'Recounting the Dead. The Rediscovery and Redefintion of Wartime Massacres in Late- and Post-Communist Yugoslavia.' In: *Memory, History, and Opposition under State Socialism*, Rubie S. Watson (ed.). Santa Fe: School of American Research Press, pp. 167–201.

———— (1996). 'Schindler's Fate: Genocide, Ethnic Cleansing, and Population Transfers.' *Slavic Review* 55: 4, pp. 728–48.

HÖPKEN, Wolfgang (1997a). ' "Blockierte Zivilisierung"? Staatsbildung, Modernisierung und ethnische Gewalt auf dem Balkan (19./20. Jhdt.).' *Leviathan* 25: 4, pp. 518–538.

———— (1997b). *War, Memory and Education in a Fragmented Society: The Case of Yugoslavia* (paper presented at the Remarque Institute, New York University, 24–27 April 1997).

HOROWITZ, Irving Louis (1997). *Taking Lives: Genocide and State Power.* New Brunswick/London: Transaction Publishers.

KADIJEVIĆ, Veljko (1993). *Moje vidjenje raspada: vojska bez države.* Beograd: Politika.

KAPLAN, Robert D. (1993). *Balkan Ghosts. A Journey Through History.* New York: St. Martin's Press.

KASER, Karl (1992). *Hirten, Kämpfer, Stammeshelden: Ursprünge und Gegenwart des balkanischen Patriarchats.* Wien: Böhlau.

KELMAN, Herbert C. and V. Lee HAMILTON (1989). *Crimes of Obedience: Toward a Social Psychology of Authority and Responsibility.* New Haven, CT: Yale University Press.

KENNAN, George F. (1993). 'The Balkan Crises: 1913 and 1993.' *The Other Balkan Wars. A 1913 Carnegie Endowment Inquiry in Retrospect with a New Introduction and Reflections on the Present Conflict.* Washington, DC: Carnegie Endowment.

KRESSEL, Neil J. (1996). *Mass Hate: The Global Rise of Genocide and Terror.* New York/London: Plenum Press.

KUPER, Leo (1981). *Genocide: Its Political Use in the Twentieth Century.* New Haven/London: Yale University Press.

———— (1985). *The Prevention of Genocide.* New Haven, CT: Yale University Press.

———— (1990). 'The Genocidal State: An Overview.' In: *State Violence and Ethnicity,* Pierre L. van den Berghe (ed.). Niwot: University Press of Colorado, pp. 19–51.

LAKE, David A, and Donald ROTHCHILD (1996). 'Containing Fear – The Origins and Management of Ethnic Conflict.' *International Security* 21: 2 (Fall), pp. 41–75.

LINDNER, Evelin (1997). *The Feeling of Being Humiliated: A Central Theme in Armed Conflicts,* unpublished manuscript, Oslo.

MANSFIELD, Edward D, and Jack SNYDER (1995). 'Democratization and the Danger of War.' *International Security* 20: 1, pp. 5–38.

MILEUSNIĆ, Slobodan (1994). *Duhovni genocid: pregled porušenih, ostečenih i obesvečenih crkava, manastira i drugih crkvenih objekata u ratu 1991–1993.* Belgrade: Muzej srpske pravoslaven crkve.

MILIVOJEVIC, Marko (1988). 'The Political Role of the Yugoslav People's Army in Contemporary Yugoslavia.' In: *Yugoslavia's Security Dilemmas. Armed Forces, National Defence and Foreign Policy,* Marko Milivojevic, John B. Allcock, Pierre Maurer (eds). Oxford/New York/Hamburg: Berg, pp. 15–59.

MITCHELL, Christopher, Michael STOHL, David CARLETON et al. (1986). 'State Terrorism: Issues of Concept and Measurement.' In: *Government Violence and Repression,* Michael Stohl and George A. Lopez (eds). Greenwood Press: New York, etc, pp. 1–44.

RHODE, David (1997). *Endgame. The Betrayal and Fall of Srebrenica. Europe's Worst Massacre since World War II.* New York: Farrar Straus & Giroux.

ROBERTS, Adam (1996). 'Communal Conflict as a Challenge to International Organization.' In: *International Perspectives on the Yugoslav Conflict,* Alex Danchev and Thomas Halverson (eds). Oxford: MacMillan, pp. 176–206.

RUMMEL, Rudolph J. (1994). *Death by Government.* New Brunswick/London: Transaction Publishers.

——— (1995). *Statistics of Democide: Genocide and Mass Murder since 1900*. Charlottesville: Center for National Security Law.

SCHMID, Alex P. (1991). 'Repression, State Terrorism, and Genocide: Conceptual Clarifications.' In: *State Organized Terror: The Case of Violent Internal Repression*, Timothy Bushnell et al. (ed.). Boulder, CO: Westview Press, pp. 23–37.

SELLS, Michael Anthony (1996). *The Bridge Betrayed: Religion and Genocide in Bosnia*. Berkeley: University of California Press.

SILBER, Laura, and Alan LITTLE (1996). *Yugoslavia. Death of a Nation*. London: Penguin.

SMAJLOVIC, Ljiljana (1995). 'Desintegration, Ethnisierung, Krieg: Der Fall Bosnien.' In: *Nationalismen im Umbruch. Ethnizität, Staat und Politik im neuen Osteuropa*, Margaditsch A. Hatschikjan and Peter R. Weilemann (eds). Köln: Verlag Wissenschaft und Politik, pp. 170–95.

STAUB, Ervin (1989). *The Roots of Evil: The Psychological and Cultural Origins of Genocide and Other Forms of Group Violence*. Cambridge: Cambridge University Press.

STOHL, Michael, and George A. LOPEZ (eds) (1986). *Government Violence and Repression*. New York: Greenwood Press.

THOMPSON, Mark (1995). *Kovanje rata. Mediji u Srbiji, Hrvatskoj i Bosni i Hercegovini*. Zagreb: Hrvatski Helsinski Odbor.

VAN CREVELD, Martin (1991). *The Transformation of War*. New York: Free Press.

VON TROTHA, Trutz (1997). 'Zur Soziologie der Gewalt.' *Kölner Zeitschrift für Soziologie und Sozialpsychologie* 37, pp. 10–56.

WALDMANN, Peter (1997). 'Bürgerkrieg – Annäherung an einen schwer faßbaren Begriff.' *Leviathan* 25: 4, pp. 480–500.

WOODWARD, Susan L. (1995). *Balkan Tragedy: Chaos and Dissolution after the Cold War*. Washington, DC: The Brookings Institution.

ZUPANOV, Josip (1995). 'Mass Media and Collective Violence.' *Politička misao* 32: 5, pp. 187–96.

PART THREE

LESSONS

CHAPTER SEVEN

The Use of Force in Minority–Majority Relations: An International Law Perspective

Rainer Hofmann

Introduction

In the perception of the general public, violence, i.e. the use of force, seems to have become again quite a common aspect of minority–majority relations in Europe. This impression is a result of, in particular, the wars fought in the former Yugoslavia, in the Transcaucasian successor states of the former Soviet Union, in Moldova and in Chechnya. The situations in Kosovo and, to a lesser extent, in the Sandžak, have been described by many observers as being on the brink of turning from 'tense' to 'violent'.[1] In addition thereto, the use of force in the form of terrorism persists in the three major West European conflict zones, i.e. the Basque Provinces, Corsica and Northern Ireland, notwithstanding all the considerable efforts made in order to end these acts of 'criminal violence', be it by legal means, notably the intensified deployment of police forces and enhanced public prosecution, or by political initiatives aiming at a negotiated solution to these conflicts.

It is true that these situations, with all their unspeakable general human suffering and the partial breakdown of public order and structures, are a part of contemporary Europe. None the less, they should not lead us to overlook the reality, i.e. that the vast majority of minority–majority

---

1   Indeed, in March 1999, the conflict which had been simmering since February 1998 between the KLA (Kosovo Liberation Army) and the forces of the Yugoslav army escalated into a full-blown armed conflict. According to the estimates of the Independent International Commission on Kosovo, about 10,000 (mostly ethnic Albanians) were killed, 863,000 sought refuge or were forced outside of Kosovo and 590,000 were internally displaced. The Commission also concluded that not only did the NATO air campaign fail to prevent massive ethnic cleansing, it might have created an environment favourable to it (see http://www.kosovocommission.org) [Editors' Note].

relations in Europe are characterised by a nonviolent coexistence between groups of the population of the states concerned and the will of the respective political leaders to bring about nonviolent solutions to existing problems.

On the other hand, there remains the undeniable fact that force has been and is being used in (some) minority–majority relations in Europe. These situations have become of utmost concern to the international community and, especially recently, to European politics. Bluntly speaking, it seems that this is not so much due to the human suffering mentioned and gross violations of fundamental human rights which, as a rule, characterise such situations; it is rather because of the seriously destabilising effects which such situations imply for the states and even the regions concerned. Therefore, it is indeed justified to raise the question of the relevance of international law for such situations in which force is used in minority–majority relations within a state.

This question will be dealt with by analysing the following issues and legal principles as to their applicability and importance for minority–majority relations: the principle of the prohibition of the use of force as enshrined in Article 2 (4) of the United Nations (UN) Charter (1945); third party intervention by means of use of force as a reaction to certain kinds of minority–majority relations; the applicability of humanitarian and human rights law to minority–majority relations; and, finally, the most controversial issue as to whether national minorities are holders of the right to (forcible) secession.

The Nonapplicability of the International Law Principle of Prohibition of the Use of Force in Minority–Majority Relations in Europe

Any international lawyer confronted with the term *use of force* will immediately think of Art. 2 (4) of the UN Charter which expressly prohibits the use of force in the following terms:

> All Members shall refrain in their international relations from the threat or use of force against the territorial integrity or political independence of any state, or in any other manner inconsistent with the Purposes of the United Nations.

This is not the appropriate place to recall the historical development of this principle.[2] Suffice it to mention that – until the First World War – the state of the law may indeed be described as being characterised by the complete discretion of any state to wage war upon any other state at any time and without any conditions. The first restrictions of this complete freedom appeared in the 1907 Hague Conventions, and were

2 But see, e.g., Randelzhofer (1994: 106–29 (109–11)).

further developed by the pertinent provisions of the League of Nations Covenant (1919). Whereas the 1924 Geneva Protocol, with its obligation incumbent upon states not to resort to war, except in self-defence or in the case of collective enforcement measures, never became binding law, a most fundamental change was brought about by the 1928 Briand-Kellogg Pact. For the first time, an international treaty formulated a general prohibition of war, and – this is important – was soon ratified by nearly all states existing at that time. The Pact suffered, however, from a severe deficiency in so far as it related, at least according to its wording, only to war, and not to the use of force in general. That particular defect of the Pact was to be remedied by Art. 2 (4) of the UN Charter. Today, this provision is generally considered as a – if not the – most important rule of public international law. It is often described as having the force of *jus cogens* and, thus, being binding also upon the few states not parties to the UN Charter and stabilised *de facto* regimes.

In our context, however, it is crucial to highlight the fact that, according to its express wording, Art. 2 (4) of the UN Charter proscribes the use of force only in international relations *between* states; consequently, it does not cover the use of force solely *within* a state. As has been rightly stated by Randelzhofer in one of the leading commentaries on the UN Charter, 'that means that the provision does not prevent insurgents from starting a civil war, nor the government concerned from using armed force against them (Randelzhofer 1994: 116).' It is further – in my view correctly – suggested that this 'legal situation changes, however, when the rebels have succeeded in establishing a stabilised *de facto* regime (Randelzhofer 1994: 116).'[3] Such regimes are likewise bound and protected by the prohibition of the use of force – now, however, based upon the customary law quality of that principle.

This does not mean, however, that international law *allows* the government or any individual to have an unconditional resort to force; it only means – and, in particular, in our context – that the principle of the prohibition of the use of force simply does not *apply* to minority–majority relations *within* a state.

Notwithstanding this clear general state of the law, there is, however, one issue of some relevance in our context that deserves to be mentioned briefly as a (possible) exception to this rule: the notion of *wars of national liberation* (Uibopuu 1982: 343–6; Randelzhofer 1994: 121–2).

The former Soviet doctrine of public international law (Zourek 1974: 108–11; Blischenko 1975: 158–78 (172–4); Tunkin 1985: 326–9), shared by a clear majority of developing countries,[4] maintained that – in

---

3 On the position of *de facto* regimes in international law, see Frowein (1992: 966–8).
4 This position led to UN General Assembly Resolution 2105 (XX), passed on 20 December 1965 by 74 votes to 6 with 27 abstentions, which reaffirmed the legitimacy of the peoples' struggle for liberation from colonial and foreign domination and alien subjugation by all means, including armed struggle.

addition to the three exceptions to this rule expressly provided for by the UN Charter, i.e. measures against former enemy states under Art. 107, Security Council Enforcement Actions under Arts. 39 *et seq.*, and the right of individual and collective self-defence under Art. 51 – there was a further exception: wars of national liberation. According to this view, such wars of national liberation by peoples under colonial or racist regimes or other forms of alien domination were claimed to be as lawful as the support, including the use of force, given to those peoples by third states. This was based upon the argument that colonialism constitutes a permanent armed attack, against which individual and collective self-defence is allowed. Since this view was continuously rejected by Western states, it does not seem possible to consider it as representing (or having constituted) customary international law (Randelzhofer 1994: 121; Malanczuk 1997: 338).

The applicability of this doctrine in minority–majority relations in Europe, i.e. in our context, is, moreover, problematic for the following two reasons: firstly, a war of national liberation may not be waged by a *minority*, but only by a *people* – an issue to which we shall return later in the context of the question as to whether minorities have a right to secession;[5] secondly, it is debatable whether there are, in contemporary Europe, peoples under colonial or other forms of suppression, although it must be recognised that this view seems to have been maintained by some quarters in the context of the war in Chechnya (Bellocchi 1995: 183–91; Tappe 1995: 255–95).

Third Party Interventions by Means of Use of Force as a Reaction to Certain Kinds of Minority–Majority Relations

As stated above, the UN Charter itself expressly provides for three exceptions to the rule on the prohibition of the use of force, one of which – Security Council Enforcement Actions – may have some relevance in our context. There are, moreover, two further issues which need to be discussed briefly – the notion of *humanitarian intervention* and the question of third party intervention in a civil war – since they, too, may be of some importance to our topic.

1. Security Council Enforcement Actions

The maintenance of international peace and security is undoubtedly the most important goal of the UN. Its preservation and restoration by all means, including the use of force, is the subject of Chapter VII of the UN

5   See footnote number 4.

Charter, which attributes the pertinent competencies to the Security Council. A precondition for any such action is, according to Art. 39, a threat to or breach of the peace as determined by the Security Council. There seems to be widespread acceptance of the view that *peace* in this context means the absence of organised use of force between states. Taken together with the aforementioned understanding of the prohibition of the use of force as applying only to the international relations of states (i.e. not to their internal situation which, according to Art. 2 (7), belongs to states' domestic jurisdiction), this means that a civil war – as a most extreme case of (violent) minority–majority relations – cannot be considered as a *breach* of international peace justifying any action by the Security Council under Chapter VII of the UN Charter (Frowein 1994: 609).

There is, however, ample – in particular recent – practice of the Security Council according to which the internal situation of a state or territory, in particular a certain form of government or a civil war, may result in a *threat* to international peace, thus indeed justifying pertinent Security Council actions. This approach, which may be traced back to the 1948 Resolution on the Indonesian Conflict and was later applied with regard to Rhodesia and South Africa (Stoll 1995: 311–29; Malanczuk 1997: 393–5), has become of specific relevance subsequent to the end of the Cold War. As has been rightly stated by Frowein, extreme violence *within* a state can generally be qualified as a threat to peace (Frowein 1994: 611). As well-known examples of this policy, one may recall numerous Security Council resolutions, such as those concerning the belligerent conflicts in Croatia and Bosnia-Herzegovina (notwithstanding some doubts as to the merely internal character of these conflicts) (Philipp 1995: 338–49; Malanczuk 1997: 409–15) and those concerning the situations in Somalia (Malanczuk 1997: 402–5), Haiti (Malanczuk 1997: 407–9), and the states in the East African Great Lakes region.[6] The rationale for these decisions seems to be the danger of third party interventions in such conflicts on the one hand, and the risk of massive flows of refugees into neighbouring states, on the other.

It is therefore justified to conclude that if minority–majority relations deteriorate in such a way as to result in the widespread use of extreme violence between minority and majority groups or even in a civil war, the international community, on the basis of a pertinent prior decision by the Security Council, *may* intervene by all means, including the use of force, in order to bring an end to such situations.

2. Humanitarian Interventions

In recent years, there has been a certain revival of the concept of *humanitarian intervention* (Lillich 1992: 557–75; Randelzhofer 1994: 123–4;

---

6 On Rwanda see Malanczuk (1997: 405–7).

Beyerlin 1995: 926–33; Murphy 1997). Usually, this term is used for forcible interventions, i.e. the use of armed force, for the prevention or discontinuation of massive violations of fundamental human rights of foreign nationals in a foreign state; in contrast to the aforementioned situation where such interventions occur on the basis of a pertinent prior decision of the Security Council, stating that the situation constitutes a threat to peace, the proponents of a wide notion of humanitarian intervention maintain that such acts by third states may be lawful even without such a Security Council decision.

From a strictly humanitarian perspective, this approach appears indeed as a possible solution to occurrences of such massive violations of fundamental human rights to which the Security Council, for political or other reasons, is incapable of reacting to in an adequate way. The conflicts in Afghanistan (Jahn-Koch 1995: 176–88), Chechnya and the states of the East African Great Lakes region may be mentioned as recent examples.

It must be stressed, however, that de lege lata[7] such forcible humanitarian interventions cannot be considered as lawful (Randelzhofer 1994: 123–4); they constitute clear violations of the territorial integrity and sovereignty of states as well as of the prohibition of the use of force, and an unlawful intervention in the states' internal affairs. Furthermore, the UN system is built upon the concept that individual states, outside the context of self-defence, are divested of the use of force as an instrument of their international policy. Finally, it must be clearly stated that there is no evidence of any state practice or any opinio juris that would allow one to conclude that the UN Charter has been, by means of the subsequent formation of customary law rules – provided that such a development is at all possible under current international law, amended or abrogated in such a way as to make it possible to consider such humanitarian interventions as lawful.

Obviously, this statement does not exclude considerations de lege ferenda[8] in order to make such humanitarian interventions lawful under future international law. However, with a view to the high risk of such a legal institution being abused by those states that hold command over the military resources needed to conduct such actions, extreme caution must be observed. In the present global situation, there is definitely no room – and no need! – for a renaissance (or a variation) of the old 'gunboat policy' by which the political interests of individual states are implemented under the pretext of serving the – doubtlessly existing – universal interest in the prevention or discontinuation of massive violations of fundamental human rights.

7   De lege lata: law that already exists [Editors' Note].
8   De lege ferenda: law that is being made [Editors' Note].

3. Third Party Intervention

If minority–majority relations have deteriorated in such a way as to result in a civil war, the question arises as to the legality of third party intervention (Malanczuk 1997: 319–24). Generally speaking, the relations between a state in which a civil war is going on and any intervening third state are always international relations. Therefore, it must be determined whether such interventions are compatible with the principles of nonintervention and the prohibition of the use of force. The traditional and supposedly still dominant view, backed by significant state practice, maintains that third states are entitled to intervene in a civil war in support of the *legitimate* government, upon its request or at least with its consent, whereas supporting the insurgents is considered to be entirely prohibited. Whereas, from a theoretical point of view, this doctrine appears to lead to clear-cut results, it does not seem to be a viable solution in practical terms. Since a state has a large measure of, or even absolute, political discretion regarding whom it wishes to recognise as a state's legitimate government, international law does not prevent the *prima facie* lawful intervention of third states in support of the different warring factions of a civil war. In order to avoid such situations, which have been quite frequent during the Cold War period, there is a growing tendency in present international law to prohibit the provision of any support to either side in a civil war (Malanczuk 1997: 324).

In our context, the legal situation is even more complex due to the fact that a civil war between a minority and the majority within a state will, as a rule, not be fought over the control of the government in that state, but will most frequently be a war of secession. Therefore, even if one subscribes to the presumably dominant view as just outlined, such third party intervention in support of the secessionist minority forces could only be considered as potentially lawful under two conditions: firstly, such a minority must constitute a *people* in the sense of the right to self-determination; and, secondly, it must be, in addition thereto, the holder of a right to secession to be implemented, if necessary, by resort to armed force (as will be shown later, it is extremely controversial whether current international law provides for such a right to forcible secession). Thus, any intervention by a third party in a civil – or rather secessionist – war will, as a rule, constitute a violation of international law and will, if at all, be lawful only under extremely unusual circumstances such as genocide or a most brutal suppression of that minority (Doehring 1994: 56–72 (71)). On the other hand, third party intervention in support of the majority, i.e. as a rule governmental, forces will be in most cases considered to be lawful – the only exception being support given to a government whose policy with respect to the minority constitutes an international crime; in this case, extending assistance to such a government should be considered as an international crime in itself.

The Applicability of Humanitarian Law Principles in Minority–Majority Relations

It has been stated above that the principle of the prohibition of the use of force, so fundamental for present international law, does not apply to minority–majority relations within a state, and that it neither prevents insurgents from taking up arms nor the government from using force in its fight against such insurgents. This does not mean, however, that international law as such is not concerned at all with the use of force in such relations. Quite to the contrary: it must be emphasised that some principles of humanitarian law may be applicable in minority–majority relations within a state that are characterised by the use of force. This fact is a result of one of the most important developments of international law after the Second World War. Some aspects of the factual situation within a state are of concern to the international community and subject to rules of international law. Thus far, the fundamental principle of the prohibition of any outside intervention in the internal, domestic affairs of a state has lost some of its previous absoluteness; examples of this development are humanitarian and human rights law (Partsch 1995: 910–12).

Before the Second World War, the laws of war applied to a civil war only if the government had recognised the insurgents as belligerents (Schlögel 1995: 531–41; Malanczuk 1997: 352–3); there was, however, no obligation for the government to do so. As regards the situation before recognition of belligerency, it was uncertain whether any of the laws of war applied. The appalling brutality of the Spanish Civil War showed how unsatisfactory this position was. The situation changed, to some extent, with the adoption of the 1949 Geneva Conventions. Since then, humanitarian law distinguishes between *international armed conflicts* to which the whole body of humanitarian law is applicable, and *noninternational armed conflicts*, i.e. internal conflicts, to which only a minimum standard applies, as laid down in common Art. 3 of the Geneva Conventions. This provision extends some of the more basic laws of war to all civil wars (or noninternational armed conflicts), regardless of recognition of belligerency; none the less, it has been judged as being completely insufficient.

This was one of the reasons for the drafting of the 1977 Additional Protocol Relating to the Protection of Victims of Non-International Armed Conflicts (Protocol II). It is, however, highly controversial whether its provisions are applicable even outside the treaty context; with a view to the still limited number of states parties to that Protocol,[9] it is doubtful whether it can be rightly considered as reflecting customary law

---

9   Whereas the four 1949 Geneva Conventions had been in force, as of 1 January 1998, for 188 states, the 1977 Additional Protocols had been ratified by only 146 states (Protocol I) and 138 states (Protocol II).

and, therefore, as binding also upon those states that have not ratified the Protocol. This is all the more regrettable since it contains a rather satisfying body of norms protecting the civilian and, to a limited extent, also noncivilian victims of noninternational armed conflicts (Eide 1979: 277–308). With a view to the factual situation of many conflicts, an important drawback of that Protocol must be emphasised. According to its Article 1 (1), it is only applicable to noninternational conflicts in which dissident armed forces or other organised groups fighting the government exercise, under responsible command, such control over part of the territory of the state concerned as to enable them to carry out sustained and concerted military operations and to implement the provisions of Protocol II. In many cases, governments tend to dispute the fulfilment of that precondition and, therefore, consider the relevant situations as internal disturbances and tensions, such as riots, and isolated and sporadic acts of violence, in the sense of Article 1 (2) of that Protocol, which results in the nonapplicability of its provisions.

The Applicability of Human Rights Law Principles in Minority–Majority Relations

As stated above, there can be no doubt as to the applicability of international human rights law also in minority–majority relations. Under current international law, the way a state treats its citizens as regards their human rights is a matter regulated by international law (Henkin 1995: 886–93 (886)). This applies also to minority–majority relations characterised by the use of force. This means that under any circumstances, a state must abide by its international law obligations in the field of human rights. Thus, nobody may be deprived of their human rights because there is force used in minority–majority relations.

Thus, in a situation short of civil war or, to put it more precisely, short of armed conflict, anyone, irrespective of their belonging to the minority or majority, is protected as concerns their human rights by international law (Meron 1987). Human rights of particular importance in this context are the prohibition of discrimination and the rights protecting an individual's life, physical integrity and personal freedom.

It is, however, essential to note that international law allows for certain limitations or restrictions to some of these human rights. In the framework of this paper it is impossible to enter into a detailed presentation of the relevant body of international law, i.e. in particular the provisions of the 1950 European Convention on Human Rights (ECHR) and the various Additional Protocols thereto and the pertinent practice of the Strasbourg organs, namely the European Commission of Human Rights and the European Court of Human Rights (Frowein 1995:

188–96).[10] They have, in my view, fully succeeded in establishing an adequate compromise between the right of all individuals to have their human rights respected even in situations in which force is used in minority–majority relations, on the one hand, and the legitimate interests and obligations of states to maintain a nonviolent public order and to prosecute and sentence those individuals who commit violent acts that break that order and, therefore, constitute crimes according to the applicable domestic criminal law, on the other hand. Thus, a person accused of, or being tried for, having committed a violent crime in the context of such minority–majority relations is, of course, still protected by the rules of international human rights law concerning, in this case, criminal procedure, namely Arts. 2 (right to life), 3 (prohibition of torture and inhuman or degrading treatment or punishment) and 5 (rights of the accused, fair trial) of the ECHR.

It is, moreover, equally essential to note that international human rights law allows a state to adopt particular measures also with regard to its international human rights obligations in specific situations characterised by the use of force: Art. 15 ECHR – and similar provisions are to be found in all other international human rights instruments – provides for the right of states to declare a situation of public emergency which, in turn, permits certain derogations from certain human rights that, without such a declaration, would constitute clear violations of that state's international human rights obligations. Obviously, if minority–majority relations are characterised by a more widespread use of force, in particular by terrorist acts committed by certain members of either group, such situations will, as a rule, justify such declarations of public emergency and, thus, also certain derogations from certain human rights.

It is, however, also essential to note that states do not enjoy – under international law – any unrestricted discretion as to which human rights they wish to derogate from and as to the extent to which they wish to do so. This is clearly reflected in the wording of Art. 15 ECHR:

(1) In time of war or other public emergency threatening the life of the nation any High Contracting Party may take measures derogating from its obligations under this Convention to the extent strictly required by the exigencies of the situation, provided that such measures are not inconsistent with its other obligations under international law.

(2) No derogation from Article 2, except in respect of deaths resulting from lawful acts of war, or from Articles 3, 4 (paragraph 1) and 7 shall be made under this provision.

(3) Any High Contracting Party availing itself of this right of derogation shall keep the Secretary General of the Council of Europe fully informed of the measures which it has taken and the reasons therefore. It shall also inform the Secretary General of the Council of Europe when such measures have ceased to operate and the provisions of the Convention are again being fully executed.

10 On 1 November 1998, the latter was replaced by a new, permanent European Court of Human Rights, also in Strasbourg. The Commission ceased to function on 31 October 1999 [Editors' Note].

Again, it is impossible to describe, in the framework of this paper, the pertinent practice of the Strasbourg organs (Frowein and Peukert 1996: 479–86; Jacobs and White 1996: 315–25). However, the essence of this jurisprudence may be summarised as follows. States parties to the Convention have quite a wide *margin of appreciation* if there exists a *public emergency threatening the life of the nation*; however, there is, in the words of the European Court, *European supervision* of this margin of appreciation which, however, is not of any considerable importance. The Commission and the Court have proceeded, however, to control whether specific derogations are indeed *strictly required*; in this context, three elements play a part: (1) the necessity of the derogations to cope with the threat; (2) the proportionality of the measures to cope with the threat; and (3) the duration of the derogations. It goes without saying that derogations from human rights which are *notstandsfest* according to Art. 15 (2) ECHR always constitute violations of a state's obligations under the ECHR, as was held, for example, with respect to certain treatment by British officials of persons who were (allegedly) members of the IRA.[11] Finally, it must be mentioned that Art. 15 (3) ECHR contains a procedural condition for a declaration of public emergency to be effective under that Convention; according to the practice of the Strasbourg organs, the notification mentioned therein has to be made *without delay*.

Minorities and the Right to (Forcible) Secession

The last issue to be dealt with in this paper concerns the highly controversial question as to whether minorities have a right to secession, or – since we are dealing with minority–majority relations characterised by the use of force – a right to forcible secession.

In my view, the answer is, from an international law point of view, quite obvious. Minorities cannot have a right to secession, be it forcible or not, because minorities do not have a right to self-determination of which the right to secession – if it exists at all – is only one aspect. This is so because the holder of the right to self-determination and, thus, also of a possible right to secession, is a *people*, not a *minority* (Thornberry 1989: 867–89 (878), 1991: 214–18; Ben Achour 1994: 321–461 (375); Lapidoth 1997: 20). Therefore, in order to avoid any misunderstanding, it is essential to stress that international minority rights law cannot and does not deal with, nor does it include, a right to self-determination which would include, under specific circumstances, a right to secede. International minority rights law consists of rules concerned with the preservation and promotion of the distinct identity of a given minority and the corresponding obligations of states (Niewerth 1996: 95–104;

11 Ireland v. United Kingdom, Judgement of 28 January 1978, Series A, no. 25.

Hofmann 1997: 420–24 (422)). If states choose to grant minorities a certain amount of territorial autonomy because they consider this to be a viable possibility to fulfil their obligations, they have opted for one possibility to preserve and promote the distinct identity of the minority concerned. It is, however, important to note that international law does not know of any such obligation of the state concerned (Hofmann 1995: 192).

It is, however, quite possible to imagine that a specific national minority claims to be a people in the sense of the international law concept of the right to self-determination. In this context, one is faced with the same problem as regards minority rights law. As yet, there do not exist any universally accepted definitions of either the term '(national) minority' or the notion 'people'; although there have been many scholarly efforts and attempts by the UN to clarify the meaning of the word *people* in the context of the right to self-determination, the results have been quite poor. The most widely accepted definitions usually include several objective criteria, such as a distinct identity based upon characteristics such as culture, language, religion, as well as subjective criteria, in particular the common wish to belong to that distinct group of persons and to preserve that distinct identity; in addition to these criteria – which, it must be stressed, also apply to national minorities – a group of persons that wishes to be recognised as forming a *people* in the context of the right to self-determination, must, as a rule, constitute the numerical majority in a geographically defined territory. Thus, some national minorities may indeed justifiably claim to constitute a *people* and, thus, to be holders of the right to self-determination under international law.

It is interesting to note that this definition complies with the historical development of the right to self-determination as a concept of international law (Doehring 1994: 58–59; Thürer 1985: 470–6). From an historical point of view, it is important to stress that the right to self-determination gained its modern relevance at the end of the First World War, in particular in the context of groups of persons who, both as regards objective and subjective criteria, distinguished themselves from other groups of persons living within the frontiers of a given state, and who constituted the numerical majority in a geographically defined part of that state. It should also be recalled that the Peace Treaties concluded subsequent to the end of the First World War provided for the creation of new states and the changing of some borders with a view to accommodate, *inter alia*, the political aims of *some* of such groups of persons, namely to live in a state of their own, their *nation-state*. It is well known, however, that the specific demographic situation of Europe, combined with the effects of political considerations of some states, resulted in the existence of ethnically heterogeneous or multinational states; this, in turn, led to the creation of the minority protection system established under the League of Nations (Capotorti 1997: 410–20 (411–14)). This system failed, however, to achieve its primary goal, namely to guarantee the protection and preservation of the distinct identities of such groups of persons, and, thus, to reduce the support, among the members of such groups, for political tendencies, based upon the claim to self-determination, aiming at the creation of new states or the 'adjustment' of borders. Obviously, this resulted in a considerable instability of the political order in Europe which considerably contributed to the developments of the 1930s leading to the outbreak of the Second World War. This development might explain why, under international law, the contents of the right to self-determination have been considerably limited after the Second World War (Oeter 1992: 741–80; Tomuschat 1993: 225–51).

In this context, it is therefore essential to stress that – notwithstanding the fact that the right to self-determination of peoples is explicitly mentioned in Articles 1 (2) and 55 of the UN Charter and the identical Articles 1 of both the 1966 International Covenant on Civil and Political Rights and the 1966 International Covenant on Economic, Social and Cultural Rights – current international law conceives this right (at least outside the decolonisation process) (Doehring 1994: 68) as embracing, as a rule, only its internal aspect (*internal self-determination*) (Rosas 1993: 1–20 (11–17)). Since this applies to all *peoples*, it applies also to such national minorities that might be considered as constituting *peoples* in this sense. The right to internal self-determination encompasses, in particular, the right of such minorities (that constitute peoples) to the preservation and promotion of their distinct identities. Therefore, as long as a government treats a national minority (that constitutes a people in this legal sense) in such a way as to respect its international law obligation to preserve and promote that minority's distinct identity, current international law does not provide for a right of that minority to exercise self-determination 'offensively', i.e. to strive for secession. This situation is considered to constitute the necessary balance between the right of any people to self-determination, on the one hand, and the right of states to territorial integrity, on the other hand (Franck 1993: 3–28 (11); Lapidoth 1997: 22). Obviously, this means – and it is most important to emphasise this in order to avoid any misunderstanding – that even those national minorities which constitute peoples in this legal sense, and which, often for accidental reasons of history, have not succeeded in founding – or living in – 'their' own state are, *de lege lata*, not entitled to secede from the state in which they live. On the other hand, it is equally important to stress that this statement does not exclude specific arrangements of domestic constitutional law providing, under certain conditions, for a right to secede for the constituent units of a federal state,[12] or the negotiated dissolution of a multinational state.[13]

12 As was the case as regards the constitution of the former Yugoslavia (Marauhn 1991: 107–14).

13 As recent examples may be mentioned the cases of the former Czechoslovakia (Hošková 1993) and the former Soviet Union (Schweisfurth 1992: 541–702).

Finally, it must be mentioned that it is increasingly being argued that current international law allows – as an exception to the above-mentioned rule – a national minority (which constitutes a people) to forcibly secede if such a minority is discriminated against by the government by means of actions consisting of widespread, persistent and gross violations of fundamental human rights such as mass killings or genocidal measures, e.g. *ethnic cleansing* (Doehring 1994: 66). This argument is – in my view rightly – based upon the pertinent wording of the most important 1970 UN General Assembly Friendly Relations Declaration.[14] In section 6 of its principle relating to self-determination, it is stated that nothing in this Declaration should be used as authorising or encouraging any action which would dismember or impair the territorial integrity of a sovereign state, or secession. However, the Declaration continues by stating that this limitation is only to be respected if the acting government is willing to observe the principle of self-determination, and if it represents the whole population of the governed territory without distinction as to race, religion or colour. Thus, governmental policies as described above, i.e. involving mass killings of and genocidal acts aimed against persons belonging to a national minority which constitutes a people in the legal sense, are considered to constitute 'discrimination' in the sense of the Declaration, and would, therefore, entitle the national minority (that constitutes a people) concerned to exercise its right to *external self-determination*, including the right to secede – if need be by resorting to force.

Concluding Remarks

Based upon the foregoing analysis, the following concluding remarks concerning the position of international law with respect to the use of force in minority–majority relations seem to be called for:

- The most fundamental principle of the prohibition of the use of force, as enshrined in Article 2 (4) of the UN Charter, is not applicable to minority–majority relations since it concerns only the international relations between states and not situations within a state.
- Situations within a state which are characterised by extreme violence may be declared by the UN Security Council to constitute a threat to international peace and security in the sense of Article 39 of the UN Charter which, thus, may justify forceful interventions by the international community if based upon a prior decision by the UN Security Council; without such prior authorisation, any third party intervention is, as a rule, to be considered unlawful unless it occurs in support of the legitimate government-provided that its policies do not constitute international crimes.

14 UN GA Res. 2625(XXV).

- If minority–majority relations have deteriorated in such a way as to have developed into an internal armed conflict, common Article 3 of the 1949 Geneva Red Cross Convention is applicable; in contrast thereto, it is highly controversial whether the provisions of the 1977 Additional Protocol Relating to the Protection of Victims of Non-International Armed Conflicts are applicable outside the treaty context; this is all the more regrettable since this Protocol contains a rather satisfying body of norms protecting the victims of such conflicts.

- Under any circumstances, governmental authorities must respect their states' treaty and customary law obligations concerning the human rights of all persons; this applies, in particular, to clauses allowing for the limitation or derogation from human rights in emergency situations such as those characterised by the use of force in minority–majority relations.

- Under current international law, national minorities as such cannot be holders of a right to secession, be it forcible or not, because national minorities do not have the right to self-determination; moreover, even those national minorities that constitute peoples in the sense of international law, do only have the right to internal self-determination which consists of the right to the preservation and promotion of their distinct identities; only under very exceptional circumstances, such as mass killings of or genocidal measures aimed at persons belonging to a national minority that constitutes a people in the legal sense, is international law increasingly accepting that the victims of such acts may exercise their right to external self-determination which includes the right to (forcible) secession.

References

BELLOCCHI, Luke P. (1995). 'Recent developments: Self-determination in the Case of Chechnya.' *Buffalo Journal of International Law* 2, pp. 183–91.

BEN ACHOUR, Yadhi (1994). 'Souveraineté étatique et protection internationale des minorités.' *Recueil des Cours de l'Académie de Droit International* 245 (1994–I), pp. 321–461.

LAPIDOTH, Ruth (1997). *Autonomy: Flexible Solutions to Ethnic Conflicts.* Washington, D.C.: United States Institute of Peace Press.

BEYERLIN, Ulrich (1995). 'Humanitarian Intervention'. In: *Encyclopedia of Public International Law, Vol. II*, Rudolf Bernhardt (ed.). Amsterdam: North Holland, pp. 926–33.

BLISHCHENKO, Igor P. (1975). 'The Use of Force in International Relations.' *Current Problems of International Law*, Antonio Cassese (ed.). Milano: A. Giuffrè Editore, pp. 158–78.

CAPOTORTI, Francesco (1997). 'Minorities'. In: *Encyclopedia of Public International Law, Vol. III*, Rudolf Bernhardt (ed.). Amsterdam: North Holland, pp. 410–20.

DOEHRING, Karl (1994). 'Self-Determination'. In: *The Charter of the United Nations. A Commentary*, Bruno Simma (ed.). Oxford: Oxford University Press, pp. 56–72.

EIDE, Asbjørn (1979). 'The New Humanitarian Law in Non-International Armed Conflicts.' In: *The New Humanitarian Law of Armed Conflict*, Antonio Cassese (ed.). Napoli: Editoriale Scientifica, pp. 277–308.

FRANCK, Thomas M. (1993). 'Postmodern Tribalism and the Right to Secession.' In: *Peoples and Minorities in International Law*, Catherine Broelmann, René Lefeber and Marjoleine Zieck (eds). Dordrecht: Martinus Nijhoff Publishers, pp. 3–28.

FROWEIN, Jochen Abr. (1992). 'De facto Régime'. In: *Encyclopedia of Public International Law, Vol. I*, Rudolf Bernhardt (ed.). Amsterdam: North Holland, pp. 966–8.

——— (1994). 'Article 39'. In: *The Charter of the United Nations. A Commentary*, Bruno Simma (ed.). Oxford: Oxford University Press.

——— (1995). 'European Convention on Human Rights (1950)'. In: *Encyclopedia of Public International Law, Vol. II*, Rudolf Bernhardt (ed.). Amsterdam: North Holland, pp. 188–96.

FROWEIN, Jochen Abr., and Wolfgang PEUKERT (1996). *EMRK-Kommentar*. Kehl am Rhein: N.P. Engel Verlag (2nd edn.).

HENKIN, Louis (1995). 'Human Rights'. In: *Encyclopedia of Public International Law, Vol. II*, Rudolf Bernhardt (ed.). Amsterdam: North Holland, pp. 886–93.

HOFMANN, Rainer (1995). *Minderheitenschutz in Europa*. Berlin: Gebr. Mann Verlag.

——— (1997). 'Minorities. "Addendum 1995" '. In: *Encyclopedia of Public International Law, Vol. III*, Rudolf Bernhardt (ed.). Amsterdam: North Holland, pp. 420–4.

HOŠKOVÁ, Mahulena (1993). 'Die Selbstauflösung der SFR.' *Zeitschrift für Ausländisches öffentliches Recht und Völkerrecht* 53 (1993), pp. 689–735.

JACOBS, Francis G. and Robin C.A. WHITE (1996). *The European Convention on Human Rights*. Oxford: Clarendon Press (2nd edn.).

JAHN-KOCH, Ingrid (1995). 'Conflicts, Afghanistan'. In: *United Nations: Law, Policies and Practice, Vol. I*, Rüdiger Wolfrum (ed.). München: C.H. Beck Verlag, pp. 176–88.

LILLICH, Richard B. (1992). 'Humanitarian Intervention through the United Nations: Towards the Development of Criteria.' *Zeitschrift für ausländisches öffentliches Recht und Völkerrecht* 53, pp. 557–75.

MALANCZUK, Peter (1997). *Akehurst's Modern Introduction to International Law*. London: Routledge (7th edn.).

MARAUHN, Thilo (1991). 'Die Auseinandersetzungen um die Unabhängigkeits bestrebungen der jugoslawischen Teilrepublik Slowenien.' *Humanitäre Völkerrecht* 4, pp. 107–14.

MERON, Theodor (1987). *Human Rights in Internal Strife: Their International Protection*. Cambridge: Grotius Publications.

MURPHY, Sean D. (1997). *Humanitarian Intervention*. Philadelphia: University of Pennsylania Press.

NIEWERTH, Johannes (1996). *Der kollektive und der positive Schutz von Minderheiten und ihre Durchsetzung im Völkerrecht*. Berlin: Duncker & Humblot.

OETER, Stefan (1992). 'Selbstbestimmungsrecht im Wandel'. *Zeitschrift für ausländisches öffentliches Recht und Völkerrecht* 52, pp. 741–80.

PARTSCH, Karl Josef (1995). 'Human Rights and Humanitarian Law'. In: *Encyclopedia of Public International Law, Vol. II*, Rudolf Bernhardt (ed.). Amsterdam: North Holland, pp. 910–12.

PHILIPP, Christiane (1995). 'Conflicts, Yugoslavia'. In: *United Nations: Law, Policies and Practice, Vol. I*, Rüdiger Wolfrum (ed.). München: C.H. Beck Verlag, pp. 338–49.

RANDELZHOFER, Albrecht (1994). 'Article 2 (4)'. In: *The Charter of the United Nations. A Commentary*, Bruno Simma (ed.). Oxford: Oxford University Press, pp. 106–29.

ROSAS, Allan (1993). 'Internal Self-Determination'. In: *The Modern Law of Self Determination*, Christian Tomuschat (ed.). Dordrecht: Martinus Nijhoff Publishers, pp. 1–20.

SCHLÖGEL, Anton (1995). 'Geneva Red Cross Conventions and Protocols'. In: *Encyclopedia of Public International Law*, Vol. *II*, Rudolf Bernhardt (ed.). Amsterdam: North Holland, pp. 531–41.

SCHWEISFURTH, Theodor (1992). 'Vom Einheitsstaat zum Staatenbund. Juristische Stationen eines Staatszerfalls und einer Staatenbundsentstehung.' *Zeitschrift für ausländisches öffentliches Recht und Völkerrecht 52*, pp. 541–702.

STOLL, Peter-Tobias (1995). 'Conflicts, Rhodesia and South Africa'. In: *United Nations: Law, Policies and Practice*, Vol. *I*, Rüdiger Wolfrum (ed.). München: C.H. Beck Verlag, pp. 311–29.

TAPPE, Trent N. (1995). 'Chechnya and the State of Self-determination in a Breakaway Region of the Former Soviet Union: Evaluating the Legitimacy of Secessionist Claims.' *Columbia Journal of Transnational Law 34*, pp. 255–95.

THORNBERRY, Patrick (1989). 'Self-Determination, Minorities, Human Rights: A Review of International Instruments.' *International and Comparative Law Quarterly 38*, pp. 867–89.

────── (1991). *International Law and the Rights of Minorities*. Oxford: Clarendon Press.

THÜRER, Daniel (1985). 'Self-Determination'. In: *Encyclopedia of Public International Law, Instalment 8*, Rudolf Bernhardt (ed.). Amsterdam: North Holland, pp. 470–76.

TOMUSCHAT, Christian (1993). 'Self-Determination in a Post-Colonial World.' In: *The Modern Law of Self-Determination*, Christian Tomuschat (ed.). Dordrecht: Martinus Nijhoff Publishers, pp. 225–51.

TUNKIN, Grigorij I. (1985). *Law and Force in the International System*. Moscow: Progress Publishers.

UIBOPUU, Henn-Jüri (1982). 'Wars of National Liberation'. In: *Encyclopedia of Public International Law, Instalment 4*, Rudolf Bernhardt (ed.). Amsterdam: North Holland, pp. 343–6.

ZOUREK, Jaroslav (1974). *L'interdiction de l'emploi de la force en droit international*. Leiden: Sijthoff Publishers.

CHAPTER EIGHT

Third Party Mediation in Violent Ethnic Conflicts[1]

Norbert Ropers

Introduction

This article will address the possibilities open to the international community for influencing violent ethnopolitical conflicts in a peaceful direction, seeking to address the question: 'What are the remedies outside actors have at their disposal to put an end to the spiral of violence, to transform protracted ethnic conflicts into nonviolent ones, even reverse them into dialogues?'

The question itself implies a considerable measure of scepticism as to what, if anything, can be achieved from the outside in these types of conflicts.[2] It is a scepticism that I share. Despite – or perhaps precisely *because* of this – it seems to me that we need to take a closer look at the possibilities for, and limits to, peaceful intervention, by setting the figure of 'third party' and the concept of 'mediation' firmly centre-stage in this process.

Let me begin by considering how these two terms are understood. According to one widely held view, the third party in a conflict situation that involves two actors ideally occupies a sort of equidistant position between the disputants. If at all possible, such a party should fulfil two preconditions. Firstly, it should be neutral – that is to say, it should not be labouring under the influence of any prior relations to either of the two parties. Secondly, it should be impartial – that is to say, it should not show any preference for either of the positions occupied by the parties to the dispute. In reality these preconditions are rarely fulfilled, particularly

1   The author wishes to thank Alexander Austin for his support in the preparation of this paper.
2   On the general topic of ethnopolitical conflict (with details of further literature), see Scherrer (1996).

since the involvement of third parties is always bound up with particular interests or a particular prior history. Therefore, it would seem more sensible to view the concept of the 'third party' as an ideal-typical one, one to which the real actors may conform to a greater or lesser degree, depending upon their own interests and their position within the web of conflictual events. Furthermore, a concern with *omnipartiality* rather than impartiality is probably a surer indication that a constructive role is being played in the conflict.

When it comes to the term 'mediation', there is even less agreement as to its sense. One broad definition takes it to mean any kind of third party intervention aimed at de-escalating a conflict, improving relations, or resolving the contentious issues. A narrower definition highlights the noncoercive, voluntary and nonviolent character of the intervention. This definition further distinguishes this type of mediation from power-based mediation and judicial-style procedures. However, in reality, the boundary between the types of mediation based on a thoroughgoing voluntary approach and those involving pressure and power, reward and punishment, or the transfer of resources, is a fluid one. This particularly applies to when it comes to identifying effective factors in mediation. Consequently, it is not sensible to opt for too narrow a definition of mediation.

Understandably as a rule, it is primarily third parties that act as mediators. The converse is not so true. I should like to say more about the 'primarily' later on. There are a number of third parties that interpret the principle of neutrality in such a way that it expressly excludes mediation on the substance of the conflict. One reason they might do this is to avoid jeopardising other endeavours such as humanitarian missions. A major exponent of this position is the International Committee of the Red Cross (ICRC).

The involvement of third parties in the settlement of conflicts is as old as conflict itself. In recent times, various factors have helped bring about a situation that we are now experiencing and that might be called a mediation boom. Consequently, there are an ever-greater number of actors involving themselves in this task. The main factors are:

- *First*, there are a number of global trends indicating a growth in conflictual potential, particularly within existing societies that are undergoing development or transformation.
- *Second*, instruments traditionally used to resolve conflict in the world of states are inappropriate to deal with the new, ethnopolitical species of conflict.
- *Third*, the 'alternative dispute resolution' movement, as developed mainly in the Anglo-Saxon world, has sharpened awareness of the need for external support in highly escalated and protracted conflicts.

The multiplicity of actors involved in this area now covers almost the entire spectrum of political operators. The so-called 'Track 1' level includes individual government representatives, diplomats, elder states-persons, delegates from various government groupings, and representatives of multilateral organisations. The 'Track 2' level – the societal level – includes representatives of the churches, human rights activists, those working for humanitarian and development NGOs, 'peace-movementeers', and academics. The overall impression is that their achievements so far have been on the modest side. To be fair, one should also add that attention always becomes focused on the conflicts that have not been resolved, those that have been dragging on for a long time, or those where violence is still being used. This runs contrary to there being no systematic review – and probably cannot be – of cases where third parties have succeeded in preventing violence.

I should like to cite three cases in which the commentators agree that the respective mediators – all very different – have succeeded in bringing about de-escalatory, problem-resolving effects:

1. The diplomatic efforts made by the OSCE High Commissioner on National Minorities and by a number of other international and transnational organisations to bring the citizenship conflicts in Estonia and Latvia to a peaceful conclusion (Zaagman 1994: 113–76).
2. The shuttle diplomacy, problem-solving workshops, and community-building and media work done by the British NGO 'Vertic' in the Georgian-South Ossetian conflict.
3. To cite an example from the field of development cooperation, and more specifically from Africa, the joint venture run by the German *Gesellschaft für Technische Zusammenarbeit* (the German bilateral development agency) together with various international and domestic NGOs in Mali. It has played a decisive role in turning the violent conflict between the Tuareg and various other ethnic groups in northern Mali until 1994 into a process of reconciliation (Papen-dieck and Rocksloh-Papendieck 1998).

However, the counter-examples are even more numerous. To stay with the same groups of actors, for instance:

1. The OSCE's 'Minsk Group', set up to mediate in the dispute between Armenia and Azerbaijan over Nagorno-Karabakh, has produced few tangible results to date. Consequently, more and more people are calling for the group to be disbanded to avoid any further damage to the OSCE's credibility.[3]

3   Further discussion on the work of the Minsk Group can be found on the OSCE web-site at http://www.osce.org

2. Almost no other trouble spot has had so many NGOs engaged in community building as the former Yugoslavia – and notably Bosnia-Herzegovina. However, the ability to influence the direction of interethnic reconciliation and understanding has so far been marginal.

3. Rwanda was a favourite target and model for the most diverse development projects, involving members of both the Tutsi and Hutu tribes. Nevertheless, both governmental and nongovernmental development organisations were surprised and hopelessly overwhelmed by the extreme violence of the 1994 genocide. A number of humanitarian organisations, after setting up numerous refugee camps in Zaire, had to accept the charge that they had de facto helped to bolster the Hutu militia.

Having outlined actual examples, what insights does the theoretical study of this area afford us?

Empirical-quantitative research into mediation has concerned itself chiefly with the prerequisites and conditions for successful intervention. In the world of states, attempts at mediation are most likely to succeed if the following conditions are met:[4]

- There is minimal internal fragmentation amongst the actors involved.
- There are only minor power-differentials between the disputants.
- Prior relations between the parties have not been marked by serious conflicts.
- There has already been some kind of trial of strength in terms of power politics, as this has made clear to the parties the consequences of not reaching a mutual settlement.
- Military hostilities have not claimed too many victims.
- The disagreements centre on ideological issues, and security and sovereignty are not at stake.

If one applies this list of criteria to the ethnopolitical conflicts we are currently faced with, it becomes clear that these are the very preconditions that are missing. In most cases, these conflicts:

- display a high degree of internal heterogeneity;
- involve an asymmetrical distribution of power;
- have a prior history of continual strife;
- involve some kind of transitional situation, in which one side or the other hopes to be able to achieve some change that will be to its advantage;
- have claimed large numbers of victims; and, most importantly,

---

4 These conditions can be found in Bercovitch and Houston (1996: 11–39).

- primarily involve issues of self-determination, autonomy or territorial integrity.

Beyond quantitative research into mediation, we also need to call on case studies of individual interventions, mediators' accounts of their experiences, conference reports, and similar material. This would aid in forming a more precise picture of the approaches to, difficulties with, dilemmas involved in, and limits to, third party mediation in ethnopolitical conflicts. At this point, I would like to focus on eight relevant features:

- Content- and relation-based mediation
- The question of neutrality in asymmetrical conflicts
- Partiality as a variable
- External and internal actors
- Mediation as an aid to bringing about change in the conflict culture
- The dissociation–association dilemma
- Mediation with or without resources?
- Mediation as a market and a growth industry

Content- and Relation-based Mediation

Mediation is essentially a process aimed at improving communication between disputing parties. It is at this point that much of the criticism of mediation arises. Where ethnopolitical conflicts are concerned, critics quite rightly point out that misunderstanding, irrationality and barriers to communication are by no means the only factors involved. Further underlying these kinds of conflicts, they say, are some thoroughly rational, systematic, power-oriented political strategies and what are at stake are the scarce resources and basic needs relating to security, identity and participation.

Mediation processes should therefore be viewed realistically. They are instruments for improving the chances of working out the practical differences more clearly. Furthermore, they aim at creating favourable conditions for a joint solution of the problems. In the best cases, they can serve to work out the interests that underlie the polarised positions. Regardless of this, mediation 'without muscle' will not work where either one or both parties have no interest in such a process.

However, especially in the case of ethnopolitical conflicts which, because of a long prior history, have developed into protracted conflicts, there is a deeper level of collective identity forming experiences, outlook and attitudes. This includes, for example, scars left by events in which a large number of members of a group have previously fallen victim to some kind of despotism, enforced expulsion, military defeat, or other forms of violence.

Working through this level of identity and attitude should therefore also be viewed as one of the tasks for third party intervention. In fact, I would go so far as to claim that, for protracted conflicts, there will be no lasting peace unless much more is done at this level. It ought to be said that the term 'mediation' is not used so frequently to describe work on this relational dimension. A more common name for it is 'consultation'. This highlights the fact that what is involved here is understanding and shared reflection rather than finding a 'solution' to a practical problem.

The Question of Neutrality in Asymmetrical Conflicts

A question that has been under discussion for some time is that of the neutrality of third parties.[5] In this context, special attention has been paid to cases where the distribution of power is extremely uneven or where one side mainly is committing massive human rights violations against the other. This is not just an ethical issue affecting the third party, as it also has a bearing on the sustainability of any resolution. The subject first began to be discussed during the Biafran war in the 1960s, when Bernard Kouchner and other doctors chose to leave the ICRC team. This was due to the feeling that they could no longer accept the organisation's attitude of passive neutrality in the face of colossal atrocities. (Kouchner later founded the rival NGO *Médecins sans frontières* – which admittedly now faces the same dilemma as the Red Cross movement.)

Since then, the issue has been discussed in numerous other permutations. This can be illustrated in the phase where one is attempting to prevent violence. For example, on the one hand, the aim is to bolster the weaker side in order to eliminate injustices. However, on the other hand, is one not thereby actually creating the potential for violent escalation? In addition to this, what about the tension that exists in postwar situations between peacemaking, reconciliation and forgiveness on the one hand, and justice and the search for truth on the other?

One answer to all these questions is to recognise that peacemaking activities by third parties require a multiplicity of actors all playing distinct roles. Thus, a clear distinction should be drawn between actors with different roles, such as between actors with advocacy and monitoring functions, for whom it is quite in order to be partial, and those actors working mainly to achieve understanding and mediation between the parties in dispute.

5 For a more in-depth discussion, see Broodmire and Sistrunk (1980: 311–28) and Smith (1985: 363–72).

Partiality as a Variable

The traditional model of mediation presupposes that the parties to a dispute are more or less homogeneous groups of actors. However, this model hardly corresponds to the reality of ethnopolitical conflicts. Firstly, one of the characteristics of ethnically defined groups is precisely their 'enforced' nature. In other words, individuals are assigned to these groups whether they want it or not. Secondly, for all the parties involved in an ethnopolitical conflict, there is a broad spectrum of political-cum-social groupings with different views and interests in relation to the conflict. In many long-standing ethnopolitical conflicts, there are often intense arguments within the two 'camps' about how the conflict should be conducted with the other side. The case of the Israelis and Palestinians is not the only one to show that these internal conflicts can themselves end up being conducted by violent means.

What conclusions should be drawn from this as far as third party intervention is concerned? There are three observations which I should like to make here:

1. The way in which the conflict is defined is influenced by how third parties involve themselves in a conflict and with whom they do so. If, for example, they give priority to negotiating with the hardliners, and adopt the latters' definition of partiality, they will, in certain circumstances, contribute to a further 'ethnicisation' of the conflict.
2. Third parties ought to be aware of the broad spectrum of actors involved in the conflictual domain. In particular, they should not indirectly help to weaken the semi-'partial' or minimally 'partial' actors further by concentrating on those who hold extreme positions. This will often only be possible if there is also a broad spectrum of third parties able to assume this task.
3. One area that has been neglected up to now is that of the role which third parties can, in certain circumstances, play in regulating conflicts *within* each respective 'camp'. Some NGOs have begun to tackle this task by conducting training sessions for influential members of individual disputant groups. Experiments have been conducted in which 'third party teams' are put together. These teams consist of members belonging to the two opposing sides as well as external actors. At present, these experiments look very promising.

External and Internal Actors

This brings me to an area upon which so far little light has been cast. It is the combined action of external third parties and those that assume, or could assume, a mediating or bridge-building function within an area of conflict. In the debate about the role of third parties, it is often assumed – as if it were inevitable – that the latter must be external actors. Yet, on closer inspection, it becomes clear that in most cases there are a number of individuals, groups and organisations fulfilling similar functions, even if they do not come under this heading. One might reasonably claim that for any peaceful settlement to be sustainable, it is of decisive importance to bolster these internal forces.

For third party intervention from the outside to be constructive, certain implications need to be addressed. These are the broadening of the internal actors' social base, enhancing their capacity for action, and putting them in a position where they can develop their own initiatives. In short, to create peace constituencies. The extent of the difficulties facing this kind of capacity building has been demonstrated by the experiences in the field of development cooperation. The challenge concerning the setting-up of internal NGOs via external initiatives lies primarily in ensuring that they are permanently anchored in the indigenous civil society.

Mediation as an Aid to Bringing About Change in the Conflict Culture

Almost all societies in which highly escalated ethnopolitical conflicts are fought out are societies undergoing development or transformation. This factor also affects the way in which social conflicts overall (and, significantly, not just ethnopolitical ones) are resolved. In other words, the conflict culture itself is in transition or consists of a juxtaposition of different conflict cultures.

At a rough glance, three models of conflict culture can be distinguished:

- command and imposition;
- bargaining and compromise;
- competition and cooperation.

A strong predominance of the first – command and imposition – model is typical of many transitional societies. For ethnopolitical conflicts to be dealt with successfully, it is necessary to bring into the area of conflict as many elements of bargaining and compromise as possible. Furthermore, it is only in the long term, within the framework of successful democratisation strategies, that one can realistically expect to establish competition and cooperation on a lasting basis.

Successful mediation can therefore be measured not only by whether the particular practical conflicts have actually been settled, but also by whether it has been possible to steer the conflict culture itself in a constructive direction. Consequently, this is a very lengthy process. This aspect also highlights the fact that even failed attempts at mediation can have a positive effect, as they provide models for a new, consensus-oriented conflict culture. (The question of whether specific traditional conflict cultures can be put to constructive use is one I should mention, though I cannot deal with it in any detail here.)

The Dissociation – Association Dilemma

In the 1970s, the Norwegian peace researcher Johan Galtung (1976: 282–304) popularised the notion of dissociation and association as two basic peace strategies. The concept states that in order to create peace, the parties to a conflict must either be kept permanently apart or be successfully reconciled with one another. This duality continues to characterise both primarily military-based 'peacekeeping' and civil-political 'peacebuilding'. Nevertheless, there is a dilemma, in that the success of each strategy is ultimately dependent on that of the other, whilst their practical implementation on the ground is often mutually exclusive.

This is currently obvious in Bosnia-Herzegovina. In order not to jeopardise the precarious peace, the peacekeeping process effectively amounts to a perpetuation of the state of ethnic separation. At the same time, it is becoming increasingly obvious that an end to the peacekeeping – at least in the sense of an honourable withdrawal – can only be expected when peacebuilding has achieved sustainable successes. Third party mediation therefore embraces much more than the negotiation of a peace treaty. Finding a solution to the dissociation – association dilemma can probably only be done on a case-by-case basis. Experience, however, shows that this task will be a very hard one without the involvement or 'god-parenting' of third parties.[6]

Mediation With or Without Resources?

One theme that was a feature of mediation literature from the very beginning was that of the distinction between the supporters of power mediation, or 'mediation with muscles', and those who hoped for more effective peacemaking through 'honest brokerage' by individuals, without the use of power, pressure or rewards. The interest in this debate

---

6   For an example of mediation work carried out in Bosnia, refer to *Assessing Conflict Management Assistance in Central and Eastern Europe and the Commonwealth of Independent States: Learnings from Projects Supported by the Charles Stewart Mott Foundation 1989–1998*, Charles Stewart Mott Foundation and the Berghof Center for Constructive Conflict Management, 1998.

has waned considerably due to two factors. First, it has become clear that both approaches can be justified and that both have their advantages and disadvantages, depending on the situation (Bloomfield 1995: 151–64). Secondly, the increased involvement of organisations engaged in humanitarian aid and development cooperation has led to the participation of third parties usually being accompanied by some change in the resource situation in the conflict region. This does not make matters any easier, but one thing remains clear: there are no longer any third party interventions of any significant time-scale that are not, in one way or another, also linked to at least the possibility of access to resources.

All third parties in conflict situations thus have to consider how they should take account of this aspect in their work. One model that has come in for increased discussion recently is that of 'peace constituencies' (Lederach 1995: 201–22). According to this, third party interventions should primarily bolster those social forces that have a lasting and practicable interest of their own in securing peace. The concept was first put into practice by American NGOs in Somalia.[7] These NGOs began to deliver their aid via local trader-networks, as a means of enlisting the support of this group in the struggle to contain clan conflict.

I have already touched upon one other aspect of this theme, namely, that many peace agreements – however well worked out with the help of third parties – will be of little worth unless there is also support at the implementation stage. To adapt a well-known formula, which says that in every conflict you have to wait for the situation to be 'ripe for resolution', it is possible to argue that 'cultivating ripeness' is a task for third parties. Experience at any rate shows that if there is no back-up in demobilising combatants, resettling refugees and rebuilding the physical and social infrastructure destroyed by war, all peace agreements will be built on sand.[8]

Mediation as a Market and a Growth Industry

The increased demand for third party mediation has led to a corresponding increase in supply. At both the 'Track 1' and the 'Track 2' levels, there is now a range of individuals and organisations seeking to make this whole field more professional. The financial involvement of charitable foundations and humanitarian aid and development programmes has produced a 'market'. In this market, conflict-resolution NGOs compete with one another for resources – albeit scarce ones. This development is necessary and desirable, but naturally it also has its negative aspects, of which the following are the most important.

---

7   This can be illustrated by the work of the Life and Peace Institute. See Heinrich (1997).
8   Examples can be found in Hampson (1996) and in Ball and Halevy (1996).

1. At least amongst the larger NGOs, there is a trend similar to that in the humanitarian aid market of wanting to show 'spectacular' success peace agreements such as the Oslo Accord. This has resulted from the increased chance of continued funding. In contrast, untiring and little publicised grass-roots endeavours, such as those engaged in by many Quaker organisations, are much less 'marketable'. This is despite the fact that securing sustainable peace is not possible without progress at precisely this level.
2. The next key concept is sustained involvement. It is precisely smaller, adaptable, external actors with good links to partners in the area of conflict which often have the greatest difficulties in obtaining the necessary resources. This is due to these actors' striving for the crucial longer-term involvement. In contrast, 'bungee NGOs', as they are often ironically termed, have an easier ride because they can offer, for example, stylish little training sessions in conflict management. This situation is further encouraged by the fact that political bodies and sponsors are interested primarily in 'quick result' projects.
3. The final aspect I should like to mention is that of legitimisation. Who and what confers legitimacy on third parties in their efforts at mediation? Up to now, the prevailing answer to this question has been 'success and acceptance on the ground'. However, given the tenacious and complex nature of most conflicts, this is not very satisfactory.

Conclusion

I should like to close this discussion with a reference to the debate about the two peace maxims – 'Si vis pacem, para bellum' and 'Si vis pacem, para pacem' – which has been recently initiated in Germany, notably by Dieter Senghaas (Senghaas and Senghaas 1992: 249). If is it true – and I am convinced that it is – that the traditional maxim 'If you want peace, prepare for war' should now be replaced by 'If you want peace, prepare for peace,' then part of this process must be the large-scale mobilisation and training of third parties to tackle the challenges of ethnopolitical conflict management.

References

BALL, Nicole, and Tammy HALEVY (1996). *Making Peace Work: The Role of the International Development Community.* Washington, D.C.: Overseas Development Council.
BERCOVITCH, J., and A. HOUSTON (1996). 'The Study of International Mediation: Theoretical Issues and Empirical Evidence.' In: *Resolving International Conflicts: The*

Theory and Practice of Mediation, J. Bercovitch (ed.). London/Boulder, CO: Lynne Rienner, pp. 11–39.

BLOOMFIELD, William P. (1995). 'Towards Complementarity in Conflict Management: Resolution and Settlement in Northern Ireland.' *Journal of Peace Research* 32: 2, pp. 151–64.

BROODMIRE, David A., and Frank SISTRUNK (1980). 'The Effects of Perceived Ability and Impartiality of Mediators and Time Pressure on Negotiation.' *Journal of Conflict Resolution* 24: 2, pp. 311–28.

GALTUNG, Johan (1976). 'Three Approaches to Peace: Peacekeeping, Peacemaking and Peacebuilding.' In: *Peace, War and Defense: Essays in Peace Research, Vol. II,* Johan Galtung (ed.). Copenhagen: Ejlers, pp. 282–304.

HAMPSON, F.O. (1996). *Nurturing Peace: Why Peace Settlements Succeed or Fail.* Washington, D.C.: United States Institute of Peace.

HEINRICH, Wolfgang (1997). *Building the Peace: Experiences of Collaborative Peacebuilding in Somalia 1993–1996.* Life and Peace Institute, Horn of Africa Series 3.

LEDERACH, J.P. (1995). 'Conflict Transformation in Protracted Internal Conflicts: The Case for a Comprehensive Framework.' In: *Conflict Transformation,* Kumar Rupesinghe (ed.). New York: St. Martin's Press, pp. 201–22.

PAPENDIECK, Henner, and Barbara ROCKSLOH-PAPENDIECK (1998). 'Vom Südrand des Azawad: Konfliktbewältigung im Norden Malis.' In: *Gewaltsame Konflikte und Ihre Prävention in Afrika. Hintergründe, Analysen und Strategien für die entwicklungspolitische Praxis.* Hamburg: Institut für Afrikakunde, pp. 77–102.

SCHERRER, Christian P. (1996). *Ethno-Nationalismus im Weltsystem: Prävention, Konfliktbearbeitung und die Rolle der internationalen Gemeinschaft.* Münster: Agenda Verlag.

SENGHAAS, Dieter, and Eva SENGHAAS (1992). 'Si vis pacem, para pacem. Überlegungen zu einem zeitgemäßen Friedenskonzept.' *Leviathan* 20: 2, pp. 230–51.

SMITH, William P. (1985). 'The Effectiveness of a Bias Mediator.' In: *Negotiation Journal,* Plenum 1: 4 (October), J. Rubin (ed.), pp. 363–72.

ZAAGMAN, Rob (1994). 'The CSCE High Commissioner on National Minorities: An Analysis of the Mandate and the Institutional Context.' In: *The Challenges of Change: The Helsinki Summit of the CSCE and its Aftermath,* A. Bloed (ed.). Dordrecht: Martinus Nijhoff, pp. 113–76.

PART FOUR

CONCLUSION

CHAPTER NINE

In Quest of Peaceful Coexistence – Strategies in Regulating Ethnic Conflicts

Ulrich Schneckener and Dieter Senghaas

Minorities and the Nation-state

Twentieth-century European history knows numerous 'tragedies'. One has become a constant 'companion' throughout the decades: the almost notorious exclusion of and discrimination against cultural minorities which to some extent undermine the concept of the 'nation-state'. Nation-states are based on the idea that state, i.e. a political entity, and nation, i.e. a certain cultural-symbolic entity, have to be concurrent. Its imperative is, according to the historian Alfred Cobban, that 'every separate national culture must, according to this theory, be a state in embryo, and the ideal of every state should be to embody a single culture-nation (Cobban 1969: 110–11).' The slogan of the nineteenth century, 'each nation, a state, each state a national character,'[1] led to the 'problem of minorities' or the 'question of nationalities', as it was called at the turn of the century. Thus, the idea of 'minorities' gained impor-tance conceptually and empirically only after the concept of 'nation-state' became the dominant principle of order, first in Europe and later on world-wide. This can be illustrated by the very fact that the term 'minority' appeared for the first time in international politics and law during Europe's reorganisation on the basis of nation-states after the First World War. As Hannah Arendt put it (Arendt 1986: 424), the Paris Peace Accords divided nations into 'peoples with a state' (*Staatsvölker*) on the one hand, and into 'minorities' on the other hand. The latter were put under special protection of the League of Nations, which again stressed their particular status.

---

1 Quote by the Swiss public lawyer Johann Caspar Bluntschli (1801–81) who himself argued strongly in favour of 'multinational' states.

This type of minority can be described as ethnonational groups that did *not* migrate, i.e. they did not leave their homelands but have come to live in a society where they are a minority in numbers, and from which they differ and, at the same time, distinguish themselves by certain cultural features as well as by their own ethnohistory. Such minority situations may be the result of: (a) border changes as stipulated in treaties; (b) territorial conquests; or (c) the creation of new nation-states.[2] Until today, these majority–minority constellations are typical of a series of ethnonational tensions which, as after 1918, have reemerged after the end of the Cold War.

On an ethnographic map of Europe there is hardly any country without a national minority and which has not undergone periods of considerable tension between the minority and the majority group in society in the past. Historically, these conflicts were by no means limited to Eastern and Southeastern Europe, where the dissolution of the Soviet Union and the break-up of Yugoslavia led to the eruption of numerous violent ethnonational conflicts. They have characterised nation- and state-building processes throughout Europe since the nineteenth century.

In dealing with ethnonational minorities, whether in Eastern or Western Europe, three different policies can be distinguished: *elimination*, *control* and *recognition* of cultural difference. The first two are regarded as *unilateral* policies on the part of a dominant majority represented by a central government; the third, in turn, is considered a *bilateral* (negotiation) process. Strategies of *elimination* aim at suppressing cultural differences within a state, i.e. at achieving greater cultural 'homogeneity' of society. Means used may range from methods of forced assimilation – especially significant with regard to language and religion[3] – forceful expulsions or forced resettlements,[4] to extreme cases of genocide and 'ethnocide'. Strategies of *control* pursue the goal of excluding a minority systematically from political and/or economic power without either denying existing cultural tensions in society or making any serious attempt to eliminate them. The majority group's primary aim is to safeguard its power in the form of a hegemonic position *vis-à-vis* the minority. This may be carried out either within an authoritarian regime or within a majority-based democratic system.[5] The third strategy implies that the

2   This type of minority differs, therefore, from the 'classical' immigrant minorities by its specific origin. Francis distinguished between 'group formation as a result of migration' and 'group formation as a result of annexation' (Francis 1965: 124; 1976: 172–213).

3   For examples of forced linguistic assimilation through particular language, school and family name laws, see Puschmann (1996: 15–31).

4   For expulsions in the twentieth century, see De Zayas (1989). Bilaterally agreed population transfers, as in the cases of Greece and Bulgaria (1919), Greece and Turkey (1923), Germany and Italy (1939), Czechoslovakia and Hungary (1946), and Yugoslavia and Hungary (1946), also fall into this category.

5   Northern Ireland (Stormont System, 1921–72) and Cyprus (1964–74) serve as two examples of hegemonic control through majority rule.

difference between majority and minority is basically 'recognised'. Unlike the strategy of control, both sides are aware that this *recognition* will lead to practical and political consequences. Its objective is to establish and to practise forms of coexistence through negotiation processes.

Elimination and *control* do not usually lead to long-lasting conflict resolution, apart from the fact that they can hardly be justified from the perspective of a liberal order characterised by the rule of law. Even if formal democratic approval exists, these policies are merely means to achieve a temporary *authoritarian containment* of a conflict and finally lead to its 'chronification'. This is demonstrated by numerous cases where ethnonational tensions have persisted and built up over generations as a result of unjust treatment in the past. Forms of containment such as attempts at forced assimilation or hegemonic control are 'reliable' (from the majority's point of view) only if the respective society or the minority concerned show a low level of politicisation. If, however, a society has already begun the process of politicisation or is already considerably politicised, authoritarian measures of containment have little chance of being successful in the long run. These conditions hardly exist in today's Europe, whereas they were the rule in large parts of the continent in the eighteenth and nineteenth centuries.

Hence, the only realistic perspective for ethnonational conflict regulation remains the mutual recognition through modes of peaceful coexistence. Central to conflict resolution is the establishment of conditions which enable a reliable realisation and maintenance of one's own (cultural) identity. This paper, therefore, points to the range of constructive means of regulation by which the escalation of ethnonational conflicts may be interrupted and finally brought to an end. The first part focuses on four requirements for coexistence which can be considered frames for gradual 'learning steps' (Senghaas 1992: 116–38). The second part presents different constitutional and institutional arrangements of coexistence whose opportunities and risks with regard to conflict regulation will be discussed on the basis of some paradigmatic cases. The underlying assumption is that these *modi vivendi* of living together allow actors to develop empathy and to broaden their perspectives. Their careful and progressive implementation may bring about processes of collective learning which, in turn, foster willingness to cooperate and, eventually, end the deadlock caused by a certain degree of autistic behaviour typical of ethnonational conflicts.

Requirements for Coexistence

In the following, four general requirements are considered which are relevant for the lengthy and painful paths leading to peaceful coexistence in ethnonational conflicts (see Senghaas 1992: 116–38). These are the establishment and practical effectiveness of (1) confidence building measures and of (2) empathy; further, the constructive consequences which result from (3) broadening the intellectual 'horizon' of the conflicting parties and from (4) achieving a problem-solving orientation shall also be examined.

1. Confidence Building Measures versus the Security Dilemma

If the escalation of ethnonational conflicts creates, in similar ways as conflicts in the international arena, a structural and fundamental security dilemma, then these can only be mitigated by confidence building and security-enhancing measures in analogy to those used in international politics. Such measures are the first steps towards establishing a certain degree of reliability. These are especially necessary where conflict parties are armed and where possibly military or quasi-military conflict has already been conducted. In this case, reciprocal information as well as supervision of both military forces, their logistics and their armament are of the same importance as mere symbolic actions to establish mutual confidence.

Again, as in international politics, peacemaking strategies, for example those incorporated in the concepts of unilateralism and gradualism, will be useful. Who will be the first to introduce confidence building actions? Who will be the first to make a move with the expectation of receiving a constructive answer? Are there further steps in the same direction that might be envisaged, even if the first move remains unanswered? When should there be a shift from mere symbolic gestures to formal binding agreements?

In international politics, confidence building measures are usually followed by arms control, disarmament and, finally, the establishment of nonaggressive defence strategies, in particular the creation of institutions of peaceful arbitration in cases of arguments and provisions for cooperative/collective security. In ethnonational conflicts, further action should be taken along these lines suggested by experience in international politics: *arms control* in the sense of surveillance of the security apparatus of the conflicting parties; *disarmament* in the sense of demilitarisation of domestic conflicts; *nonaggressive defence mechanisms* in the sense of mutually acceptable security arrangements; *forms of peaceful arbitration* as a means for nonviolent conflict management; and *measures of collective security* as a last resort in case violence erupts again. All these steps are precautionary measures that support the de-escalation of ethnonational conflicts and offer potential for demilitarisation.

2. Empathy versus Ethnocentrism

To expect empathic understanding while ethnocentrism is increasing is paradoxical and contradicts the actual process of escalation. Coexistence, however, cannot be achieved without a minimum of shared understanding of the prevailing problems and the specific interests of the communities concerned.

While ethnonationalism often creates a sense of overestimation and infallibility, coexistence demands the recognition of the other communities and their identities as well as their right to exist which, in turn, has the effect of seeing one's own position in more relative terms. The extreme opposite of this attitude often manifests itself in the politics of elimination. The promotion, encouragement and extension of empathy is therefore a fundamental requirement for coexistence in a constructive way (not coexistence in the sense of a master coexisting with his subjects). Empathy should not be confused with sympathy: empathy and sympathy might go together, but sympathy is not necessarily a precondition of empathic understanding. Empathy is, nevertheless, a requirement for a constructive political culture in dealing with conflicts which allows for fair conflict management without attempting to contain conflicts in an authoritarian manner.

3. Broadening the Actors' Intellectual 'Horizon' versus Autistic Behaviour

The escalation of ethnonational conflicts quickly leads to a form of 'group narcissism' and narrow-mindedness. A combination of both provides the autistic background for such conflicts. It does not allow for learning processes beyond the experiences of the parties themselves and will therefore lead to the automatic exclusion of conflict regulation mechanisms from the actors' considerations. The constitutional instruments and principles for ethnic conflict regulation which have been successful in several cases remain, very often, more or less unknown to the conflicting parties.

Pluralist societies are equipped with a great variety of conflict management mechanisms which could be used as an inspiration for new attempts to solve ethnonational conflicts. But very often the knowledge of their existence is missing. This reinforces the lack of perspective for a realistic conflict solution scenario. The perceptions of possible strategies, thus, remain limited in scope and extent and are, at most, lacklustre. The general lack of perspective often serves as a background for increasing power politics and power fantasies with the consequence of militarisation.

4. Problem-Solving Orientation versus Zero-Sum Mentality

The promotion of empathy and the opening of new perspectives are the basis for positive actions with regard to solving problems; they are the very opposite of a zero-sum mentality which so often seems to govern ethnonational conflicts. Empirical evidence shows that solutions will be more easily achieved if the right to existence is mutually recognised, if the possibility of organising coexistence in the long run is not denied from the very beginning and if the gross national product grows, i.e. if the surplus that can be distributed is enlarged. The concentration on joint tasks, such as improving the economic situation, is in many cases helpful for instilling a problem-solving attitude. This implies a more productive use of common (human as well as other) resources and the end of the destructive, vicious circle of zero-sum games. If one side perceives gains by the other side as losses, then there will be no mutual process of learning. If, however, constructive conflict management leads to a shared benefit, i.e. a win-win situation for all parties involved, the vicious cycle will be replaced by a virtuous cycle. This process will be the basis for a self-sustaining cooperative behaviour.

Confidence building measures, empathy, broadening the 'horizon' and a problem-solving orientation are pillars of a *productive conflict culture*, i.e. the ability to contain and manage conflicts in a constructive and nonviolent manner through institutional arrangements accepted by all parties involved. In other words, a corresponding mentality, the willingness to compromise, the ability to form coalitions for a certain length of time and the compliance with institutionalised rules are needed. This necessarily implies, in cases of ethnonational conflicts, the recognition of cultural difference which can be achieved by different modes.

Modes of Coexistence and Ethnic Conflict Regulation

The following modes are based on a policy of *recognition of cultural difference*. This point of departure is challenged by a general critique which practically denies the peacebuilding effect of these modes. According to this critique, a political system whose organisation and guarantee of rights is based on cultural cleavages of society reproduces and consolidates these differences as it ignores existing cross-cutting cleavages. Thus, a plural, ethnically segmented society becomes a self-fulfilling prophecy. The cause of conflicts is limited to the cultural dimension which, in turn, gains in conflict potential because of this very approach. These modes are, therefore, not suitable for containing a conflict permanently because they tend to deepen cultural frictions and to divide society rather than foster political integration.

The implied alternative of the critics, however, which is to ignore or at least not to give sufficient recognition to the political dimension of articulated cultural difference, will hardly solve the problem. The 'politics of difference', according to Michael Walzer (Walzer 1992: 229), start already 'when a group of people insists on their value as a group, on the solidarity of its members and demanding some kind of public recognition.' The difference articulated is 'real', 'it is a characteristic of the social world, and from now on every denial to recognise this fact will become an act of suppression itself (Walzer 1992: 230).' The prime objective of these modes is to initiate learning processes through recognition, negotiations and regulations among the parties concerned which, firstly, increase the will-ingness to cooperate and, secondly, minimise the political importance of cultural differences recognised before. In other words, the recognition, rather than the denial, of cultural differences within the public arena, offers some prospect of their depoliticisation or at least of their 'dedramati-sation' in the mid-term.

1. Minority Rights

Special provisions for minorities can be considered the most basic form of recognition. Minority rights can be legally guaranteed by the constitu-tion, by a special minority law and/or by various single laws (i.e. laws on language, education, media, etc.). They are special rights in the sense that they go beyond the scope of classical liberal freedoms. They rather form the legal basis of cultural and political (self-)organisation of minorities. This instrument's main advantage is its flexibility because it is possible to reflect both the particular ethnographic situation of the country concerned as well as the demands of minority groups. Minority rights depend neither on the size nor on the kind of settlement of a group. Basically, they are applicable to all minority situations (to a certain degree this applies also to immigrant groups), and one can specify these rights in detail as well as tailor them to the needs of different groups. In fact, empirical variation is enormous, regulations differ from state to state, both in form and in content.

Problems, however, may arise with respect to normative as well as practical aspects. On the normative side, two main reservations exist. First, there is the fear that special rights for certain groups may violate the principle of equality of all citizens, i.e. the ability to claim certain rights based on group membership rather than on the recognition as equals before the law. The second argument is that some minority rights may conflict with norms of 'classical' liberal individual rights. This applies above all to the right to preserve one's own culture which may include practices and rules considered as illiberal or even inhuman by the majority (e.g. religious rituals, penal norms, forms of ownership, atti-tudes on education and family life).[6]

But it has to be pointed out that both arguments are based on an unnecessary dichotomy between individual and group rights combined

6 Examples for such normative conflicts are usually taken from the North American context and are related to religious groups (e.g. Amish communities) or the traditional lifestyles of indigenous peoples.

with a misunderstanding of what minority rights imply in detail. Minority rights complement (rather than substitute) classical liberal rights. On the one hand, they serve to ensure equality and justice, i.e. structurally disadvantaged groups are granted special privileges in compensation for inequality. On the other hand, they contribute to the recognition of cultural identity of individuals as an inherent value. As in liberalism, the argument here is: the protection of personal identity is a prerequisite of a functioning democratic society. While the former tends to be taken for granted by the majority population (e.g. the unrestricted use of one's mother tongue), minority groups may need special protection in order to preserve their identity.

Hence, in general, minority rights may be defined as positive and negative 'protection measures' *vis-à-vis* the majority society. Will Kymlicka distinguishes between minority rights that contribute to the *external protection* or the *internal restriction* of a group (Kymlicka 1995). Only in the latter scenario might a conflict with basic individual rights arise. If this is the case, individual rights are to be given preference as a group member must not be forced to comply with certain practices although the group as such has been granted the right to follow them. Empirical evidence of national minorities in Europe, however, shows that the danger of *internal restriction* on the basis of granted special rights is extremely low. Nobody is forced by law to practise a certain culture, to learn or to use one's mother tongue, to participate in the election of self-administration bodies, etc., but every member of the minority in question has the possibility to share these activities with other members of the group. According to this understanding, minority rights are both individual rights of *members of a minority* and 'collective' rights, in the sense that certain rights are only meaningful when practised 'collectively' (e.g. the right to one's own culture, the right to self-government bodies, etc.). In this respect, minority rights hardly differ from classical liberal rights whose very aim is to enable the formation of groups (right of assembly, right of association) and to protect them in their substance, i.e. their identity (freedom of religion and of conscience).

The following list will make it even clearer what is understood by minority rights here, namely *group-related rights* (rather than *group rights* in a stricter sense) that have both an individual and a collective point of reference.

1. *Right to existence*, i.e. the existence of one (or several) national minorities is explicitly recognised and put under special protection by the state. Italy's constitution, for example, states: 'The republic protects the linguistic minorities through special provisions' (Art. 6). A more profound statement of recognition is made by the new Hungarian constitution (1989) which not only promises minorities special protection, but in Article 68 (1) considers them 'constituent elements of the state.'

2. *Right to nondiscrimination and equal treatment.* Minorities are granted this right on the analogy with other groups in society. All constitutions in Europe contain an article on nondiscrimination even if its legal interpretation may differ from country to country.

3. *Right to protection against forced assimilation,* i.e. protection against government measures aimed at assimilating a minority into the majority population. It is also prohibited to change a country's ethnographic situation in favour of the majority by a state-controlled settlement policy.[7]

4. *Right of using names in one's own language and spelling.* This provision is, like the former, also based on negative experience. In the past, many governments forced members of national minorities to change their names according to the majority's language and spelling.[8]

5. *Right to maintain and develop one's own cultural identity.* This provision is often mentioned in constitutions or minority laws without further specification. This right may provide for linguistic and religious rights, for customs, as well as for the protection of traditional legal systems. It implies certain protection and support measures by the government.

6. *Right to use one's own language in private and in public,* i.e. special laws on language that take into account the particular interests of national minorities. This above all applies to regulating the use of a minority's language in public offices and courts of law.[9]

7   E.g. because of the forced assimilation policy against Turkish and Pomak minorities after 1945, Bulgaria's new constitution (1991) contains the 'prohibition of assimilation' (Art. 29 (1)). It is also explicitly stated that this clause remains in force in a state of emergency (Art. 57 (3)).

8   This practice of 'nationalising' names of minorities is a common pattern and could be found, for example, in the German Kaiserreich towards the Polish minority, in Mussolini's Italy towards the German minority in South Tyrol, in post-1945 Greece towards Slav minorities (Greek-Macedonians), in post-1945 Bulgaria towards the Turkish, the Pomak and the Roma minorities, or in post-1945 Czechoslovakia towards the Hungarian minority. Even today, there is a debate in Slovakia about the new names law (1993), which only provides rules for the use of first names in minority languages without Slovak endings while the question of surnames is not explicitly regulated. This implies no legal guarantee for minorities (Hošková 1994a: 134–5).

9   Oellers-Frahm distinguishes three forms of regulation: (a) national and official language are identical, i.e. no minority language obtains the status of an official language (this is the case in France, Turkey, Romania, Bulgaria and Greece); (b) multilinguistic regimes through the existence of two or more official languages (Belgium, Switzerland, Finland), through equal treatment of the minority languages and the official language (e.g. in Italy's regions such as the Valle d'Aosta, South Tyrol and Friuli-Venezia Giulia), and through the right of individuals to use their mother tongue in official communication (e.g. Austrian and Hungarian minority laws); and (c) minority language as the only official language in certain regions (e.g. Swedish-speaking Åland Islands in Finland, Swiss canton of Grisons (Graubünden) with Italian- and Romansh-speaking districts) (Oellers-Frahm 1994: 387–98).

7. *Right to one's own education and cultural policy* to enable a minority to learn and preserve its language as well as its culture, identity and history (education and cultural autonomy). A key issue here is the question of education in the mother tongue, which can be provided in different ways (e.g. minority schools, bi- or multilingual schools, minority language as a compulsory or a voluntary subject).[10]

8. *Right to information*, i.e. general access to media as well as radio, TV broadcasts and press publications in a minority's language. Furthermore, it includes the duty of the government and of local officials to provide correct, accessible and timely information important for minorities.

9. *Right of access to the public sector.* This implies that members of a minority must not be excluded from public service in principle (anti-discrimination). In order to achieve this aim, quota systems may be introduced in regions and communes where the minority is primarily settled in order to guarantee its appropriate representation in relation to the overall population. An example would be the detailed regulations for 'ethnic proporz' in South Tyrol's public policy.[11]

10. *Right of organisation and association*, i.e. minorities are explicitly granted the right to found cultural, historical, scientific, etc., associations and political parties for which they may receive financial support from the government. The creation of associations may result in the transfer of official functions and duties from the central government to the minority, i.e. these associations are charged with providing certain services for their members.

11. *Right to political representation.* This implies special rules in favour of national minorities in executive and legislative bodies. On the executive level, this may include government institutions (ministries, commissions, representatives) or special councils dealing with minority issues such as the Ethnic Advisory Councils in Austria where government officials and minority representatives meet jointly. On the legislative level, special voting regulations which, to a certain extent, privilege minorities, may be necessary. Examples are abolishing thresholds or lowering the number of votes required for obtaining a seat in parliament,[12] allowing joint voting lists and election coalitions as well as guaranteeing a minimum of one parliamentary seat.[13]

10 For the different models in language education, see Marauhn (1994: 410–50).

11 Art. 89 autonomy statute (Oellers-Frahm 1993: 200–3).

12 E.g. voting regulation in Hungary where the leader of a minority list is elected to parliament when he collects at least 3,000 votes; normally candidates have to gain 30,000 to 40,000 votes to obtain a seat (Nolte 1993: 526–7).

13 Slovenia's constitution (1991) guarantees a single mandate in the first chamber of parliament for the Italian and the Hungarian minorities (Marko 1994: 333).

12. *Right to self-government bodies* (personal autonomy). Independently of their settlement, minorities are given the possibility of forming self-government bodies at communal, regional and/or national level (councils or elected 'minority parliaments'). These bodies represent the minority's interests and fulfil certain functions which, in some cases, may be state functions.[14]

13. *Right to free contacts* allows minorities to maintain contacts with citizens, organisations and institutions at the domestic and international level. This right is of particular importance for cross-border cooperation and relations between a minority and an external 'patron state', but also for minority groups dispersed throughout different countries such as Sámi and Roma groups.

14. *Right to appropriate international representation*, i.e. a minority's direct and indirect representation at the international level, either within the framework of a country's foreign policy or independently.[15]

What becomes clear from this list is that minority rights entail political and practical problems which tend to result from shortcomings during implementation. First, the guarantee of minority rights may prove to be *insufficient* in solving an existing conflict. This may have several reasons: (a) a central government limits itself to granting only the most basic provisions (e.g. right to existence, right to nondiscrimination) without conceding more substantial protection measures, not to mention self-government rights; (b) Minority rights are granted 'too late', i.e. a central government had to be persuaded, in some cases through violent means, to concede rights to a minority group. What may have served as a preventive measure before violence erupted looks like a half-hearted and belated step, since a minority's demands become more radical as a conflict intensifies so that they are no longer satisfied with certain concessions. Typical examples of such a development during which a government progressively lost credibility while demands of the opposing side increased are the events in Northern Ireland in the 1960s and the ongoing conflict with the Kurds in Turkey; and (c) Minority rights are not the appropriate nor the only response to a given minority situation. This above all applies to groups whose settlement is concentrated in a certain area where they are clearly in the majority (e.g. Albanians in Kosovo, Hungarians in southern Slovakia) and to so-called 'nations without a state' (e.g. Scots, Welsh, Basques, Catalans, Flemings and Walloons). These groups tend to demand more extensive political and economic rights of autonomy than can be granted within the framework of minority rights.

14 E.g. the 'Community's Council' of the German-speaking population in Western Belgium, the Sámi parliaments in Finland, Norway and Sweden, as well as the newly established institutions of minority self-government in Hungary.

15 One example is the representation of Greenland, the Danish Færø Islands and the Finnish Åland Islands in the Nordic Council with two seats each.

The second problem during implementation is that interpretation and development of minority rights may lead to a permanent dispute between the central government and a minority, especially when one side does not comply with its duties or when perceptions of these duties differ. Such typical points of dispute are: financial resources (e.g. for education in the minority's mother tongue), extension of rights, the demand for concrete protection measures by the state, and, vice versa, the minority's 'loyalty' which is often questioned by a central government. Generally, the situation remains especially delicate during implementation. In the worst case, these debates may revive the mutual distrust which has characterised minority–majority relations – in particular in Central, Eastern and Southeastern Europe up to the very recent past.

In order to prevent failure, the extent to which the actors concerned are prepared to learn from comparable 'successful' or 'promising' cases during the implementation process is of particular importance. An instructive example of disputes on minority protection is Austria, where the adoption of a minority law (Ethnic Group Act) in 1976 did by no means solve all problems, but gave rise to protests of the Croat and Slovene minorities, which, in turn, resulted in amendments.[16] Further examples of comprehensive minority laws in Europe are the so-called Sámi laws in Norway (1986), Finland (1992) and Sweden (1993); the new minority laws in Lithuania (1989), Ukraine (1992), Estonia (1993) and Hungary (1993); as well as the special provisions for the Hungarian and Italian minorities in the Slovenian constitution (1991). Provisions range in all cases from linguistic and cultural rights to rights of political representation – the Hungarian minority law and its well-defined system of minority self-government being the most

16 Austria had to acknowledge special rights for the Slovene and Croat minorities in the Vienna State Treaty of 1955 (Art. 7). But the implementation of these rights did not always prove sufficient, in particular with regard to the Slovenes in Carinthia, where ethnic tensions became apparent in 1972 with the clashes over bilingual place-name signs ('Ortstafelstreit'). With the Ethnic Groups Act (1976), the government tried to provide a more comprehensive solution but created new problems also and caused serious criticism by the minority groups. In particular, the so-called '25 percent rule' caused major public debates. The rule said that a minority can be seen as 'considerable' only if they represent 25 percent of the population in a district. This would guarantee them considerable rights in education and language as well as the chance to opt for bilingual place-name signs. For implementing this numerical approach, the members of the minority had to be counted. This aim was strongly opposed by the Slovene organisations. Thus, the so-called 'secret survey on the mother tongue' of 1976 failed because Carinthian Slovenes broadly boycotted the census. The '25 percent rule' was weakened step by step, especially after the constitutional court declared parts of the Ethnic Groups Act as unconstitutional (Marauhn 1993: 160–91). For the historic and legal background of the long-standing Austrian-Slovenian conflict, see Veiter (1980).

comprehensive one.[17] Whereas in Austria, Scandinavia, Hungary and Slovenia the size of minorities with special rights is relatively small, minorities in Lithuania, Ukraine and Estonia are far larger.[18] From this follows that a minority's size is not the only factor that induces a government to offer concessions. This is further confirmed by the fact that countries with few or no minority rights include states comprising both large and smaller minority groups, such as France, Greece, Albania and Croatia with small minorities, as well as Turkey, Serbia, Romania, Slovakia and Bulgaria with relatively large groups. It can be concluded that, in particular in Southeastern European countries with a high potential for ethnic conflict, the negation or the extremely slow introduction of minority rights is most common. In other words: in those areas where minority rights are most urgently needed, central governments are least willing to grant them, with reasons differing from country to country. But what most of these countries have in common is that their political culture is based on the idea of a central-ist state and of 'the indivisible nation', which does not allow any 'derogation' from this norm. This is especially true for France, Turkey, Greece, Romania and Bulgaria. It may to a lesser extent apply to Croatia, Serbia and Slovakia where the negative attitude towards minorities is, on the one hand, related to the special circumstances under which these states where founded and, on the other hand, connected to the Croatian, Serbian and Slovak 'nation building' process in which hostile images of the past play a major role: in Croatia against Serbs; in Serbia against Croats, Muslims and Albanians; in Slovakia against Czechs and Hungarians. Unfortunately, members of these nationalities which serve as negative points of reference for the development of the new state's national identity constitute minorities in the respective countries. Conceding special rights to these minori-ties is unthinkable for large parts of their society, including their political elite.

2. Bilateral Minority Protection

The existence of so-called 'patron states' requires a special regulation mechanism which constructively integrates such states into the solution process. To illustrate the basic problem, it is sufficient to refer to the

17 The Hungarian minority law establishes a country-wide self-government body for each minority. The different groups have, additionally, the right to various forms of local self-government according to the ethnographical situation in each village, town and/or district. This guarantees a considerably high level of autonomy despite the fact that the minorities in Hungary live, with minor exceptions, intermingled with the majority population (Sitzler and Seewann 1995: 352–87).

18 In Lithuania, 20 percent of the population belongs to an ethnonational minority, in Ukraine 30 percent, and in Estonia about 39 percent.

ethnographic picture of Southern and Central Europe. All states in this region contain minorities for which a neighbouring state could 'assume' a 'patron function' while, in turn, members of their own titular nation live as minorities in a neighbouring country. In principle, each state in this region is a potential 'patron state'.[19]

As a result of this situation, minority conflicts can easily degenerate into interstate conflicts where at least one side believes that it has to represent the interests of its conationals across the border. Often, national minorities become innocent victims of long-standing hostilities and may even be drawn into other conflict issues (economic questions, territorial and border disputes) that are not related to the minority problem as such.[20] Moreover, minorities may be accused of 'working' for the 'other' side, of being disloyal towards the state where they live, while the neighbouring state may be accused of pursuing irredentist goals or interfering in domestic affairs. On the other hand, minorities sometimes, in fact, use their 'big brother' as a threat in order to improve their bargaining position. However, central governments are not prepared to offer concessions but instead opt for a policy of 'preventive repression' (Offe 1994: 160) in order to counter such tendencies. This, in turn, encourages neighbouring states in their efforts to protect their 'conationals'. This progressive escalation, typical of bilateral minority problems, also applies to Northern Ireland and Kosovo, albeit with differing intensity.

One approach that may practically stop such a process of escalation between two neighbours and contribute to the gradual settlement of historical enmities is a bilateral minority protection regime on the basis of agreements or treaties under international law. Such attempts at bilateral conflict regulation are extremely numerous in Europe although they differ strongly from one another. In some cases no more than minimum standards were achieved after a difficult negotiation process, as with the Basic Treaties between Hungary and Slovakia, as well as between Hungary and Romania (both 1996). These treaties grant the respective Hungarian minorities some basic rights with respect to language and education but contain no rights of political self-government or forms of territorial autonomy.[21] Other agreements led to more comprehensive

19 Austria, Albania, Bosnia, Bulgaria, Croatia, Greece, Hungary, Italy, Moldova, Poland, Romania, Serbia, Slovakia, Slovenia, Turkey and Ukraine share a bilateral minority problem with at least two, sometimes even three or more, neighbouring states.

20 E.g. the Turkish minority in Greece and the Greek minority in Turkey are indirectly involved in other conflict issues between the two countries, such as Cyprus and the Aegean dispute (Meinardus 1985).

21 A footnote at the very end of the Romanian-Hungarian Basic Treaty states explicitly that this agreement recognises neither any 'collective rights' nor 'any right to a special status of territorial autonomy based on ethnic criteria.' During the ratification process of the Hungarian-Slovak treaty, Slovakia's parliament adopted a resolution which made clear that the Hungarian minority has only 'individual', but no 'group rights'.

provisions and duties, as in the German-Danish case where the Bonn-Copenhagen Declarations of 1955 served as a starting-point. Another type of case is where two neighbouring states jointly assume responsibility for regulating an ethnonational conflict in a particular region. This is the case for Italy and Austria with respect to South Tyrol,[22] as well as for the United Kingdom and Ireland with respect to Northern Ireland.[23] Here it is not only a question of negotiating a solution, but – as in South Tyrol – of maintaining a dialogue while agreements are being implemented. Similar approaches which, however, presuppose that both states renounce territorial claims could be applied to a series of other bilateral minority conflicts and may even be the only way towards their peaceful settlement, e.g. in the cases of Cyprus and Kosovo.

The decisive effect that bilateral conflict treatment produces is 'that a certain minority receives a patron in the form of a treaty state which is in a position to criticise the other party's unfair treatment of its minorities as a violation of the treaty without being charged with violating the principle of non-interference in domestic affairs as enshrined in international law (Brunner 1986: 238).' In other words: bilateral treaties allow for a departure from the principle of noninterference in minority protection and its implementation becoming a topic of international relevance. Minorities concerned can thus no longer be accused of being a 'fifth column' of the neighbouring state. Equally, minorities may well find that their officially recognised 'patron state' is not always willing to give in to each and every one of their demands, which may in turn lead to a more moderate policy on all sides.

For such a development to occur, certain principles need to be agreed upon, as was the case with the German-Polish Treaty (1990). These comprise (Barcz 1996: 281–310): (a) commitments by the two states to protect their national minorities, if possible, in such a way that they can be reliably monitored. These commitments may range from the prohibition of forced assimilation through concrete measures that support a minority in preserving its cultural identity, to forms of political participation and consultation; (b) cooperation on all questions of minority

---

22 The bilateral conflict management started with the De Gasperi-Gruber Agreement (1946). In the 1960s this was followed by trilateral negotiations (Italian and Austrian governments as well as South Tyrol's people's party) on a new autonomy statute. The statute finally came into force in 1972 after both the Italian and the Austrian parliament approved the so-called 'Package Agreement' in 1969. Further, both countries agreed to appeal to the International Court of Justice in cases of disagreement. In 1992, both governments officially stated in a letter to the UN Secretary-General that the conflict over South Tyrol had been solved (Oellers-Frahm 1993: 196).

23 Since the Anglo-Irish Agreement of Hillsborough (1985), Ireland is officially part of the Peace Process in Northern Ireland. The bilateral attempts were continued by the Downing Street Declaration (1993) and are now official peace talks with the relevant parties in Stormont. On the Anglo-Irish cooperation, see McGarry and O'Leary (1996: 242–76, 327–55).

protection considered an integral part of good and friendly relations between neighbouring states; (c) the introduction of 'safety clauses', on the one side guaranteeing that the claim to minority rights is in keeping with international law and cannot be granted to an individual, and on the other side committing minorities to remaining loyal towards the state where they live since 'states will not agree to advance with the process [...] unless it is guaranteed that it does not pose a bigger threat to their political independence and territorial integrity (Barcz 1996: 303);' and (d) the principle of 'cooperative mutuality' which may be established in a reciprocal minority situation (Barcz 1996: 303), e.g. in the German-Danish case both sides introduced analogous provisions.

The signature of such treaties is facilitated by two main factors. The first is the successful linkage of the minority issue with other areas of bilateral cooperation from which both governments expect positive effects. Thus, minority protection is 'embedded' in the general context of bilateral relations resulting in its partial 'depoliticisation' (Barcz 1996: 303). The proposition is that cooperation of mutual benefit, e.g. in economic respect, will, in the mid-term, ease minority-related tensions. The second factor is the regulation's international dimension. When formulating minority rights, the negotiating parties often refer to international standards of the Council of Europe or of the OSCE, thus turning them into common international law. A general reference to the respective documents may save parties lengthy negotiations on the definition of groups as well as on their rights, although it does not guarantee more than minimum standards. Pressure on the part of European institutions that expect their new member states to have regulated their relations with their neighbours also has a positive effect.[24] This integration process was particularly effective with regard to Poland and Hungary, who concluded treaties on minority protection with almost all of their neighbours.

However, the danger remains that the two sides can agree on no more than the smallest common denominator, which may lead to protraction of the minority problem. This above all applies to asymmetric constellations as in the Slovak-Hungarian case, where the Hungarian minority in Slovakia is much bigger than the Slovak group in Hungary. Here, the treaty's analogous commitments have had a rather negative effect on the situation of the Hungarians in southern Slovakia, because their more far-reaching demands for territorial autonomy were not taken into account.

---

24 The EU made some attempts within the framework of the 'Stability Pact' (Balladur Plan) to encourage bilateral agreements between Eastern and Central European countries. Already in the German-Danish case, international integration had some impact, albeit to a lesser extent. The Bonn-Copenhagen Declarations were signed the same year West Germany became a member of NATO (1955) and it was seen as a precondition of membership to solve bilateral problems with other NATO partners beforehand (Ipsen 1996: 272).

In addition, the Slovak government does not see any reason why it should now extend minority protection beyond the agreed minimum standards.

3. Territorial Solutions

A higher degree of self-government rights is offered by territorial solutions. Here, two concepts have to be distinguished: *territorial autonomy* and *federalism*. The former involves specific regulations for certain regions of a country while the latter deals with the territorial and political organisation of the entire state. While territorial autonomy represents a form of decentralisation, ideal-type federalism is based on a noncentralised structure. According to Elazar, the systematic difference is that 'decentralisation implies the existence of a central authority, a central government that can decentralise or re-centralise as it desires. [...] In a non-centralised political system power is so diffused that it cannot be legitimately centralised or concentrated without breaking the structure and spirit of the constitution (Elazar 1979: 14).' In other words: territorial autonomy can be described as the delegation of powers and responsibilities to a lower level, safeguarded by a simple law (autonomy statute) as well as by a 'constitutional right to autonomy'.[25] Federalism, on the other hand, implies a constitutionally guaranteed division of power between the central government and the federal components.

The concept of *territorial autonomy* refers to self-government of a certain territory, in most cases a 'historical region' where a national minority forms a local majority. This model is used relatively often in Europe. Examples are South Tyrol (autonomy statutes of 1948 and 1972), the Finnish Åland Islands (Self-Government Act of 1991), the Danish Færø Islands (autonomy statute of 1948), Greenland (autonomy statute of 1978), Corsica (autonomy laws of 1982 and 1991), the Crimean Republic in the Ukraine,[26] as well as the autonomy for the Trans-Dniester region and the Gagauz people in Moldova.[27] The question of autonomy is still very much disputed in Georgia (Abkhazia, South Ossetia, Ajaria), in Azerbaijan (Nagorno-Karabakh), in Russia (Chechnya) and in Yugoslavia (Montenegro, Kosovo, Vojvodina). Territorial autonomy has also been demanded (but denied by the central

25 See, e.g., Art. 143 of the Spanish constitution as well as Art. 52a of Finnish constitutional law which in 1994 granted the autonomy of the Åland Islands.
26 The regulations concerning Crimea are defined by the 'Law on the Status of the Autonomous Republic of Crimea' (1992) as well as in Ch. 17 of the new Ukrainian constitution (Hošková 1994b: 359).
27 Moldova's constitution (1994) provides a special status for the Trans-Dniester region in Art. 111, although the process of negotiating its status is still going on. In 1994, Moldova's parliament passed an autonomy law for the Gagauz areas which were defined as an 'autonomous territorial unity' (Troebst 1995: 560–84).

government) by the Russian-speaking community in northeastern Estonia,[28] by Hungarians in southern Slovakia and by some activists of the Albanian minority in Macedonia.

A comparison of regulations demonstrates that both powers and structure of self-government bodies (executive and legislative), as well as the territory's administrative status (district or region), may vary from case to case. Suksi regards the following as important criteria for the degree of autonomy: the existence of elected decision makers, legislative power and independent financial administration (e.g. the right to raise taxes) (Suksi 1997: 225). While all cases of territorial autonomy mentioned have their own elected bodies, legislative power exists only partially (not at all in Corsica) or to a very limited extent (e.g. Crimean Republic in Ukraine). In South Tyrol, Greenland, the Spanish 'Communities' or the Åland Islands, in turn, autonomy statutes contain detailed regulations and relatively comprehensive competencies. The right to levy taxes, however, hardly exists. A significant exception is the Basque Country which, due to traditional privileges (fueros), is the only Spanish Comunidad with its own constitutionally guaranteed tax and financial sovereignty (Oeter 1993: 402–3). In other cases, finances for autonomous territories may be raised by one of the following means (Suksi 1997: 229): (a) through general taxes that are directly levied by the state in an autonomous territory (e.g. Corsica); (b) through taxes levied by the state to which autonomous regions have a legal right (e.g. interterritorial redistribution fund in Spain); (c) through specific budget allocations by the state (e.g. in the case of the Åland Islands). This analysis shows that the majority of autonomous regions are financially dependent on the central government, which has been a bone of contention between the two levels time and again.[29]

Federalism involves the organisation of the entire state, of which several types can be distinguished. One is that each part, even if the units differ in size, has the same rights and responsibilities vis-à-vis the central government, i.e. a symmetrical state structure (federal state or federation). Another variant is called cantonisation, regionalisation or semi-federal structure. The difference essentially consists in the fact that the subunits' relations to each other and to the central government are organised asymmetrically, i.e. their powers vis-à-vis the centre differ. With respect to ethnic conflict regulation, the aim in both cases is to

---

28 In July 1993, referenda organised by the Russian-speaking minority took place in Narva and Sillamäe in Northern Estonia. A great majority voted in favour of the establishment of a 'national-territorial autonomy' within Estonia (turnout between 55 and 61 percent). Estonia's Supreme Court ruled the referenda unconstitutional since, firstly, the foundation of autonomous entities is not a matter of local municipalities but of national legislation, and, secondly, the constitution contains no provisions for territorial autonomy at all (Suksi 1997: 244).

29 E.g. the disputes over Spain's financial constitution (López Pina 1993: 37–46).

create a state's territorial and constitutional polity according to the given territorial distribution of groups so that, ideally, political structure coincides with ethnic boundaries. The practical relevance of federal structures is highlighted both by the current peace plans for divided Cyprus ('bicommunal federalism') and the solution for Bosnia-Herzegovina (1995) to end the conflict by dividing the state into two 'entities', a Muslim-Croat federation and a Serb republic.

The paradigmatic case of *symmetric federalism* is Belgium's progressive development towards a federal state comprising three regions: Flanders (Flemish), Wallonia (French) and Brussels (bilingual). In Czechoslovakia, the ethnoterritorial structure was similar, but there efforts after 1989/90 to federalise the state failed, leading to its final break-up. At least from a purely legal perspective, the Soviet Union and ex-Yugoslavia also belong to this type, where different groups became titular nations of the republics in which they represented the majority (with the exception of Kazakhstan).

A characteristic example of *asymmetric federalism* is Spain, where competencies are unevenly distributed among the seventeen 'autonomous communities'. Only seven communities possess the highest possible level of autonomy: four of them (Catalonia, Basque Country, Galicia and Andalusia) by their statutes, Navarre on the basis of historical rights, and the Canary Islands as well as Valencia by devolved powers from the central government.[30] A similar process could be observed in Great Britain, when in 1999 Scotland and Wales received their own elected assemblies which have, however, different powers. If, in the future, England also gets its own parliament, then the political system will have been entirely transformed from a centralised to a (semi-) federal state. To a much lesser extent than Spain, Italy is also shaped by an asymmetric structure since five out of twenty regions have a special status which – with the exception of the more far-reaching statute in South Tyrol – essentially grants them specific cultural and linguistic rights.[31]

The imperative inherent in territorial autonomy and federalism, namely establishing borders that reflect ethnic distribution, is by no means an easy undertaking. Empirical evidence shows that in none of the above-mentioned examples, with the possible exception of autonomous islands, could the minority problem be avoided. With each new border that is drawn, 'new' minorities are created. These may consist of members of the majority group or other ethnonational minorities. If the former occurs, a 'double minority situation' results which may

---

30 Within these groups, however, there are still differences as highlighted by the above-mentioned example of the Basque fiscal and financial autonomy. For the development of the Spanish 'autonomy state', see Nohlen and Hildenbrand (1992: 9–44).

31 The five regions with a special status are Sardinia, Sicily, Valle d'Aosta (French-speaking minority), Friuli-Venezia Giulia (Slovenian minority, Friulian language group) and Trentino-Alto Adige (South Tyrol).

aggravate a conflict since both sides consider themselves the discriminated group and both fear marginalisation. This perception may considerably limit their readiness to offer concessions and accept compromises. The conflict in South Tyrol, for example, was strongly affected by such a constellation.[32] The opposite problem may arise when a new region established under the principle of ethnoterritoriality does not include all members of the group concerned, thus causing permanent irredentism within a state. Spain is one such example, where a Catalan-speaking population exists outside Catalonia in the neighbouring province of Valencia and on the Balearic Islands. A similar case is the Basque Country and the western part of Navarre with its Basque-speaking inhabitants.[33]

Although in practice it is generally impossible to draw borders strictly respecting the ethnographic situation, these concepts to a certain extent convey the idea that a group's political, cultural and economic autonomy can only be fully realised within its 'own' territory. Focusing a policy on territorial questions only may, however, have fatal consequences. At worst, as happened in Bosnia, conflicting parties anticipate this territorial logic by creating facts on the ground for later border settlements through 'ethnic cleansing'. We have observed similar developments in Cyprus. This very experience has given rise to the argument that territorial solutions do not procure domestic peace but sow the seeds of discord, because the whole conflict focuses on territoriality. Thus, cleavages are rendered political and associated with a territory whereas possible common interests are played down. Moreover, groups without a territory have to fear further discrimination, when such great importance is attached to its possession. Critics of the territorial principle also denounce the fact that it encourages existing or emerging secessionism and that the recognition of territoriality as a legitimate political boundary only reinforces separatist demands for national sovereignty.

From a peace/political perspective, these concepts can indeed be considered a political minefield. Firstly, it has to be assured that the parties concerned do not stick to the impression that minority protection

---

32 In the province of Bolzano the German-speaking population represents the majority, the Italians are the local minority, while in the whole region of Trentino-Alto Adige the situation is the other way round. The autonomy statute of 1948 referred only to the region as a whole, which caused considerable tension between the linguistic groups. Only with the second statute of 1972 has the problem of 'double minority situation' been solved, when the institutions of the province of Bolzano gained more power and independence from the regional government.

33 In Spain, the borders between the autonomous communities do not exactly match the linguistic ones because they refer to historical administrative units. During the reform of 1977/78, nevertheless, this territorial status quo was disputed. In the Basque Country as well as in Catalonia (concept of the 'Catalan countries'), territorial claims were made towards the neighbouring regions. The constitution, however, expressly prohibits territorial changes or the unification of regions (Art. 145 (1)).

is only a question of territoriality. Moreover, territorial solutions have to include specific regulations for 'new' minorities. In this respect, South Tyrol is again a good example: here, the Italian and, to a lesser extent, the Ladinian minorities in the province of Bolzano possess specific rights, above all with regard to language, education and culture.

Secondly, with territorial solutions more than with minority rights, it is a question of reconciling two conflicting aspects: unity and diversity. With reference to federalism, although it basically also applies to territorial autonomy, Elazar states that 'federalism involves both the creation and maintenance of unity and the diffusion of power in the name of diversity [...], the effective combination of unity and diversity (Elazar 1979: 28).' He goes on to say that a territorial solution requires a combination of 'self-rule' and 'shared rule' with slightly more emphasis on the first element. Hence, federal structures have to be considered a 'continuing seminar in governance' (Elazar 1979: 41–42) with the aim of obtaining compromises which are acceptable and advantageous to all territorial units.

In order to achieve this, two conditions seem to be of major importance. One is concerned with the existence of cross-cutting cleavages or overlapping loyalties. This point is also stressed in the 'Charter of Basel for federalist conflict solution' set up by a group of scientists: 'In a federation socio-economic, religious, and ethnic rifts must not be allowed to coincide in one wide rift. It can thus be avoided that conflicts always arise along the same lines and that one group feels constantly and intolerably ignored (Bächler 1997: 320–1).' With different actors attempting to find compromises in several policy areas, the potentially permanent conflict between central government and constituent parts or autonomous regions may be somewhat eased. At the same time, it becomes apparent that issue-related viewpoints do not always follow ethnoterritorial lines. Belgium and Switzerland, where both religious and party-political differences exist diagonally to language groups, serve as proof. However, it has to be pointed out that in almost every conflict cross-cutting cleavages could be detected, if only the actors concerned showed some good will. There are nevertheless historical situations when a society's central cleavage became the dominating issue.[34] This was above all the case with the collapse of post-communist federations, despite the fact that cross-cutting cleavages had existed there as, for example, loyal to versus critical of a regime, religious versus nonreligious identity, national versus federal identity (i.e. Yugoslav or Soviet identity).

34 Even in the cases of Belgium and Switzerland there was considerable tension. The Swiss civil war of 1848 between Protestants/Progressives and Catholics could have led to the end of the Confederation. In Belgium, the linguistic issue became the most prominent domestic issue in the 1960s and was accompanied by the rise of Flemish and Walloon parties.

From this follows that the question of cross-cutting cleavages has to be further qualified. Therefore, the second condition is concerned with the point of time and the way a territorial solution is implemented. This implies that a state's territorial reorganisation has to take place 'in time' and on the basis of democratic procedures. In other words: the territorial principle offers a chance of conflict regulation as long as a minority is still wavering between autonomy and secession and the majority or the dominant elite has not yet decided, for whatever reason, to steer a secessionist cause. A territorial solution, in particular involving the creation of new internal borders, has to be legitimised democratically either via a referendum or via a parliamentary procedure. While, for example, these preconditions were more or less fulfilled both in Belgium and in Spain, they were completely ignored in Yugoslavia and in the USSR. In both cases, the state-ordained federal structures and borders were not submitted to a democratic review or reform, while at the same time the ethnonational groups' interest in maintaining the federal state vanished *grosso modo*.

For a concept of territorial autonomy to be successful a third condition applies if the minorities concerned are not 'nations without a state' but groups with a neighbouring 'patron state'. Developments in the Åland Islands and in South Tyrol suggest that in such cases territorial autonomy is feasible only when both states are integrated into the solution.[35] It follows that the introduction of territorial autonomy for the Kosovo Albanians and the Hungarians in southern Slovakia requires bilateral negotiations between Albania and Serbia and Hungary and Slovakia respectively.

4. Power Sharing (Consociationalism)

The key idea of consociational democracy is to provide a means of power sharing between two or more groups, which implies that one side cannot rule without the consent of the other side. In cases of disagreement, a lasting compromise, generally among the different elites, has to be found. From the viewpoint of democratic theory, this kind of polity is often labelled as 'consensus democracy', as distinct from the majority rule of the Westminster model.[36] The obligation of consensus can be achieved through five institutional arrangements which, in reality, are used in combination (see also Schneckener 2000):

35 The Åland Islands' autonomy is based on an agreement between Sweden and Finland in 1921. In the case of South Tyrol, since the 1960s trilateral negotiations between the German-speaking population, the Italian and the Austrian governments took place which finally resulted in the 'Package Agreement' (1969).
36 For a distinction between the two concepts, see Lijphart (1984).

1. *Power sharing executive* (e.g. grand coalition, all-parties government or temporary roundtables) such as the Swiss Federal Council which has been ruled since 1959 by a stable coalition ('magic formula'), incorporating the four major parties as well as the three main language groups.
2. *Proportional representation* of groups in parliament, government, courts and administration (quota system for seats and posts). This is, for example, the case in Belgium with the parity of French- and Flemish-speakers among government ministers, judges at the three highest courts and office holders in key positions within the state administration.
3. Either *veto rights* for the minority, i.e. for certain decisions the consent of the minority is essential, or *mutual veto* in cases of groups relatively equal in numbers. The latter form is practised in Belgium in the framework of two laws: firstly, the 'community majority law' which states that, on certain questions (like changes of the linguistic border or the community's powers), a qualified majority is necessary; secondly, the so-called 'alarm clock procedure' which *de facto* allows for a veto with a delaying effect for both Walloons and Flemings.[37]
4. *Segmental autonomy*, i.e. each group enjoys far-reaching autonomy in specific policy areas and has its own elected bodies and administration. Only a few issues have to be coordinated with other segments of society. If this kind of power sharing is based on territorial borders, this mechanism is basically identical to territorial autonomy or federalism.[38] Nevertheless, in cases of nonterritorial groups, the segmentation of political powers is also feasible. These groups form public organisations based on the principle of personality, independently of the residence of their members (see e.g. the model of communal chambers in Cyprus from 1960 to 1963).
5. *Arbitration.* In addition to the former instruments, specified regulations and procedures are necessary in the case of disagreements. This includes the establishment of mediation committees or arbitration commissions in which all sides are equally represented, as well as more formal arbitration courts and ombudspersons.

Apart from the paradigmatic cases of Belgium and Switzerland, there have been only a few attempts in Europe to regulate ethnonational

37 In order to pass the 'community majority law' it is necessary that the majority of each language group within both houses of parliament give their approval and, furthermore, that the total number of 'yes' votes reaches a quorum of two-thirds of all delivered votes. The 'alarm clock procedure' takes place when three-quarters of the parliamentary members of one language group have signed a resolution in order to stop a particular law or draft law. The Council of Ministers then has to table a compromise within thirty days (Alen 1990: 501–44, esp. 510).
38 For the conceptual link between consociational democracy and federalism, see Lijphart (1979: 499–515).

conflicts through consociational elements. South Tyrol serves as another relatively successful example since in the province of Bolzano a system of ethnic proportional representation in elected bodies and public administration has been established.[39] There are also failed power sharing experiments such as in Cyprus (1960–63/64)[40] and in Northern Ireland ('Sunningdale Agreement', 1973–4).[41] The most recent cases where success or failure remains to be seen are Bosnia-Herzegovina (since 1995) and, again, Northern Ireland (since 1998). In the first case, the Dayton Peace Accords (14 December 1995) provided a new constitutional structure. Most notably, each group is represented in a three-member state presidency; the presidents are directly elected and enjoy comprehensive veto rights. In the government (Council of Ministers) each group *de facto* holds one-third of the posts and in the two chambers of the parliament two-thirds of the seats are reserved for the Muslim-Croat part and one third for the Serbian republic. In the second case, the Good Friday Peace Agreement (10 April 1998) resulted in a power sharing executive, comprising of Unionists and Nationalists; furthermore, the First Minister is a Unionist, the Deputy First Minister a Nationalist, and both have to be elected by the assembly.[42]

The power sharing concept, however, has been criticised for different reasons. From the viewpoint of democratic theory (Barry 1975: 393–412; Lustick 1979: 325–44), critics especially emphasise the danger that the establishment of consociational elements may lead to anti-democratic and manipulatory techniques in order to keep certain elites in power. In other words: the various instruments will either be used by the dominant group in order to control and assure their superior position (e.g. in the

39 The posts of the president and the vice-president of the regional parliament rotate after thirty months between representatives of the Italian- and the German-speaking population (Art. 30, autonomy statute). Further, each language group holds one of the two vice-presidencies of the regional government. The size of the two groups in parliament determines the composition of the regional government (Art. 36). Similar regulations apply to the bodies of the Bolzano province. (Art. 49, 50).

40 The Cypriot constitution provided for the establishment of two presidencies with equal rights, including a veto power on specific issues, as well as for a quota system within the Council of Ministers and the House of Representatives.

41 The power sharing executive, established in December 1973, failed in May 1974 after strong Protestant/Unionist opposition. During the past three decades, several attempts were made by the British and the Irish governments to persuade the conflicting parties of the merits of the power sharing idea (e.g. initiatives in 1975–6, 1977–8 and 1982–4) (Darby 1996: 199–209).

42 The implementation of the agreement, however, proved to be rather difficult. After lengthy negotiations, a compromise led to the establishment of the power-sharing executive in December 1999. However, after repeated disputes over the decommissioning of paramilitary groups, the British Northern Ireland Minister suspended the regional body in early February 2000 in order to prevent the formal resignation of First Minister David Trimble (UUP). New guarantees by the IRA, however, made the executive's reestablishment possible in May 2000.

case of fixed quotas) or can be abused by a certain clique consisting of leading figures from different segments (sometimes in order to exclude other elites). Both variants give rise to the development of patronage and nepotism, which exist beyond any democratic control. Against this criticism, it can be argued that the misuse of democratic procedures and the problem of nepotism can hardly be entirely avoided by any kind of democratic model. The misuse simply indicates the 'wrong' implementation of consociational democracy which is, as Lijphart pointed out (Lijphart 1977: 1), not only an empirical but also a normative concept, i.e. the aim of power sharing is to favour groups which are structurally in a permanent minority situation and have therefore no opportunity to come to power under simple majority rule. If this basic norm is not respected by all parties concerned, it seems no longer accurate to call a particular political system consociational.

More serious questions are the following. How can the institutional arrangements achieve their objective? And moreover, is it possible to 'transfer' regulations which have developed in a specific historical context, such as in Belgium and in Switzerland, to other multinational societies? The dilemma of consolidating unity and diversity at the same time is even more apparent within consociational arrangements than in the case of territorial solutions since the conflicting parties have to rely much more on cooperation in order to maintain the political system. The rationale of territorial solutions is above all to separate the groups to a certain extent and to solve a range of issues through allowing for the group's self-determination within its territory. In contrast, consociational democracy compels the different parties to sit permanently at the same table and, ideally, to make any decisions via consent. In extreme cases, such as in Bosnia today or in Cyprus in the future, these same actors who beforehand did everything to divide the state into its constituent parts must now govern the state jointly.

The key precondition of this model – even more important than in the case of territorial solutions – is the renunciation of separatist threats. Otherwise, there is the danger that common institutions and complex mechanisms (e.g. mutual veto) could be abused to the benefit of secessionism, resulting in a permanent blockade of any politics. This lesson can be drawn from Cyprus and Northern Ireland, where at least one side wanted to change the territorial status quo. In contrast, in South Tyrol consociationalism works not least because of the consensus among the main local parties to keep the autonomy status.[43]

A combination of federalism and consociationalism is generally more promising since not everything has to be agreed upon by all groups, but each group can decide in as many areas as possible independently from

---

43 This consent might be challenged if the neofascist party MSI (Movimento Sociale Italiano/Italian Social Movement), which wants to abolish autonomy, gains more support amongst the Italian-speaking population (Alcock 1994: 51–53).

the other. This assumption, which to a high degree mirrors the cases of Belgium and Switzerland, increases at least theoretically the prospects of succeeding in today's Bosnia and Cyprus, whereas in Northern Ireland such a combined effort is obviously not feasible since territorial groups are lacking. If, however, one takes into account other factors favouring consociationalism (Lijphart 1977: 53–103; 1991: 497–9), the prognosis for Bosnia and Cyprus is far more pessimistic.

Cross-cutting cleavages and multiparty systems which are not solely shaped by ethnonational membership exist in Belgium and in Switzerland, but not in Northern Ireland, Cyprus and Bosnia where political parties are strongly linked with one ethnonational segment of society, although one may distinguish, as in Northern Ireland, between extreme and moderate forces.

To a certain degree, numerical aspects such as the number of groups and the proportions between the groups, also have an impact. According to Lijphart (Lijphart 1977: 55–61), neither a clear majority position for one group nor two relatively equal groups are optimal for achieving a 'balance of power'. The former allows for a hegemonic position of the majority if the constitutionally agreed consociational democracy faces its first serious crisis. This was the case in Cyprus in 1963/64 when, after a long blockade by the Turkish-Cypriot minority, the Greek-Cypriot side simply declared the end of the experiment. The latter position refers to the growing danger of a zero-sum game between equal groups in which both sides perceive gained rights or privileges by the other side as losses by one's own camp. This situation is characteristic of Belgium and a reason for the difficulties of various negotiation processes in the 1970s and 1980s. Whereas in Belgium, however, this aspect can be more or less 'neutralised' by other positive factors, it intensifies the conflict in Northern Ireland or Bosnia. In both cases a zero-sum mentality, which was more and more reinforced during the conflict, dominates. Each group, not just one, as in the case of the Turkish-Cypriots, fears marginalisation by the other side.

Nevertheless, the above-mentioned factors (territoriality of groups, cross-cutting cleavages, multiparty system, number and size of groups) should rather be seen as secondary conditions, which only partly explain the strength and persistence of consociational systems. The crucial aspect seems to be the existence of an overarching loyalty to which all groups have a certain feeling of belonging. A very strong loyalty would be the common expression of belonging to the same 'nation' which gives the common state its name. If, however, one group tries to monopolise the position of the titular nation, the whole system will face considerable difficulties, i.e. other groups will no longer accept the state and the existing institutional framework as their 'own' but as a means of controlling them. The empirical evidence for this assumption is fairly strong: neither in Switzerland nor in Belgium is there a titular nation; instead, there are the Swiss and, probably less obviously, the Belgians in an emphatic sense, apart from their attachment to a particular language group. The opposite has happened during the conflicts in Bosnia, Cyprus and Northern Ireland. The Greek-Cypriots and Muslim Bosniaks attained more or less the role of the titular nation while in Northern Ireland the word 'Ulster' has been appropriated by the Unionists, which excludes any positive identification with the province as such by the Irish Nationalists. In other words: while in Belgium and Switzerland a widespread self-awareness of living in a multinational or multilingual state exists, the elites in the three other cases are much more addicted to the concept of the 'nation-state' which will be achieved through forced assimilation or through hegemony over minorities (see e.g. the politics by Greek-Cypriots and Northern Irish Protestants) or, moreover, through attempts to bring a territory under control in order to create their 'own' state (see e.g. Turkish-Cypriots and the Bosnian War). It is, in particular, the aspect of overarching loyalty which, in fact, constrains the possibility of 'transferring' the model, since Belgium and Switzerland are, to a certain extent, unique cases in Europe where cultural pluralism became part of the *raison d'état*.

5. Secession and Partition

Secession or partition of a territory can be seen as the most far-reaching way of recognising cultural difference.[44] Central to this approach is a procedure which allows for peaceful territorial change. Such a procedure, however, is based on the precondition that, firstly, the conflict has not yet turned into massive violence, and that, secondly, all parties concerned, and in particular the central government, take into account secession as a legitimate form of conflict management. As long as secession is portrayed as 'destabilising' and 'dangerous', it will be difficult to negotiate openly about secession or partition. Secession, then, can hardly be an instrument of peaceful conflict resolution. However, its nonacceptance will not prevent cases of secession which then may be achieved through violence and, in extreme cases, through long-standing wars of independence.

The attempt to constrain secessionism by setting up a regulated procedure allows for a different argument: only if one does not exclude secession as an option and try to counter secessionism with violent means, might one have the possibility of avoiding such territorial changes through a negotiation process, simply because it may occur during the public debate that there are indeed more arguments in favour of staying together than falling apart. But even if secession cannot be prevented by argument, the opportunity remains to soften the political,

44 For the following see also Schneckener (1997: 458–79).

economic and social consequences for both sides through various agreements (e.g. financial questions, common use of natural resources,
common administration of cultural sites as well as of economic and
strategically important territories such as ports). This kind of fair divorce
settlement is very unlikely in the case of a full-scale independence war.
What would an ideal procedure look like? The most basic requirement
would be that the members of an ethnonational group vote in a referendum in favour of secession by a large majority (e.g. two-thirds). The
main problem, however, remains: how to prevent the independence of
one group from causing the suppression of another (sub-)group? Recent
examples of this pattern are Croatia, Slovakia, the Baltic States or
Moldova – although the extent of discrimination against the 'new'
minorities differs from case to case. In these cases, secession as such did
not change the general problem of a majority–minority conflict. Therefore, an additional requirement seems to be necessary in order to
strengthen the legitimacy of secession decided by a large majority. If a
majority of a group votes for secession, then, in turn, the minority (if this
subgroup is territorially concentrated) has the right to decide either to
remain within the previous state or to found its own state. Beran (1984:
29) calls this measure 'recursive use of the majority principle'. In other
words: a secession can only be legitimate if the seceding group allows, if
demanded, for the secession of a subgroup. If not, the first group will lose
its right to secession.

An example where this method was used is the Jura conflict in
Switzerland, although the separatism of the *Rassemblement Jurassien* was
a case of internal secessionism in order to gain a new canton (Beran
1984: 30). With a 'cascade system' of different referenda the respective
minority (subgroup) was permitted to express its will in an additional
voting which finally allowed for a very differentiated drawing of borders
between the two cantons of Jura and Berne.[45]

45 Since 1815 the seven French-speaking districts of the Jura region have belonged to the
German-speaking canton of Berne. Between 1945 and 1970 the conflict resulted in
political protest and several terrorist acts by Jura separatists. The case became more
complicated, since not all, but only the Catholic Jura, districts wanted to secede from
Berne. The French-speaking Protestants of southern districts preferred to stay with
Protestant Berne. In 1970 the parties agreed to launch several referenda which were
held in 1974/75. The first referendum on building a new canton covered the whole Jura
region. This proposal was approved by a large majority of 75 percent in the northern
districts while the three southern districts rejected the proposal by a two-thirds majority.
The electorate of these districts had to vote again in a second round and decided to stay
with Berne. Only within one district was there a considerable minority of one-fifth of the
voters who wanted to live in the new Jura canton. Thus, in a third round, the people of
this area could vote another time on the level of municipalities in order to draw the new
border carefully according to the wishes of the population. Finally, in 1978 the Jura
canton was recognised as the 26th Swiss canton by a country-wide referendum (McRae
1983: 185–212; Linder 1994: 25–27, 65–68; Wiegandt 1993: 221–47).

The result of the procedure is that the 'domino effect', which is feared by critics of the right to secede, will be consciously drawn into the actors' calculation. The principle is: whoever demands secession should know that he, too, must acknowledge the secession of others.

This logic was based on a law from the final phase of the Soviet Union in 1990 which tried to establish certain procedures for the secession of Union republics.[46] Art. 3 of this law called not only for a republic-wide referendum on independence but also for separate voting in the different autonomous entities within the republic: 'The peoples of autonomous republics and autonomous formations shall retain the right to decide independently the question of staying in the USSR or in the seceding Union republic, as well as to raise the question of their own legal state status.' Thus, the regions, often composed of an ethnic group distinct from the republic's titular nation, obtained an independent right of self-determination with the possibility to make a different decision from that of the majority. The eventual secession of an ethnonational subgroup was therefore anticipated and built into the procedure. To a certain extent, this also applied to territorial groups lacking an autonomous status.[47] During the dissolution process of the USSR, however, this law was simply disregarded. It would otherwise have resulted in some border changes that would have decreased the number of ethnonational conflicts and separatism which occurred after the demise of the Soviet Union.

Who knows, for example, how the Moldovan government would have acted if, in order to achieve Moldova's independence, it had had to recognise at the same time the right of self-determination for the Gagauz minority in the south and for the Russian-speaking population of the Trans-Dniester region? This logic would not have prevented the foundation of a Moldovan State but would probably have led before independence to negotiations between the government and the various ethnonational groups in order to convince them to stay in the new state and to meet some of their demands on special autonomous rights. After this formal recognition of ethnic pluralism the idea of a

---

46 'Law on Procedures for Resolving Questions Related to the Secession of Union Republics from the USSR' (3 April 1990) (Hannum 1993: 753–60). This law referred to Art. 72 of the Soviet constitution (1977) which allowed every Soviet republic to freely leave the Union. This article, whose application was never considered seriously by any Soviet leader, later served as the legal basis of the USSR's dissolution.

47 Art. 3 stated: 'In a Union republic whose territory includes areas with concentrations of national groups that make up the majority of the population in a given locality, the results of the voting in these localities shall be considered separately during the determination of the referendum results.'

Moldovan nation-state would have been obsolete.[48] The principle of *recursive use* can therefore demonstrate that the separatists' blueprint of achieving their 'own' homogenous nation-state is simply an illusion.

The proposed procedure is based on the assumption that, in a negotiation process, the parties take the option of secession hypothetically into consideration before they later on, and in full knowledge of eventual consequences, make a decision through referenda in favour of or against secession. One way of institutionalising such a procedure is through a 'constitutional right of secession' (Buchanan 1991: 127–49) which, however, is no guarantee that the actors will respect the constitutional provisions as the examples of Yugoslavia and the USSR have shown. Another way is the example of the peaceful secession of Norway from Sweden in 1905. In this case, the referendum was only the final stage of a long process in which Norway gained more and more sovereignty over its domestic affairs and, since the 1890s, also over its international political and trade relations. Because of this kind of 'silent secession' over decades, the dissolution of the Norwegian-Swedish Union did not come as a surprise to either side, but was generally expected.[49]

The attempt to always take into account the ensuing secession might work if there are territorial subgroups that have already articulated their demands before the first group secedes. But what should be done in the case of nonterritorial minorities within the *seceding group*? Before gaining independent statehood, the *seceding group* has to be forced to respect human and minority rights, otherwise it will not be recognised as a new member by the international community. The member states of the EU established such rules in 1991 when they adopted special 'Guidelines on the Recognition of the New States'[50] in response to the

48 Instead, the opposite happened. In September 1989, the Republic's government declared Moldovan as the official state language, including the obligation for all inhabitants of the Republic to pass a language test by 1994. This provision caused protests by the linguistic minorities. They feared, moreover, that a new Moldovan state would eventually aim at unification with Romania. The Moldovan declaration of independence in August 1991 was therefore followed by similar declarations by the people of the Trans-Dniester region and by the Gagauz. Neither group recognised the authority of the new state. The final result was two ethnic conflicts lasting many years, with a solution reached only in 1994 after painful negotiations and mediation by the OSCE (Hausleitner 1995: 105–23).

49 The Union of Norway and Sweden was established in 1814/15; before that, Norway was ruled by Denmark. During the nineteenth century, the Norwegian constitution of 1814 and the Norwegian parliament (*Storting*) were kept in force and Norway achieved a high degree of autonomy. After several constitutional crises, mainly on the issue of international representation, dissolution became an option for Norwegian as well as Swedish politicians. In the referendum of 1905, Norway's population voted almost unanimously in favour of separation (Lindgren 1959).

50 For the full document, see Heintze (1994: 230–2).

dissolution of the USSR and Yugoslavia. As a necessary precondition for recognition, these provisions call for respect for the rule of law, democracy and human rights as well as for guarantees on the rights of 'ethnic and national groups and minorities'.[51]

To summarise, secession can only serve as a mode of conflict regulation if beforehand all parties concerned, i.e. central government, seceding group and ethnonational subgroups, have negotiated the consequences of secession and have agreed how they will handle their legal and political relations in the future. The precondition for such a negotiation process is the acceptance of secession as one option of conflict management among others. To achieve this, it is important that a 'domino effect' or the suppression of 'new' minorities be avoided. Otherwise, secessions will just reproduce the old problem, as demonstrated in the cases of the successor states of the USSR and former Yugoslavia.

Conclusion: Coexistence through Learning Processes

The implementation of the various modes of ethnic conflict regulation differs enormously according to the degree of difficulty. The guarantees of minority rights and bilateral agreements are comparatively simple to carry out, despite the problems when it comes to details. The other three modes – territorial solutions, consociationalism and secession – give rise, however, to rather complex requirements, even if the actors show some good will which, in general, is not the case. The problem becomes even more challenging because of the fact that the most intractable and lengthy conflicts, such as in Northern Ireland, Bosnia, Cyprus, Kosovo or the Trans-Dniester region, have to be regulated by one of these more complex modes in order to achieve lasting coexistence, since minority protection alone does not meet the demands of any group. Furthermore, the analysis of regulated cases shows that in particular the *combination of different modes* may lead to success. The best example is the South Tyrol conflict where minority rights, bilateral conflict management (Italy and Austria), territorial autonomy as well as elements of power sharing contributed to conflict regulation. Similar combinations are applied in the Finnish Åland Islands, the Swiss cantons and the Spanish 'Autonomous Communities'. However, the 'good news' is that, in fact, the great majority of minority situations in Europe could generally be

---

51 In reality, however, the EU did not act in accordance with its own rules, but gave recognition because of political opportunity despite the fact that in the case of Croatia a legal commission, set up by the EU, expressed considerable criticism of the insufficient regulations for minority rights (Heintze 1994: 155–9).

eased through specific legislation in favour of ethnonational groups or through bilateral agreements although, as indicated above, in particular in the most critical cases, the governments' readiness to grant such concessions is rather limited.

All modes depend, therefore, on the willingness of the groups' elites to cooperate, albeit to a different degree. Without the concerned parties' will to make concessions and compromises, the modes will fail. Critics of these concepts, in particular of the *power sharing* approach, stress that a cooperative attitude of the actors is more important for achieving peaceful coexistence than the various mechanisms of conflict regulation.[52] If the parties want to reach an agreement anyway, then the described modes stand a chance of being implemented; if not, even the most sophisticated institutional arrangement will not help. Instances for this thesis are the failed attempts at conflict regulation in Northern Ireland and in Cyprus. So far, this standpoint has, at least at first glance, some plausibility.

However, the opposite point of view emphasised in this paper is that *readiness to cooperate* originates in the process of implementing politics of recognition; it must not be given *a priori*. The outlined modes offer the chance to start an institutionalised negotiation process in which the results achieved have to be constantly examined and the actors have to struggle continually for compromise. Readiness to cooperate is therefore based on *collective learning processes* which are initiated and accompanied by procedures and rules as suggested by the modes, although the danger of failure or the breakdown of learning processes can never be completely excluded.

Three types of collective learning processes can be principally distinguished: (a) *learning because of 'good will'*; (b) *learning because of cost-benefit assessments*; and (c) *reluctant learning* (i.e. learning through procedures). The first type is based on the assumption that the parties involved generally show 'good will' and are willing to cooperate from the very beginning. The second type refers to a learning process and the resulting cooperation which follows cost-benefit considerations. In this case, the actors come step by step to the conclusion that respect for certain rules is of mutual benefit, or that other strategies such as forced assimilation or hegemonic control cause, in the long run, considerable 'high' costs, in particular because of rather limited success. The third type is somewhat curious since the groups' elites are drawn into learning processes within the framework of an institutionalised procedure despite their original refusal to cooperate, and may finally make concessions to which they would never have given their consent before.

The crucial distinction between the third and the first two types is that in (c) the actors' preferences are gradually changing in the direction

---

52 See criticisms by Barry (1975: 393–412); Lustick (1979: 325–44).

of a problem-solving orientation,[53] while in types (a) and (b), in contrast, the preferences do not generally alter. This does not present a problem in the case of (a), since the parties involved have a preference for a constructive solution anyway, whereas in the case of (b) the means to achieve the existing objective may change and thus ease conflict regulation.[54]

A closer examination of comparatively well-regulated cases shows that, in most conflicts, learning processes occurred in the form of variants (b) and (c). 'Good will' was hardly ever shown from the beginning of conflict management; this attitude developed only in the process of regulation and its implementation. This assumption is valid for certain regions with territorial autonomy as well as for the political systems of Belgium or Spain. In particular, processes of reluctant learning, notably in the case of South Tyrol, indicate that willingness to cooperate can be a result of this process.

This will, however, only happen if it is possible, over time, to broaden the 'horizon' of the parties concerned. The described modes and procedures suit this purpose in two ways. Firstly, they offer an organised framework in which majority and minority can discuss and reevaluate their preferences and interests (*hermeneutic dimension*). Secondly, the knowledge of different *modi vivendi* increases the possibilities of looking beyond their own conflict and of 'learning' from comparative cases in which similar modes of coexistence proved to be successful.[55] The main objective is to finally enter a learning process which leads from broadening the intellectual perspectives to confidence building measures (and vice versa) and to a growing degree of empathy until a more pragmatic problem solving attitude prevails within the political elites.

In the long run, success or failure of institutional arrangements depends on the concrete course of the learning process: the more actors

53 For a well-researched example of reluctant learning, see the gradual policy shifts by the British Thatcher government in the case of Northern Ireland. The conflict was first seen as an internal British problem to be solved by strengthening the integration of the province into the United Kingdom. After several setbacks, the government officially recognised the 'Irish dimension' and started joint conflict management with Ireland (Anglo-Irish Agreement of 1985). At the same time, the previously rejected concepts of power sharing and devolution were reconsidered. According to O'Leary, these inconsistencies between the conservative agenda and actual policy can be explained by processes of 'slow and painful learning' (O'Leary 1997: 663–76).

54 One example is the Hungarian minority law (1993) whose general generosity towards minorities in Hungary can be partly explained by the aim of achieving better conditions for the larger Hungarian minorities in the neighbouring states. The Hungarian government wanted to design a positive model which could be used as a reference for regulations in these cases. The learning process is demonstrated by the fact that, during the interwar period, the Hungarian government was not prepared to make any concessions, but treated its own minorities as badly as others treated Hungarians abroad.

55 This point is developed in more detail in Senghaas (1996: 1–4).

are prepared to follow the outlined way in the direction of problem solving, the more the stability of the chosen mode of coexistence increases. But – and this is the crucial point – the modes define an institutional framework in which sustainable learning processes are possible; they often even force the parties to learn in the first place. Learning is difficult to imagine if the parties are not compelled to meet each other regularly on an institutionalised basis and to settle the conflict constructively at the negotiation table. Ethnic conflict regulation, therefore, has to be understood as a gradual process in which institutional modes of coexistence and collective learning processes presuppose and reinforce each other mutually. If this development is accompanied by external facilitation and mediation, all the better.

References

ALCOCK, Anthony E. (1994). 'South Tyrol'. In: *Minority Rights in Europe*, Hugh Miall (ed.). London: Pinter, pp. 51–53.

ALEN, André (1990). 'Belgien: Ein zweigliedriger und zentrifugaler Föderalismus.' *Zeitschrift für ausländisches öffentliches Recht und Völkerrecht* 50, pp. 501–44.

ARENDT, Hannah (1986). *Elemente und Ursprünge totaler Herrschaft*. München: Piper.

BÄCHLER, Günther (ed.) (1997). *Federalism against Ethnicity*. Zürich: Verlag Rüegger.

BARCZ, Jan (1996). 'Den Minderheitenschutz betreffende Klauseln in den neuen bilateralen Verträgen Polens mit den Nachbarstaaten.' In: *Friedenssichernde Aspekte des Minderheitenschutzes in der Ära des Völkerbundes und der Vereinten Nationen in Europa*, Manfred Mohr (ed.). Berlin: Springer, pp. 281–310.

BARRY, Brian (1975). 'The Consociational Model and Its Dangers.' *European Journal of Political Research* 3:4, pp. 393–412.

BERAN, Harry (1984). 'A Liberal Theory of Secession.' *Political Studies* XXXII, pp. 21–31.

BRUNNER, Georg (1986). 'Die Rechtsstellung ethnischer Minderheiten in Südosteuropa.' *Südosteuropa* 35:5.

BUCHANAN, Allen (1991). *Secession – The Morality of Political Divorce from Fort Sumter to Lithuania and Quebec*. Boulder, CO: Westview Press.

COBBAN, Alfred (1969). *The Nation-State and National Self-Determination*. London: Collins.

DARBY, John (1996). 'An Intractable Conflict? Northern Ireland: A Need for Pragmatism.' In: *Ethnicity and Power in the Contemporary World*, Kumar Rupesinghe and Valery A. Tishkov (eds). New York: United Nations University Press, pp. 199–209.

DE ZAYAS, Alfred-M. (1989). 'A Historical Survey of Twentieth Century Expulsion.' In: *Refugees in the Age of Total War*, Anna Bramwell (ed.). London: Unwin and Hyman, pp. 15–37.

ELAZAR, Daniel (1979). 'The Role of Federalism in Political Integration.' In: *Federalism and Political Integration*, Daniel Elazar (ed.). Tel Aviv: Turtledove Publishing, pp. 13–57.

FRANCIS, Emerich (1965). *Ethnos und Demos*. Berlin: Dunker & Humblot.

———— (1976). *Interethnic Relations*. New York: Elsevier.

HANNUM, Hurst (ed.) (1993). *Documents on Autonomy and Minority Rights*. Dordrecht: Martinus Nijhoff.

HAUSLEITNER, Marianna (1995). 'Nationalitätenprobleme in der Moldaurepublik und die Beziehungen zu den Nachbarstaaten.' In: *Nationalismen im Umbruch: Ethnizität, Staat und Politik im neuen Osteuropa*, Magarditsch Hatschikjan and Peter Weilemann (eds). Köln: Wissenschaft und Politik, pp. 105–23.

HEINTZE, Hans-Joachim (1994). *Selbstbestimmungsrecht und Minderheitenrechte im Völkerrecht*. Baden-Baden: Nomos.

HOŠKOVA, Mahulena (1994). 'Der Minderheitenschutz in der Slowakischen Republik.' In: *Der Minderheitenschutz in der Republik Polen, in der Tschechischen und in der Slowakischen Republik*, Peter Mohlek and Mahulena Hoškova. Bonn: Kulturstiftung der Vertriebenen, pp. 134–5.

————— (1994). 'Die rechtliche Stellung der Minderheiten in der Ukraine.' In: *Das Minderheitenrecht europäischer Staaten, Vol. 2*, Jochen Frowein, Rainer Hofmann and Stefan Oeter (eds). Berlin: Springer, pp. 352–82.

IPSEN, Knut (1996). 'Die Minderheitensituation im dänisch-deutschen Grenzraum.' In: *Friedenssichernde Aspekte des Minderheitenschutzes in der Ära des Völkerbundes und der Vereinten Nationen in Europa*, Manfred Mohr (ed.). Berlin: Springer, pp. 267–80.

KYMLICKA, Will (1995). *Multicultural Citizenship: A Liberal Theory of Minority Rights*. Oxford: Clarendon Press.

LIJPHART, Arend (1977). *Democracy in Plural Societies*. New Haven, CT: Yale University Press.

————— (1979). 'Consociation and Federation: Conceptual and Empirical Links.' *Canadian Journal of Political Science* 12, pp. 499–515.

————— (1984). *Democracies: Patterns of Majoritarian and Consensus Government in Twenty-One Countries*. New Haven/London: Yale University Press.

————— (1991). 'The Power-Sharing Approach'. In: *Conflict and Peace-making in Multiethnic Societies*, Joseph V. Montville (ed.). New York: Lexington Books, pp. 497–9.

LINDER, Wolf (1994). *Swiss Democracy*. London: Macmillan.

LINDGREN, Raymond (1959). *Norway-Sweden: Union, Disunion and Integration*. New York: Praeger Publishers.

LÓPEZ PIÑA, Antonio (1993). 'Die Finanzverfassung Spaniens.' In: *Föderalismus zwischen Integration und Sezession*, Jutta Kramer (ed.). Baden-Baden: Nomos, pp. 37–46.

LUSTICK, Ian (1979). 'Stability in Deeply Divided Societies: Consociationalism Versus Control.' *World Politics* Vol. XXXI, pp. 325–44.

MARAUHN, Thilo (1993). 'Die rechtliche Stellung der walisischen Minderheit in Großbritannien.' In: *Das Minderheitenrecht europäischer Staaten, Vol. 1*, Jochen Frowein, Rainer Hofmann and Stefan Oeter (eds). Berlin: Springer, pp. 160–91.

————— (1994). 'Der Status von Minderheiten im Erziehungswesen und im Medienrecht.' In: *Das Minderheitenrecht europäischer Staaten, Vol. 2*, Jochen Frowein, Rainer Hofmann and Stefan Oeter (eds). Berlin: Springer, pp. 410–50.

MARKO, Joseph (1994). 'Die rechtliche Stellung der Minderheiten in Slowenien.' In: *Das Minderheitenrecht europäischer Staaten, Vol. 2*, Jochen Frowein, Rainer Hofmann and Stefan Oeter (eds). Berlin: Springer, pp. 320–51.

MCGARRY, John, and Brendan O'LEARY (1996). *The Politics of Antagonism: Understanding Northern Ireland*. London: Athlone Press (2nd edn.).

MCRAE, Kenneth D. (1983). *Conflict and Compromise in Multilingual Societies: Switzerland*. Waterloo: Wilfrid Laurier University Press.

MEINARDUS, Ronald (1985). *Die Türkeipolitik Griechenlands: Der Zypern-, Ägäis- und Minderheitenkonflikt aus der Sicht Athens (1967–1982)*. Frankfurt: Peter Lang.

NOHLEN, Dieter, and Andreas HILDENBRAND (1992). 'Regionalismus und politische Dezentralisierung in Spanien.' In: *Der Staat der Autonomen Gemeinschaften in Spanien*, Dieter Nohlen and José Juan Gonzáles Encinar (eds). Opladen: Leske & Budrich, pp. 9–44.

NOLTE, Georg (1993). 'Die rechtliche Stellung der Minderheiten in Ungarn.' In: *Das Minderheitenrecht europäischer Staaten, Vol. 1*, Jochen Frowein, Rainer Hofmann and Stefan Oeter (eds). Berlin: Springer, pp. 526–27.

O'LEARY, Brendan (1997). 'The Conservative Stewardship of Northern Ireland, 1979–97: Sound-bottomed Contradictions or Slow Learning?' *Political Studies* 45:4, pp. 663–76.

OELLERS-FRAHM, Karin (1993). 'Die rechtliche Stellung der Minderheiten in Italien.' In: *Das Minderheitenrecht europäischer Staaten, Vol. 1*, Jochen Frowein, Rainer Hofmann and Stefan Oeter (eds). Berlin: Springer, pp. 200–3.

———— (1994). 'Der Status der Minderheitensprachen vor Behörden und Gerichten.' In: *Das Minderheitenrecht europäischer Staaten, Vol. 2*, Jochen Frowein, Rainer Hofmann and Stefan Oeter (eds). Berlin: Springer, pp. 387–98.

OETER, Stefan (1993). 'Die rechtliche Stellung der Minderheiten in Spanien.' In: *Das Minderheitenrecht europäischer Staaten, Vol. 1*, Jochen Frowein, Rainer Hofmann and Stefan Oeter (eds). Berlin: Springer, pp. 402–3.

OFFE, Claus (1994). *Der Tunnel am Ende des Lichts*. Frankfurt: Campus.

PUSCHMANN, Claudia (1996). 'Zur historischen Dimension der Sprachunterdrückung in Europa vom 18. bis 20. Jahrhundert.' In: *Unterdrückte Sprachen*, Karin Bott Bodenhausen (ed.). Frankfurt: Peter Lang, pp. 15–31.

SCHNECKENER, Ulrich (1997). 'Leviathan im Zerfall. Über Selbstbestimmung und Sezession.' *Leviathan* 25:4, pp. 458–79.

———— (2000): 'Making Power-Sharing Work. Lessons from Successes and Failures in Ethnic Conflict Regulation,' Working Paper no. 19/2000. Bremen: Institute for Intercultural and International Studies.

———— (2002). *Auswege aus dem Bürgerkrieg. Modelle zur Regulierung ethno-nationalistischer Konflikte in Europa*. Frankfurt: Suhrkamp.

SENGHAAS, Dieter (1992). *Friedensprojekt Europa*. Frankfurt: Suhrkamp.

———— (1996). 'Provocative Mediation. A Suggestion.' *Peace and the Sciences* 47, pp. 1–4.

SITZLER, Kathrin, and Gerhard SEEWANN (1995). 'Das ungarische Minderheitengesetz: Vorbeeitung, Inhalt, öffentliche Diskussion.' In: *Minderheiten als Konfliktpotential in Ostmittel- und Südosteuropa*, Gerhard Seewann (ed.). München: Oldenbourg, pp. 352–87.

SUKSI, Markku (1997). 'Rechtliche Regelung der Autonomie – Die autonomen Ålandinseln und weitere europäische Beispiele.' In: *Selbstbestimmungsrecht der Völker – Herausforderung der Staatenwelt*, Hans-Joachim Heintze (ed.). Bonn: Dietz, pp. 222–47.

TROEBST, Stefan (1995). 'Die bulgarische Minderheit Moldovas zwischen nationalstaatlichem Zentralismus, gagausischen Autonomismus und transnistrischen Separatismus (1991–1995).' *Südosteuropa* 44: 9–10, pp. 560–84.

VEITER, Theodor (1980). *Verfassungsrechtslage und Rechtswirklichkeit der Volksgruppen und Sprachminderheiten in Österreich 1918–1938*. Wien: Braumüller.

WALZER, Michael (1992). *Zivile Gesellschaft und amerikanische Demokratie*. Berlin: Rotbuch.

WIEGANDT, Ellen (1993). 'The Jura Question: A Challenge to Swiss Ethnic Peace.' In: *Roots of Rural Ethnic Mobilization*, D. Howell (ed.). New York: New York University Press, pp. 221–47.

INDEX

A

Abkhazia, 9, 74, 77, 80, 181
   Abkhaz conflict, 73, 74
   Abkhaz minority in Georgia, 38, 44
Adams, Gerry, 95, 99
Afghanistan conflict, 81, 138
African National Congress (ANC), 98, 99, 102, 103
Ahern, Bertie, 86
Ajaria, 181
Agarians in Georgia, 44
Åland Islands, 173n. 9, 175n. 15, 181, 182, 186, 195
   Åland Self-Government Act (1991), 181
Albania, 21, 42, 44, 177, 178n. 19, 186
Albanian, Albanians
   Albanian diaspora, 45
   Albanian minority in Macedonia, 44, 45, 182
   Albanian party in Macedonia, 41n
   Albanians in Kosovo, 42, 133n, 175, 186
   Albanians in Serbia, 44, 177
Algeria, 59n. 6, 60, 126
Alsace and Lorraine, Alsatians, 65
Alter, Peter, 2, 7, 21
Amnesty International, 94, 101
Andalusia, 183
Anglo-Irish Agreement (1985), 85, 91, 97, 101, 179n. 23, 197n. 53
Angolan civil war, 93
Aosta Valley, Valle d'Aosta, 7, 25, 173n, 183n
Apartheid, 92, 96, 98, 103
   anti-apartheid activists, 93
Arkan (Željko Ražnatović), 114
Armenia, 5, 34, 44, 73, 74, 152
Armenian, Armenians
   Armenian intellectuals, reform movement, 74
   Armenian minority in Azerbaijan, 44, 74
   Armenians in Georgia, 44
Armscor (South African armaments corporation), 93
Army of the Republika Srpska / Vojska Republike Srpske (VRS), see Republika Srpska

assimilation, see forced assimilation
Austria, 27, 176n, 177, 178n. 19
   ethnic advisory councils, 174
   Ethnic Group Act (1976), 176
   Vienna State Treaty (1955), 176n
   Austrian-Slovenian conflict, 176n
   Austrian minority law, 173n. 9
   and South Tyrol, 179, 186n. 35, 195;
   see also South Tyrol
Autonomous Republic of North Ossetia, see North Ossetia
autonomy
   territorial/political autonomy, 6, 7, 12, 14, 23, 25, 26, 27, 32n, 42, 43, 50, 51, 73, 74, 100, 144, 154, 175, 177n. 17, 178, 180–87, 189, 194n. 49, 195, 197
   cultural autonomy, 7, 26, 74, 174, 184
   personal autonomy, 175
   segmental autonomy, 187;
   see also Spanish Autonomous Communities
autonomy statutes, 181
   of the Åland Islands (1991), 181, 186n. 35
   of Corsica (1982, 1991), 181
   of Crimea (1992), 181n. 26
   of the Færø Islands (1948), 181
   of Gagauzia (1994), 181n. 27
   of Greenland (1978), 181
   of South Tyrol (1948, 1972), 43, 174n. 11, 179n. 22, 181, 184n. 32, 188n. 39
Azerbaijan, 34, 43, 44, 73, 74, 77, 152, 181;
see also Nagorno-Karabakh

B

Balearic Islands, 184
Balkan, Balkans, Balkan States, 1, 11, 31, 40, 47, 49, 51, 106, 114
   Balkan peoples, 106, 113, 114
   Balkan epic poetry, 114
   Balkan wars of 1912/13, 106
Balladur Plan, see Stability Pact
Baltic
   Baltic peoples, 38
   Baltic States, 31, 35, 37, 39, 192

Baltic Sea, 31
Barrès, Maurice, 66
Basic Treaty
   between Hungary and Slovakia, 14, 178
   between Hungary and Romania, 178
Basque
   Basque fiscal and financial autonomy, 68, 183n. 30
   Basque identity, culture, 9, 57, 58, 59, 64, 67
   Basque language (Euskara), 57, 68
   Basque language schools (ikastolak), 67
   Basque nation, people, 9, 25, 57, 64, 175
   Basque nationalist movement, nationalism, nationalists, 9, 24, 58, 59n. 6, 60, 63, 64, 65, 67, 68, 98
   Basque Nationalist Party (PNV), 59n. 6;
   see also Euskal Herritarrok, Herri Batasuna
Basque Provinces, Basque Country, 1, 3, 6, 7, 9, 23, 24, 25, 41, 57, 133, 182, 183, 184
   Euskadi (Basque Country), 9, 57, 58, 59, 60, 61, 62, 63, 64, 67, 68, 69
Begin, Menachem, 68
Belarus, 9, 44, 47
Belarusians in Estonia, Latvia, Lithuania, 44
Belfast, 84, 85, 89
Belgium, 23, 24, 27, 42, 61, 173n. 9, 175n. 14, 183, 185, 186, 187, 189, 190, 191, 197
Belgrade, 38, 121, 114
Berne canton, 192
Biafran war, 155
bilateral minority protection, bilateral conflict management, bilateral negotiation process, 14, 166, 177–81, 186, 195
bilateral treaties, bilateral agreements, 46, 179, 180n, 195, 196;
   see also Basic Treaty
Bilbao, 58, 60, 67

Black Sea, 31
Blair, Tony, 85, 86, 103n
Bolzano province, 184n. 32, 185, 188;
    see also South Tyrol
Bonn-Copenhagen Declarations (1955), 179, 180n
Bosnia-Herzegovina (BiH), Bosnian conflict, 1, 7, 11, 14, 37, 40, 43, 44, 49, 50, 105–30, 137, 153, 158, 178n. 19, 183, 184, 188, 189, 190, 191, 195
Bosnian, Bosnians
    Bosnian Croat armed forces, 112
    Bosnian Croat leadership, 111, 123
    Bosnian Croats, 44, 109, 111, 123
    Bosnian Muslims, Bosniaks, 33, 37, 41, 44, 109, 191
    Bosnian Serb armed forces, 112, 124; see also Army of the Republika Srpska (VRS)
    Bosnian Serb paramilitary groups, 37
    Bosnian Serb parliament, 123
    Bosnian Serbs, 37, 40, 44, 109, 111, 121, 123, 124
    Croat community of Herceg-Bosna, 123;
    see also Croatian Democratic Union (HDZ), Dayton Peace Accords, Muslim-Croat federation, Party of Democratic Action (SDA), Republika Srpska, Serb Democratic Party (SDS)
Briand-Kellogg Pact (1928), 135
British
    British state, government, 8, 25, 26, 197n. 53
    British government and Northern Ireland, 84–86, 90–91, 93–98, 100, 101, 102, 188n. 41
    British government and Libya, 92
    British identity, 26
    British Isles, 10, 89, 91, 96, 99
    British foreign policy, 49
    British politicians, 26
    British Conservatives, 32n
    British socialists, 59
    British imperialism, 89, 101
    British officials' treatment of alleged members of the IRA, 143;
    see also Great Britain, London, Northern Ireland, United Kingdom
Bulgaria, 21, 33, 40, 44, 45, 46, 166n. 4, 173nn. 8, 9, 177, 178n. 19
Bulgarian, Bulgarians
    Bulgarian constitution, 173n. 7
    'Bulgarian horrors' of the nineteenth century, 4

Bulgarians in Moldova, 44;
    see also Movement for Rights and Freedoms (MRF)
Bulgarian Communist Party (BCP), 45
Burgos Trial (1970), 63
Burundi, 126

C
Calic, Marie-Janine, 3n, 11, 105, 107
Canary Islands, 183
cantonisation (symmetrical federal state structure), 111, 182
Carinthia, Carinthian Slovenes, 176n
Carlsson, Ingmar, 48
Carrero Blanco, Luis, 64
Carter, Jimmy, 94, 97
Catalonia, 3, 7, 9, 25, 64, 65, 67, 183, 184
Catalan, Catalans
    Catalan movement, Catalan nationalism, Catalan resistance, 5, 67, 69
    Catalans, 25, 175
    Catalan-speaking population outside of Catalonia, 184
Catholicism (Roman), 31
Catholic, Catholics
    Catholic Church in Croatia, 47
    Catholic churches, Catholic cultural heritage in Bosnia, 118, 119
    Catholic Jura, 192n
    Catholics, Catholic minority in Northern Ireland, 85, 86, 89, 93, 97, 100
    Catholics in 1848 Swiss Civil War, 185n
    Catholics in Spain, 63
Caucasus, 1, 3n, 8, 10, 38, 41, 71, 72, 73, 76, 77, 78, 80
Caucasian, Caucasians
    anti-Caucasian language, action, 78
    Caucasian conflicts, 9, 81
    'Caucasian Revolution', 79
    Caucasians, 78n. 9
    North Caucasians, 74
    'person of Caucasian nationality', 78
    Russia's Caucasian periphery, 78
Ceauşescu, Nicolae, 36
Central Asia, Central Asian republics, 31, 34, 36, 38, 77
Central European Free Trade Area (CEFTA), 49
Četniks, 125
Chechnya, Chechnya conflict, 3n, 7, 9, 10, 38, 43, 71–83, 133, 136, 138, 181
Chechen
    Chechen independence movement, 79
    Chechen National Congress, 75

Chechen National Guard, 76
Chechens, 9, 34, 71, 72, 75, 77, 78, 79, 80, 81, 82
Christianity, 114
Chuvash, 44
Ciorbea, Victor, 46
citizenship, 50, 51, 65
    citizenship conflicts in Estonia and Latvia, 37, 13, 152
    Czech citizenship law (1993), 39
citizens' rights, 33
civil society, 7, 35, 157
civil war
    Spanish Civil War, 58, 60, 140
    in Bosnia, 11, 126
    Swiss civil war of 1848, 185n
    in Georgia, 74
Clausewitz, Carl von, 118
Clinton, Bill, 10, 48, 85, 87, 88, 89, 94, 95, 96, 97, 102
Cold War, 22, 59, 88, 102, 108, 137, 139, 166
collective learning processes, 196, 198
collective rights, 52, 172, 178n. 21
colonialism, 68, 79, 101, 136
Commonwealth of Independent States (CIS), 1, 32, 44
communist, communism, 8, 21, 31, 34, 35, 36, 37, 43, 45, 47, 50, 52, 75, 106, 108, 109, 111, 114, 115
    Bulgarian Communist Party (BCP), 45
    Communist Party of Kyrgyzstan, 36
    Kazakh Communist Party, 73
    Soviet Communist Party, 72;
    see also ex-communist elites, ex-communists
Conference on Security and Co-operation in Europe (CSCE), see OSCE
confidence building, 14, 46, 77, 78, 168, 170, 197
'conflict entrepreneur', 125
consociational democracy, consociationalism, 14, 186–91, 195;
    see also power sharing
Constantinescu, Emil, 46
Conversi, Daniele, 9, 24, 57, 59, 60n. 9
Cook, Robin, 49
Corsica, 1, 24, 25, 41, 133, 182
    autonomy laws of 1982 and 1991, 181
    Corsican nationalists, 98
Council of Britain and Ireland, 86
Council of Europe, 8, 22, 39, 42, 43, 49, 52, 79, 142, 180
    European Commission of Human Rights, 141
    European Convention on the Protection of Human Rights and Fundamental Freedoms/European Convention on Human Rights

(ECHR) (1950), 43, 141, 142, 143
European Court of Human Rights, 141, 142n, 143
Framework Convention for the Protection of National Minorities (1995), 52n. 16
Recommendation 1201 (1993) of the Parliamentary Assembly of the Council of Europe (PACE), 43
Crimean Republic, 181, 182
Crimean Tatars, 34
Croatia, 3, 8, 37, 38, 43, 44, 47, 48, 49, 108, 137, 177, 178n. 19, 192, 195n
Croat, Croatian
  Croat nationalists, 50
  Croat parties in Yugoslavia, 36
  Croatian state, Croatian government, Croat leadership, 38n. 6, 40, 50
  Croatian Army, 112
  Croatian Information Centre, 121n. 13
  Croatian nation-building, 177
  'Greater Croatia', 108, 111
  Croat community of Herceg-Bosna, Croatian para-state, Croat leadership in Bosnia, Croat armed forces in Bosnia, see Bosnian, Bosnians;
  See also Eastern Slavonia, Krajina, Ustaša
Croatian Defence Council (HVO) (Croatia), 108
Croatian Democratic Union (HDZ) (Bosnia-Herzegovina), 111
Croats, 111, 114, 123
  Croats in Austria, 176
  Croats in Bosnia-Herzegovina, 44, 109, 111
  Croats in Serbia and Montenegro, 44, 177
  Croats in Yugoslavia, 114
  Croats in Slovenia, 44
Cuba, Cuban experience, 59n, 60
Cyprus, 1, 14, 166n. 5, 178n. 20, 179, 183, 184, 187, 188, 189, 190, 191, 195, 196
  Cypriot constitution, 188n. 40
Czech Republic, 8, 39, 40, 43, 44
  Czech citizenship law (1993), 39
Czechoslovakia, 3, 21, 39, 43, 145n. 13, 166n. 4, 173n. 8, 183
  1968 Soviet invasion, 115
  break-up of Czechoslovakia, 39, 43, 145n. 13, 183
Czechs, 177

D
Daftary, Farimah, 1
Daghestan, 71
Dayton Peace Accords (1995), 127, 188
de-escalation, 1, 3, 5, 6, 92, 168;

see also escalation
de facto regime, 135
de Klerk, Willem, 102
Declaration on the Rights of Persons Belonging to National or Ethnic, Religious and Linguistic Minorities, see United Nations
'decommissioning' of weapons (in Northern Ireland), 10, 86, 88, 95, 103, 188n. 42
Decree on the Rehabilitation of the Repressed Peoples (1991), 75
Democratic Alliance of Hungarians in Romania (UDMR) (Romania), 41–42, 49
Democratic Unionist Party (DUP) (Northern Ireland), 86
democratisation, 15, 111, 157
deportation, deported peoples, 34, 75, 77, 79, 124, 126;
  see also expulsion
devolution, 7, 26, 27, 88, 197n. 53
Dole, Bob, 48
Donostia, 60
Dresden, 71, 82
Dublin, 91
Dudaev, Dzhokhar, 75, 76, 79

E
Eastern Slavonia, 38n. 6
economy, economic situation, 28, 40, 82, 170
  corrupt economic activity, 35
  economic action, protests, 4, 61, economic arguments of regionalism, 28
  economic autonomy, sovereignty, 81, 184
  economic blockade, isolation, pressure, 10, 40, 61, 76, 79
  economic cooperation, ties, integration, 22, 34, 48, 49, 51, 52
  economic oligarchies, economic-political groupings, economically motivated entrepreneurship, 8, 15, 22, 35
  economic reform, transition, development, 15, 39, 47, 51, 82, 110
  economic rights, 175
  socioeconomic factors in the Bosnian conflict, 107–10;
  see also International Covenant on Economic, Social and Cultural Rights
elimination (as a strategy for dealing with minorities), 13, 117, 166, 167, 169
escalation, 1, 3, 4, 5, 43, 105, 113, 155, 167, 168, 169, 178;
  see also de-escalation
Estonia, 3, 13, 37, 44, 49, 75, 79, 80, 152, 176, 177, 182
  Estonian constitution, 182n. 28
Estonian Popular Front, 75
ethnic cleansing, ethnic

purification, 11, 14, 15, 33, 40, 105, 118, 120, 122, 124, 133n, 146, 184
ethnic entrepreneurs, 1, 5, 8, 11, 36, 112
ethnic homogenisation, 8, 34, 117
ethnic identity, see identity
ethnocentrism, 168
ethnogenesis, 9, 64
ethnoradicalism, ethnic radicalism, ethnoradical movements, 4, 7, 39, 50, 57, 71
ethnoregional movements, 1
ETA, see Euzkadi 'ta Askatasuna
Etxebarrieta, Txabi, 62
European Commission of Human Rights, see Council of Europe
European integration, 9, 22, 23, 51, 101
European Union (EU), European Community, 1, 46, 49, 50, 88, 113, 180n, 194, 195n
  European Coal and Steel Community, European Economic Community (EEC), 22
  Guidelines on the Recognition of the New States (1991), 194; see also Stability Pact (Balladur Plan), Stability Pact for Southeastern Europe
European Convention on Human Rights (ECHR), see Council of Europe
European Court of Human Rights, see Council of Europe
Euro-region, 27, 28, 49
Euskadi, see Basque Country
Euskal Herritarrok (EH), 23n, 98n. 11;
  see also Herri Batasuna
Euskara, see Basque language
Euzkadi 'ta Askatasuna/Euskadi 'ta Askatasuna (ETA), 4, 9, 23, 41, 57, 59, 60, 61, 62, 63, 64, 65, 68, 98
  ekintzak (ETA armed actions), 64
  etarras (ETA members), 63
ex-communist elites, ex-communists, 45–47
expulsion, expulsions of minorities, 32, 33, 37, 41, 117, 126, 155, 166

F
Færø Islands, 175n. 15, 181
  autonomy statute of 1948, 181
Fair Employment (Northern Ireland) Act (1989), Fair Employment Commission, 97
Falangism, 65
Fanon, Franz, 60
fascism in Spain, 63, 65, 67;
  see also neofascist
Federal Republic of Yugoslavia (FRY), see Yugoslavia
federalism, 7, 14, 27, 111, 181, 182, 183, 185, 187, 189

asymmetric federalism, 183
symmetric federalism, 183
Finland, 21, 42, 173n, 175n, 176,
186n. 35;
see also Åland Islands
First World War, 31, 134, 144, 165
FitzGerald, Garret, 90, 91, 94n
Flanders, 183
Flemings, 24, 175, 187
Flemish
Flemish parties, 185n
Flemish region, Flemish speakers,
183, 187
Flynn, Bill, 95
forced assmiliation, 45, 166, 167,
173, 179, 191, 196
Framework Convention for the
Protection of National
Minorities, see Council of Europe
France, French government,
authorities, 1, 7, 15, 23, 24, 25,
51, 61, 63, 92, 93, 173n. 9, 177
French, 65
French Revolution (1789), 5, 31,
66
French nationalists, nationalism,
66, 67
French speakers in Belgium, 183,
187; see also Walloons
French-speaking minority in the
Valle d'Aosta, 183n. 31
French-speaking districts of the
Jura region, 192n
Franco, Francisco, 9, 25, 57, 58, 59,
64
Francoism, 59, 65, 67
Friends of Ireland, 97
Friuli-Venezia Giulia, 7, 25, 173n. 9,
183n. 31
Friulian language group, 183n. 31
Frunda, György, 40n, 46, 47
fueros (traditional privileges in
Spain), 182

G
Gagauzia, Gagauz people, minority,
44, 181, 193, 194n. 48
Galicia, Galicians, 7, 25, 183
Gallagher, Tom, 8, 9, 31, 36n, 45, 51
Gandhi, Mahatma, Gandhism, 59,
61
Geneva Conventions, see
International Committee of the
Red Cross (ICRC)
genocide, genocidal policies,
genociders, 106, 107, 117, 121,
122, 124, 126, 127, 139, 153,
166;
see also UN Genocide
Convention
Georgia, 3, 37, 38, 43, 44, 73, 74,
75, 77, 181
Georgians, 38, 74, 75
Georgian language, 74, 75
Georgian reform movement, 74;
see also South Ossetia, Abkhazia,

Ajaria, Armenia, Armenians
Germany, 22, 27, 33, 46, 51, 52n,
65, 66, 99, 101, 160, 166n. 4,
180n
German, 2, 24, 60, 118, 152
German nationalism, 66, 67
German occupation, 11, 115
German Romantic intellectual,
66
German speakers in Alsace and
Lorraine, 65
German speakers/German
minority in South Tyrol, 43,
173n. 8, 184n. 32, 186n.35,
188n. 39
Germans in Kazakhstan, 44
Germans in Poland, 44, 46, 49
German-speaking canton of
Berne, 192n
German-speaking minority in
Belgium, 24, 175n. 14
German-Danish case, 179, 180
German-Polish Treaty (1990),
179
German bilateral development
agency Gesellschaft für Technische
Zusammenarbeit, 152;
see also Bonn-Copenhagen
Declarations
Ghadaffi, Moammar, 91, 92
glasnost, 72, 76
Gligorov, Kiro, 45
Good Friday Agreement (1998),
10, 11, 84, 88, 90, 99, 102, 103,
188
Gorbachev, Mikhail, 9, 72
Gore, Al, 95
Government of Ireland Act (1920),
86
Great Britain, 183
Great Lakes region, 137, 138
Greece, 33, 49, 51, 166n, 173nn. 8,
9, 177, 178nn. 19, 20
Greek, Greeks
Greek language, 31
Greek-Cypriots, 190, 191
Greek-Macedonians, Slav
minority in Greece, 173n. 8
Greeks in Albania, 44, 45
Greek minority in Turkey, 178n.
20
Greek lobby in Washington,
DC, 45
Greenland, 175n. 15, 181, 182
autonomy statute (1978), 181
Grisons/Graubünden canton, 173n.
9
Grozny, 71, 78, 80, 81, 82
Guardia Civil, 58, 62
Guelke, Adrian, 10, 84, 97n, 102n
guerrilla warfare, 60, 79
Guidelines on the Recognition of
the New States, see European
Union
Gypsy, see Roma

H
The Hague, 38n. 6, 105, 114, 116;
see also International Criminal
Tribunal for the former
Yugoslavia (ICTY)
Hague Conventions (1907), 134
Hajduks, 114
hegemonic control, 166n. 5, 167,
196
Helsinki Committees, 48
Herder, Johann Gottfried, 64, 66,
66n. 24
Herderian, Herderianism, 64,
65, 67
Herri Batasuna, 23, 98;
see also Euskal Herritarrok
Ho-Chi-Minh, 61
Hofmann, Rainer, 12, 133, 144
Horn, Gyula, 46
human rights, 10, 11, 12, 36n, 37,
38n, 39, 40, 48, 49, 50, 52, 63,
75n, 78, 79, 88, 89, 94, 97, 101,
102n, 105, 118, 119, 120, 124,
134, 138, 141, 142, 143, 146,
147, 152, 155, 195
international human rights law,
12, 134, 140, 141, 142
human rights activists, 13, 152
humanitarian intervention, 12,
136, 137, 138
Hungary, Hungarian government,
21, 42, 44, 45, 46, 47, 48, 166n.
4, 174n. 12, 175n. 14, 176, 177,
178, 180, 186, 197n. 54
Hungarian, Hungarians, 8, 32, 37,
40, 46, 47
Hungarian constitution, 172
Hungarian minority law (1993),
173n. 9, 176, 177n. 17, 197n.
54
Hungarian Socialist Party, 46
Hungarians in Romania, 34, 36,
41, 43, 44, 46, 47, 49, 178;
See also Democratic Alliance of
Hungarians in Romania
(UDMR)
Hungarians in Serbia and
Montenegro, 44, 46
Hungarians in Slovakia, 44, 47,
173n. 8, 175, 177, 178, 180,
182, 186
Hungarians in Slovenia, 174n.
13, 176;
see also Basic Treaty between
Hungary and Slovakia, and
between Hungary and Romania
Huntington, Samuel P., 109
Hutu, 153

I
identity, 50, 51, 57, 58, 59, 64, 67,
77, 114, 118, 119, 120, 143,
144, 145, 154, 155, 167, 172,
173, 174, 177, 179, 185
ethnic identity, 1, 50
identity politics, 64

ikastolak, see Basque language
  schools
Iliescu, Ion, 36
Ingushetia, Ingush Republic, Ingush
  people, 75, 80
Internal Macedonian Revolutionary
  Organisation, 4n
International Committee of the Red
  Cross (ICRC), 151
  Additional Protocol Relating to
  the Protection of Victims of
  Non-International Armed
  Conflicts (1977), 12, 140, 141,
  147
  Geneva Conventions (1949), 12,
  124, 140, 147
  Red Cross movement, 155
International Criminal Tribunal for
  the former Yugoslavia (ICTY),
  38n. 6, 105, 106, 114, 119n,
  123n. 15, 124nn. 16, 17, 18
Ireland, Republic of, 10, 26, 85, 87,
  88, 89, 90, 92, 96, 97, 98, 99,
  100, 101, 103n, 143n, 179, 197n.
  53
  united Ireland, 85, 100, 101
  Irish constitution, 85, 86, 90, 91;
  see also Anglo-Irish Agreement,
  Good Friday Agreement,
  Government of Ireland Act,
  Joint Declaration, Northern
  Ireland, Sunningdale Agreement
Irish National Caucus (INC), 97
Irish-American lobby, 94, 95, 96,
  97n
Irish Republican Army
  (IRA)/Provisional IRA, 4, 41,
  84, 86, 87, 88, 91, 92, 95, 96, 98,
  99, 100, 101, 188n. 42
  'Provisionals', 96, 98, 99, 102;
  see also Real IRA
Iron Curtain, 22
irredentism, 42, 89, 90, 184
Islam, 31, 114
Israel, Israelis, 59n. 6, 156
Italy, 7, 23, 24, 27, 28, 33, 42, 101,
  166n. 4, 172, 173nn. 8, 9, 178n.
  19, 183, 195
  and South Tyrol, 25, 179, 186n.
  35;
  see also South Tyrol
Italian
  Italian constitution, 172
  Italian occupation, 11, 115
  Italian regions, 25, 173n. 9,
  (north Italian) regionalism,
  northern Italians, 27, 28
  Italian-speaking district in
  Switzerland; *see also*
  Grisons/Graubünden canton,
  173n. 9
  Italian minority in Slovenia,
  174n. 13, 176
  Italian minority in South Tyrol,
  Bolzano province, 184n. 32, 185,

188n. 39, 189n;
  see also South Tyrol

J
Jacobinism, 63, 67
Jaszi, Oscar, 8, 37
Jáuregui Bereciartu, Gurutz, 58, 67,
  68
Jews, 33, 44
Joint Declaration (1993), 84, 95
Jura conflict, 192
  Rassemblement Jurassien, 192

K
Kadijević, Veljko, 112
Karadžić, Radovan, 11, 114, 119n,
  123, 123n. 124nn. 16, 17, 18
Kazakh Communist Party, 73
Kazakhs in Turkmenistan,
  Uzbekistan, 44
Karakalpaks in Uzbekistan, 44
Kazakhstan, 44, 72, 183
Kedourie, Elie, 66
King, Peter, 89
Kissinger, Henry, 91
Klaus, Václav, 39
Koschnick, Hans, 50
Kosovo, 1, 5, 14, 41, 42, 45, 48, 133,
  175, 178, 179, 181, 195
  Kosovo Albanians, 47
Kosovo Liberation Army (KLA), 6,
  42, 133n
Kouchner, Bernard, 155
Krag, Helen, 9, 10, 71, 75
Krajina, 38n. 6, 44
Krosigk, Friedrich von, 24
Krutwig, Federico, 60, 61, 62, 68
Kurdistan, Kurds, 9, 44, 175
Kyrgyzstan, 36, 44;
  see also Communist Party of
  Kyrgyzstan
Kyrgyz in Tajikistan, 44

L
Ladinian minorities in Bolzano
  province, 185
Latvia, 13, 37, 44, 49, 152
League of Nations, 33, 144, 165
League of Nations Covenant
  (1919), 135
  Geneva Protocol (1924), 135;
  see also Paris Peace Accords,
  Treaty of Lausanne
Lebed, Aleksandr, 71
Lega Nord, 28
Lezgins in Azerbaijan, 44
liberal, liberal traditions, liberalism,
  29, 35, 37, 38, 39, 47, 65, 172
  liberal ethnic policies of Tito, 45
  liberal EU norms for minority
  rights, 47
  liberal democracy, 50
  liberal minority policies, 46n, 51
  liberal freedoms, liberal
  individual rights, 171, 172

Liberals (in Northern Ireland), 63,
  100
Libyan involvement in Northern
  Ireland, 91–92
Lithuania, 44, 73, 177
  Lithuanian minority law, 176
Lithuanians in Latvia, 44
Lockerbie, 92
London, 26, 27, 85, 91, 92, 95, 99,
  101
Loyalist Volunteer Force (LVF), 86

M
MacBride principles, 97
Macedonia, 4n, 5, 41n, 44, 45, 182
Macedonians in Bulgaria, 44
Maharaj, Mac, 99
Mali, 152
Mallon, Seamus, 85
Mandela, Nelson, 98, 99n
Manzanas, Melitón, 62, 63
Mao-Tse-Tung, 61
  Maoist, 61n. 11
Marxism-Leninism, Marxist,
  Marxists, 34, 35, 60, 63
Maurras, Charles, 66
Maze prison (Northern Ireland), 87,
  99
McCartney, Robert, 86
Meãiar, Vladimír, 47
Médecins sans frontières, 155
'Memorandum' of the Serbian
  Academy of Arts and Sciences
  (1986), 113
Middle East peace process, 102
Milošević, Slobodan, 6, 37, 40, 42
Milward, Alan, 22
minority
  international minority rights law,
  12, 143–44
  minority conflicts, 9, 14, 76, 178,
  179, 192
  minority languages, 42, 173nn. 8,
  9
  minority parties, 41, 43
  minority rights, 8, 14, 33, 42, 48,
  51, 52, 79, 171–77, 180, 185,
  194, 195
  Minority Rights Group
  International, 44
  minority rights norms of the EU,
  46
  minority status, 32, 38n. 6
minority–majority relations, 9, 51,
  52, 76, 79, 176
  and international law, 12, 133,
  134, 135, 136, 137, 139, 140,
  141, 142, 143, 146, 147
'Minsk Process', 'Minsk Group', *see*
  OSCE
Mitchell, George, 87
Mitchell, Robert, 103n
Mladić, Ratko, 119n, 123n. 15, 124
Moldova, 3, 43, 44, 45, 133, 178n.
  19, 181, 192–94

Moldovan constitution, 181n. 27
Moldovan language, 194n. 48
Montenegro, 44, 181
Moscow, 9, 10, 73, 75, 76, 78–82
Mostar, 50
Movement for Rights and Freedoms
(MRF) (Bulgaria), 42
Mowlam, Marjorie ('Mo'), 87
Mtintso, Thenjiwe, 99
multiculturalism, 38
multiethnic, multinational
states, empires, 21, 25, 31, 50,
110, 111, 113, 144, 145, 165n,
189, 191
societies, 14, 189
Muslim
armed forces in Bosnia-
Herzegovina, 50, 125
cultural heritage in Bosnia-
Herzegovina, 118
fundamentalists, extremist
norms, 82, 83
populations, 33
states, 10, 82
Muslim-Croat federation (Bosnia-
Herzegovina), 183, 188
Muslims, 33, 44, 114, 177;
see also Bosnian Muslims

N
Nagorno-Karabakh conflict, 9, 43,
73–74, 77, 80, 152, 181
Narva, 182n. 28
nation building, 32, 65, 67, 68, 177
National Committee on American
Foreign Policy, 95
National Salvation Front
(Romania), 36
Nationalists (in Northern Ireland),
85, 86, 96, 100, 103, 188, 191
nationalities, 25, 32, 34, 108, 114,
123, 165, 177
nation-state, nation-states, 1, 2, 7,
21, 22–25, 27–29, 32, 122, 144,
165, 166, 191, 194
Navarre, 57, 183, 184
Nelson, Rosemary, 88
neofascist, 98, 189n
New Ireland Forum, 94, 97
nomenklatura, 8, 47
nomenklatura nationalism, 8, 9,
35–37, 45–46
nongovernmental organisations
(NGOs), 13, 15, 48, 82, 101,
105, 152, 153, 155–57, 159–60
'bungee NGOs', 13, 160
noninternational armed conflicts,
140–41
NORAID, 96, 97
Nordic Council, 175n. 15
North Atlantic Treaty Organisation
(NATO), 22, 45, 47, 48, 133n,
180n
Partnership for Peace (1994), 48

North Caucasians, see Caucasians
North Ossetia, Autonomous
Republic of North Ossetia,
Republic of North Ossetia-
Alania, 72, 75
Northern Ireland, 1, 6–10, 14, 27,
41, 48, 84–104, 133, 166n. 5,
175, 178, 179, 188–91, 195–97
Northern Ireland Assembly,
86–88, 103n
Northern Ireland Minister, 188n.
42;
see also Anglo-Irish Agreement,
Fair Employment (Northern
Ireland Act), Fair Employment
Commission, Friends of Ireland,
Good Friday Agreement, Joint
Declaration, New Ireland Forum,
Stormont parliament,
Sunningdale Agreement;
North—South institutions, 86, 88
Norway, 175n. 14, 176, 194
Norwegian constitution, 194n. 49
Norwegian-Swedish Union, 194

O
O'Dowd, Niall, 95
Omagh bombing (1998), 88
Orange Order, 84, 86, 87
Organization for Security and Co-
operation in Europe (OSCE)
(formerly CSCE), 8, 42, 43, 71,
74, 82, 152, 180, 194n. 48
Copenhagen Meeting (1990),
43
High Commissioner on National
Minorities, 13, 48, 152
Minsk Process, Minsk Group,
74, 152
Ortega y Gasset, José, 65
Orthodox Church, Orthodoxy, 31,
47
Ossetians in Georgia, see South
Ossetia
Ottoman rule, 106, 114

P
Padanian Republic, 28
Paisley, Ian, 86
Palestine Liberation Organization
(PLO), 98, 102
Palestinian state, 98, 102
Palestinians, 156
Pan Am Flight 103, 92
paramilitary groups, paramilitaries
in Northern Ireland, 86, 87, 88,
91, 92, 93, 96, 188n. 42
in Bosnia-Herzegovina, 37, 108,
112, 119, 120, 126
in Spain, 62
Paris, 25, 93, 127
Paris Peace Accords (League of
Nations), 165
partisan, partisan warfare, resistance,

11, 115
partition, 14, 100, 191
and Bosnia-Herzegovina, 123
of Chechnya and Ingushetia, 75
of Czechoslovakia, 43
and Northern Ireland, 88, 98,
100
Partnership for Peace, see NATO
Party of Democratic Action (SDA)
(Bosnia-Herzegovina), 111
peace constituencies, 157, 159
peacebuilding, 158
peacekeeping, 158
peacemaking, 155, 158, 168
perestroika, 9, 72, 73, 76
Plaid Cymru (Party of Wales), 26
Poland, 4n, 21, 44, 46, 49, 178n. 19,
180
Poles, 44
Pomak minority in Bulgaria, 173nn.
7, 8
Portadown, 86
Portugal, 101
postnationalist model, strategy, 51,
52
power sharing, 1, 7, 14, 84, 86, 100,
186–91, 195–96, 197n. 53;
see also consociational democracy
Prigorodny conflict, Prigorodnyi
rayon, 9, 73, 75
proportional representation, 187–88
Protestantism, 31
Protestants
in Northern Ireland, 88, 89, 97,
188n. 41, 191
in Swiss civil war (1848), 185n
in Berne, 192n
Provisional Irish Republican Army
(IRA), Provisionals, see Irish
Republican Army (IRA)
Putin, Vladimir, 83

Q
Quaker organisations, 160
Quebecois movement, 5

R
Ramaphosa, Cyril, 99
Reagan, Ronald, 94
Real IRA, 88
recognition (strategy for dealing
with minorities), 13–14, 32, 42,
77, 98, 102, 140, 166–67,
169–72, 193
Recommendation 1201, see Council
of Europe
Red Army Faction, 101
Red Brigades, 101
regionalist, regionalists, regionalism,
regionalization, 7–8, 21–30, 182
Renan, Ernest, Renanian,
Renanianism 60, 64–68
Republic of North Ossetia-Alania,
see North Ossetia

Republika Srpska (Bosnia-
Herzegovina), 112, 121, 123
Army of the Republika Srpska
(VRS), 121
constitution, 123
Rhodesia, 137
Roma (Gypsy), 8, 39, 40, 41, 44, 50,
52n. 15, 173n. 8, 175
Romania, 21, 33, 34, 36n, 40, 41, 43,
44, 45–48, 49, 51, 173n. 9, 177,
178, 194n. 48;
see also Democratic Alliance of
Hungarians in Romania
(UDMR), National Salvation
Front
Romanian Constitutional Court, 49
Romanians, 36, 40, 46
Ropers, Norbert, 13, 150
Royal Ulster Constabulary (RUC)
(Northern Ireland), 87, 94, 97
Russia, Russian Federation, 38, 42,
44, 45, 71, 73, 74, 75, 77, 78, 79,
80, 81, 82, 181
Russian constitution, 76
Russian language, 78
Russians, 32, 34, 71, 78
Russians in the Baltic States, 37,
44, 50
Russian-speaking community in
Estonia, 182
Russians in Azerbaijan, Belarus,
Georgia, Kazakhstan, Kyrgyzstan,
Tajikistan, Turkmenistan,
Uzbekistan, 44
Russians minority in Ukraine, 44,
45
Russians minority in Moldova,
44, 45, 193
Rwanda, 126, 137n, 153

S
Sámi parliaments (Finland, Norway,
Sweden), 175n. 14
Sarajevo, 109, 113
Sardinia, 7, 25, 183n. 31
Sartre, Jean-Paul, 63
Schneckener, Ulrich, 13, 14, 165,
186, 191n
Scotland, Scots, Scottish
regionalism, 7–8, 25–27, 32n,
175, 183
Scottish National Party (SNP),
26
Scottish Parliament, 8
secession, secessionism, secessionist,
10, 12, 14, 42, 50, 77, 102, 134,
136, 139, 143, 145–47, 184, 186,
189, 191–95
Second World War, 11, 21, 22, 71,
79, 109, 114, 115, 125, 126, 140,
145
self-determination, 10, 29, 31, 33,
38, 66n. 23, 73, 76, 77, 82, 102,
126, 139, 143–47, 154, 193

external self-determination, 146,
147
internal self-determination, 12,
145, 147, 189
self-determination and minorities,
12, 139, 143–47
Senghaas, Dieter, 13, 14, 160, 165,
167, 197n. 55
separatism, separatist, 1, 14, 15, 22,
42, 47, 77, 80, 184, 189, 192–94
Serb Democratic Party (SDS)
(Bosnia-Herzegovina), 111, 112
Serbia, Serbian state, 9, 33, 36, 40,
44, 46–48, 108, 111, 113, 123,
177n, 186, 188
'Greater Serbia', 40, 108, 111
Serbs, 38, 44, 109, 111, 114, 121,
123, 177;
see also Bosnian Serb armed
forced, Bosnian Serb paramilitary
groups
Shevardnadze, Eduard, 74
Sicily, 7, 25, 183n. 31
Sillamäe, 182n. 28
Sinn Féin, 84–88, 95, 96, 98–99
Sládek, Miroslav, 39
Slovakia, 9, 39–40, 41n. 11, 43, 44,
46, 47, 173n. 8, 175, 177, 178,
180, 182, 186, 192
Slovak, Slovaks
Slovak nation building, 177
Slovaks in the Czech Republic,
44
Slovaks in Hungary, 44, 180;
see also Basic Treaty between
Hungary and Slovakia
Slovenia, 44, 102, 177, 178n. 19
Slovene, Slovenian
parties, 36
minority in Austria, 176
minority in Italy, 183n. 31
Slovenian constitution, 174n. 13,
176
Social Democratic and Labour Party
(SDLP) (Northern Ireland), 85,
97, 98
Socialist Federal Republic of
Yugoslavia, see Yugoslavia
Somalia, 137, 159
South Africa, South African
transition, 10, 91–93, 96–99, 102,
103, 137
South Ossetia, South Ossetian
conflict, 9, 73, 75, 152
Ossetians, Ossetian minority in
Georgia, 38, 44, 75
South Slavs, 33
South Tyrol, 6, 7, 25, 41, 43, 173n. 9,
174, 179, 181–86, 188, 189, 195,
197
Autonomy Statutes (1948, 1972),
43, 181, 184n. 32
Trentino-Alto Adige, 6, 183n. 31,
184n. 32;

see also Bolzano province
South-East European Cooperation
Initiative (SECI), 49
sovereignty, 12, 13, 27, 38, 43, 51,
73, 74, 81, 138, 153, 182, 184,
194
Soviet
bloc, 31, 35, 39, 50
constitution, 193n. 46
identity, 185
law, legislation, 73–74
post-Soviet, 3n, 10, 79
special forces in Georgia, 74, 75
Soviet Communist Party, 72
Soviet Union, 21, 31, 33, 34, 41, 43,
73, 75, 93, 102, 133, 145n. 13,
166, 183, 193
former Soviet Union, empire, 37,
38n. 7, 39
break-up, 41, 43, 73
Spain, Spanish state, 1, 7, 9, 15, 23,
24, 25, 27, 42, 51, 57, 182, 183,
184, 186, 197
Spanish
Autonomous Communities
(Communidad), 43, 182, 195
Civil War, 140
constitution, 181n. 25, 184n. 33
fascism, 65
language (Castilian), 65
nation, 64
politics, 64n
regions, 25
Srebrenica, 105, 124, 125, 127
Stability Pact (Balladur Plan) (EU),
180n
Stability Pact for Southeastern
Europe (EU), 49
Stalin, Josef, 59
state building, 32, 33, 166
State Department (US), 94, 95, 97,
102
Stavropol, 72
Stormont parliament (Northern
Ireland), 90, 166n. 5, 179n. 23
Sunningdale Agreement (1973), 85,
188
Sweden, 48, 175n. 14, 176, 186n. 35,
194
Swedish
Swedish politicians, 194n. 49
Swedish-speaking Åland Islands,
173n. 9;
see also Norwegian-Swedish
Union
Switzerland, Swiss cantons, 173, 185,
187, 189–92, 195

T
Tajikistan, 44
Tajiks in Uzbekistan, 44
Talysh in Azerbaijan, 44
Tatars in Kyrgyzstan, Russian
Federation, Tajikistan,

Uzbekistan, 44
Taylor, John, 84
territorial integrity, 12, 13, 52, 61, 134, 138, 145, 146, 154, 180
Thatcher, Margaret, 91, 94, 197n. 53
third party intervention, 12, 134, 136, 137, 139, 146, 151, 155–57, 159
third party mediation, 13, 15, 150, 154, 158, 159
Tîrgu Mureş, 36
Tito, Josip Broz, 45, 108, 112, 115
Tolstoy, Leo, 7
'Track 1', 'Track 2' levels, 13, 152, 159
Transcaucasus, 31
Trans-Dniester region, 14, 181, 193, 195
Transylvania, Transylvanian, 34, 46
Treaty of Lausanne (1923) (League of Nations), 33
Trentino-Alto Adige, see South Tyrol
Trimble, David, 85, 188n. 42
Troebst, Stefan, 1, 4n, 5, 181n. 27
Trotskyite, 59
'Troubles' (Northern Ireland), 27, 89, 90, 94, 96, 97, 100
Tuareg, 152
Tudjman, Franjo, 38, 47
Turkey, 33, 45, 166n. 4, 173n. 9, 175, 177, 178nn. 19, 20
Turks, 123
    Turks in Bulgaria, 41, 44, 173nn. 7, 8
    Turkish minority in Greece, 41, 178n. 20
    Turks in Macedonia, 44
    Turkish-Cypriot minority, Turkish-Cypriots, 190, 191
Turkmenistan, 44
Tutsi, 153

U
Ukraine, 3, 31, 44, 45, 176, 177, 178n. 19, 181, 182
    Ukrainian constitution, 181n. 26
Ukrainian Military Organisation/Organisation of Ukrainian Nationalists in Poland, 4n
Ukrainians, 44
Ulster Democratic Party (UDP) (Northern Ireland), 87
Ulster Freedom Fighters (UFF) (Northern Ireland), 87
Ulster Resistance (Northern Ireland), 93
Ulster Unionist Party (UUP) (Northern Ireland), 84
Union of Soviet Socialist Republics (USSR), 9, 72, 186, 193–95
Unionist, Unionists (in Northern Ireland), 10, 85, 86, 88, 90, 96, 98, 100, 103, 188, 191

United Kingdom, 1, 10, 23, 25, 26, 27, 86, 88, 89, 90, 93, 94, 100, 101, 143n, 179, 197n. 53; see also Great Britain
United Kingdom Unionist Party (UKUP) (Northern Ireland), 86, 96
United Nations (UN), 42, 74, 92, 121n. 12, 134, 136, 138, 144
    Charter (1945), 134–38, 145–46
    Commission of Experts to investigate war crimes in former Yugoslavia, 120, 123n. 14, 124
    Commission on Global Governance, 48
    Declaration on the Rights of Persons Belonging to National or Ethnic, Religious and Linguistic Minorities (1992), 42
    General Assembly, 118n. 7
    General Assembly Resolution 2105, 135n. 4
    General Assembly Friendly Relations Declaration (1970), 146
    Genocide Convention (1948), 122
    hostage crisis, 120
    Human Rights Committee, 39n. 9
    International Covenant on Civil and Political Rights (1966), 145
    International Covenant on Economic, Social and Cultural Rights (1966), 145
    peacekeepers, 105
    protected areas, 125
    Secretary-General, 179n. 22
    Security Council, 12, 118nn. 7, 8, 121n. 10, 123n. 14, 124n. 19, 136–38, 146
    Security Council Resolution on the Indonesian Conflict (1948), 137; see also International Criminal Tribunal for the former Yugoslavia (ICTY)
United Nations Educational, Scientific and Cultural Organization (UNESCO), 119
United Nations High Commissioner for Refugees (UNHCR), 39, 105
United States, USA, 21, 31, 49, 59, 66, 87, 90, 94, 96, 102, 113
United States Congress, 121n. 13
Ustaša, 4n, 125
Uzbek people, 36
    Uzbeks in Kazakhstan, Kyrgyzstan, Tajikistan, Turkmenistan, Uzbekistan, 44

V
Valencia, 183, 184
Valle d'Aosta, see Aosta Valley
'Vertic' (British NGO), 152

veto rights, mutual veto, 187, 188, 189
VRS: Vojska Republike Srpske / Army of the Republika Srpska, see Bosnian Serb armed forces
Vojvodina, 46, 181

W
Wales, 8, 25, 26, 27, 42, 183
    Government of Wales Act (1998), 27n;
    see also Plaid Cymru
Wallonia, Walloons, 24, 175, 183, 187
    Walloon parties, 185n
Welsh, 25–27, 175
    regionalism, 7, 26
    Assembly, 27
    devolution, 26–27
Western European Union, 22
Westminster parliament, model, 27, 186
Wilson, Woodrow, 31
Wright, Billy, 86–87

Y
Yandarbiev, Zelimkhan, 71
Yeltsin, Boris, 38, 71, 75, 76, 79
Yugoslav
    case, 3n, 117
    break-up, 10, 11, 43, 45, 73, 102, 110, 119, 126, 166, 194, 195
    constitution, 111, 145n. 12
    identity, 114, 185
    military doctrine of all-peoples' defence, 11, 112, 115
    wars of succession, 52, 106, 126
Yugoslav People's Army (JNA), 108, 112, 133n
Yugoslavs, 11
    in Bosnia-Herzegovina, Croatia, 44
Yugoslavia
    (Socialist Federal Republic of), former Yugoslavia, ex-Yugoslavia, 8, 21, 36, 40–42, 45, 46, 48, 52n. 16, 105n, 109, 110, 111, 115, 118n. 7, 123, 166n. 4, 186, 194–95
    Federal Republic of Yugoslavia (FRY), rump Yugoslavia, 38, 42, 108, 121, 120–22, 124, 133, 153, 181, 183, 195;
    see also International Criminal Tribunal for the former Yugoslavia (ICTY)

Z
Zaire, 153
Zalbide, José Luís, 61, 62
Zanzibar, 126
zero-sum games, zero-sum mentality, 169–70, 190
Zionist, 68